An Introduction to the Study of Public Policy *2nd edition*

The Duxbury Press Series on Public Policy

Charles O. Jones, University of Pittsburgh
General Editor

An Introduction to the Study of Public Policy, 2nd edition
    Charles O. Jones

The Domestic Presidency: Decision-Making in the White House
    John H. Kessel (Ohio State University)

Forthcoming—

Public Policy and Politics in America
    James E. Anderson, David W. Brady and Charles L. Bullock, III
    (University of Houston)

Understanding Intergovernmental Relations
    Deil Wright (University of North Carolina)

Of related interest—

A Logic of Public Policy: Aspects of Political Economy
    L. L. Wade (University of California, Davis)
    Robert L. Curry, Jr. (California State University, Sacramento)

Democracy in America: A Public Choice Perspective
    L. L. Wade (University of California, Davis)
    R. L. Meek (Colorado State University)

Politics, Change, and the Urban Crisis
    Bryan Downes (University of Oregon)

Charles O. Jones

Maurice Falk Professor of Politics
University of Pittsburgh

AN INTRODUCTION TO THE STUDY OF

Public

Policy Second Edition

Duxbury Press   North Scituate, Massachusetts

Library of Congress Cataloging in Publication Data

Jones, Charles O.
  Introduction to the study of public policy.

  Bibliography: p.
  Includes index.
  1. United States—Politics and government.   2. Decision-making in
public administration.   I. Title.
JK271.J62   1977   353   76–48140
ISBN 0–87872–130–4

DUXBURY PRESS
A DIVISION OF WADSWORTH PUBLISHING COMPANY, INC.

© 1977 by Wadsworth Publishing Company, Inc., Belmont, California
94002. All rights reserved. No part of this book may be reproduced, stored
in a retrieval system, or transcribed, in any form or by any means, electronic
mechanical, photocopying, recording, or otherwise, without the prior
written permission of the publisher, Duxbury Press, a division of Wadsworth
Publishing Company, Inc., Belmont, California.

An Introduction to the Study of Public Policy was edited and prepared for
composition by Eleanor Gilbert. Interior design was provided by Dorothy
Booth, and the cover was designed by Garrow Throop.

L. C. Cat. Card No.: 76–48140
ISBN 0–87872–130–4
PRINTED IN THE UNITED STATES OF AMERICA
3 4 5 6 7 8 9 — 81 80 79

To the late John Merriman Gaus—
above all he had compassion

To the Students

In the following pages I seek to provide a basis for describing, explaining, and evaluating the policy process in the United States. One of my main concerns is to ask the right questions. Let me emphasize that I don't have all of the answers—and that you probably have more than you know. Most problems in political science and public policy have not been resolved; and though trained political scientists have thought a great deal about these problems, students can and should be actively involved in analyzing the central issues of political study.

Though I always draw a great deal from my colleagues in political science, in this effort I owe a particular debt of gratitude to my students at Wellesley College, the University of Arizona, and the University of Pittsburgh. They suffered me while I struggled to develop my ideas and added to my education by sharing their experiences and insights into ordinary, everyday policy situations. I want to continue talking with students here—examining various analytical concepts and practical case studies, raising questions, and writing in a more or less conversational style. I invite you to join in the discussion and to challenge my understanding of concepts from your own experience and from your study of policy problems in this course. The process of education is, and must be, a process of exchange—between you and the professor, between you and the written word, between you and your colleagues. It would please me a great deal to be told by your professors that this book was torn apart and reassembled in more intelligent form by their respective classes. I ask only that you let me know what you know. Nothing would be more unfair than for a student who has something to teach to keep his knowledge from a teacher who has something to learn.

Acknowledgements

I wish to acknowledge the assistance of several persons who helped put these words together and get them printed. Bernard C. Hennessy, California State University, Hayward, and Randall B. Ripley, Ohio State University, read the manuscript and contributed helpful comments and suggestions for improvement. My colleagues at the University of Pittsburgh educate me on a daily basis and I know their ideas have entered these pages without proper acknowledgement. Mr. Robert Gormley encouraged me to write such a text in the first place and I have found his staff at Duxbury Press most cooperative and helpful. Mrs. Kendall Stanley and Mrs. Janet Altenbaugh typed the manuscript with care and assisted in other ways as well. Dieter Matthes brought the bibliography up-to-date. And Vera, Joe B. and Danny helped me maintain perspective.

One final word. In the original development of this book, I often consulted Professor John M. Gaus, a frequent winter visitor in Tucson. Always willing to give of his time, Professor Gaus taught me much about the policy process. His power in teaching came from a unique ability to create conditions under which students could reach the right conclusions on their own. John M. Gaus relied on humility and understanding in his relationships with students, but above all he had compassion. He set a standard that none will reach and few will even understand.

CONTENTS

Introduction and General Framework of Analysis

Comprehending the work of government has come to be a monumental, if not impossible, task. Consider the major public problems being worked on in Congress during a not untypical week (June 2-7, 1975): appropriation for emergency jobs (president's veto sustained), military procurement, foreign aid, air pollution control, strip mining controls, copyrights, food safety, emergency livestock loans, equal credit opportunity, developmental disabilities assistance (mentally retarded, epilepsy, cerebral palsy), energy supply and demand, a deadlocked U.S. Senate election (Wyman versus Durkin in New Hampshire), multiyear financing for public broadcasting, promotion of tourism, and extension of the Voting Rights Act.[1] I emphasize that these were items for *major* action in Congress—not the executive. Individual committees and offices were working on literally hundreds of other matters of public concern. Each of those identified above, however, varies in terms of the nature of the problem, what constitutes a reasonable solution, the extent and kind of existing government involvement, the level of government involved, the extent and kind of private involvement, the program targets, and the impact of government action. And we have here only a small slice of public policy making taken from one institution at one level of government.

One is justified then in conceptualizing a veritable constellation of perceptions, receptions, pressures, demands, cues, and responses operating as a dynamic set of interactions on problems, issues, and policies. Somebody always wants somebody else to do something and that something is normally specific—not general. Further, the target for these demands, pressures, and cues has a designated role to play in some phase of the policy process. Governmental response to these pressures will vary markedly and a simple understanding of the institutions—legislative, executive, bureaucracy, and courts—as compartmentalized units is not sufficient to encompass this mosaic of interactions on public problems and policy. Clearly, a method is required for studying policy development and implementation in other than strictly institutional settings.

The principal purpose of this book is to offer just such a method. Rather than proposing the more traditional *institutional process approach* in which one studies decision making in the legislature, executive, and the courts, I offer a set of concepts to encourage students to consider cross-institutional and interlevel policy relationships. In this second approach, the central question is simple: How is the problem defined and acted on in government? To respond comprehensively, one must trace a set of actions—permitting the problem to take you where it will rather than limiting the analysis to one institution. With this approach, the student will discover that those vitally involved in acting on the problem in various ways are drawn from several institutions. This mode of study may properly be called a *policy process approach* and it will serve as the orienting purpose for this book.

I have organized the material as follows. The remainder of this chapter will be devoted to other important introductory matters—definition of terms, identification of what I call "initial realities" (including my own preferences in the study of public policy), and an overview of the framework of analysis. The next chapter will briefly discuss the nature of public problems. The other chapters follow the sequence identified in the framework—providing elaboration of the concepts introduced and illustrating each with case materials.

What Is Policy?

The term "policy" gets used in many different ways to refer to highly diverse sets of activities or decisions. In a single day one can hear a United States senator proclaim that "the United States no longer has a foreign *policy* in the Far East," a mayor announce a change in traffic control *policy* for the central business district, the gas man tell you that company *policy* now requires that the meter be near the road, and a clerk declare, "Sorry, store *policy* does not permit the exchange of swimming suits once they've been worn." Listen to S. David Freeman as he discusses energy policy in this country.

> America's energy policy amounted to a blind act of faith that the oil companies and the utilities would indefinitely continue to deliver the goods. . . . Even after the fuel shortages became a reality in the winter of 1972–73, the federal government played down the seriousness of the problem. "Praying for mild weather" was the government energy policy. . . . Government policy was to rely on the oil companies, and their policy was to put profits ahead of the public interest.[2]

Freeman uses the term rhetorically to characterize failure to act and accusingly to condemn the oil companies. Some clarification is needed since these various uses imply differences in the substance, scope, form, and processes of policy.

One is not assisted very much by turning from how the term is used in common parlance to how it is defined by social scientists. H. Hugh Heclo found agreement that "at its core, policy is a course of action intended to accomplish some end." But he concluded that "there is nevertheless a certain ambiguity as to whether or not policy is more than the *intended* course of action. . . . The term policy needs to be able to embrace both what is intended and what occurs as a result of the intention. . . ."[3] By Heclo's analysis, one can conceive of a whole series of actions from the initial definition and setting of goals as an official surveys a problem to the results of any official intervention to solve the problem. Then of course, as Freeman suggests above, conscious decisions *not* to intervene also get called policy by some.

Well, this is a broader spectrum of meaning than is suitable for present purposes. What is needed is a breakdown of the components of public policy behavior, many of which get called "policy" when in fact other terms are more appropriate. Consider, for example, the distinction among the following policy ingredients:

> *Goals:* the desired ends to be achieved.
> *Plans or Proposals:* specified means for achieving the goals.
> *Programs:* authorized means for achieving goals.
> *Decisions:* specific actions taken to set goals, develop plans, implement and evaluate programs.
> *Effects:* the measurable impacts of programs (intended and unintended; primary and secondary).

One can reasonably use "policy" as an adjective with each of these components, but it does become somewhat confusing if the term "policy" is used interchangeably with all of them.[4]

Note should also be taken of the more legal terms associated with public policy making—legislation, laws, statutes, executive orders, regulations, legal opinions. These too are often called "policy." For our purposes, however, they are simply the formal ingredients or legal expressions of programs and decisions.

So what, then, is policy? First, let me emphasize that my use of the term is only to introduce order and clarity into this discussion, not to set down immutable formulations. Words have the meanings we give them for the purposes we specify. In this case, I reserve the term "policy" for my personal use as an analyst to characterize what it is I have found in studying government action on a public problem. In other words, policy is what the findings lead me to conclude in respect to the questions I have asked.

Heclo puts it this way:

> Thus, policy does not seem to be a self-defining phenomenon; it is an analytic category, the contents of which are identified by the analyst rather than by the policy maker or pieces of legislation or administration. There is no unambiguous datum constituting policy and waiting to be discovered in the world. A policy may usefully be considered as a course of action or inaction rather than specific decisions or actions, and such a course has to be perceived and identified by the analyst in question.[5]

In their massive study of city politics and policies in the San Francisco Bay region, Heinz Eulau and Kenneth Prewitt come to much the same understanding of policy.

> Policy is a strictly theoretical construct inferred from the patterns of relevant choice behavior. Policy is distinguished from policy goals, policy intentions, and policy choices. Policy is defined as a "standing decision" characterized by behavioral consistency and repetitiveness on the part of both those who make it and those who abide by it.[6]

It is in these senses of the word that this book is "an introduction to the study of public policy." The purpose here is to provide a basis for understanding the "behavioral consistency and repetitiveness" associated with efforts in and through government to resolve public problems. Used in this way, policy is a highly dynamic term. As Eulau and Prewitt point out: "What the observer sees when he identifies policy at any one point in time is at most a stage or phase in a sequence of events that constitute policy development."[7] Put another way, we stop the action and hold it in place for purposes of analysis. Whatever we learn must be specified in terms of the questions we sought to answer, the time frame within which our research was conducted, the institutional units studied, etc. Therefore, any reference to "defense policy," "farm policy," or "social security policy," should lead us to ask: "What do you mean by that? Are you speaking of national goals? current statutes? recent decisions? Or are you characterizing certain behavioral consistencies by decision makers?" The point of asking these questions is not to enforce one particular definition of the term policy, but rather to clarify meanings and therefore improve understanding.

Some Initial Preferences and Realities

Increasingly I have come to believe that authors of texts should identify their own biases or preferences, at least to the extent that they can identify them. In my own case, I have no doubt that I have through the years consistently had a "process" bias. There are two dimensions to this bias. First, I tend to emphasize the study of processes in political science. As will become evident in this book, I stress the importance of understanding the "how" of public policy—how problems get to government, how they are defined there, how they are acted on, etc. As I have pointed out, the nature of problems themselves—for example, energy, environment, defense, labor, agriculture—comes to influence how various processes develop and work. Therefore, I encourage the study of public problems and policies as an important supplement to the study of political institutions. Briefly stated, it is my contention that problems influence the processes designed to solve them, the processes in turn help to explain programs and policies, and the policies affect what problems emerge in society and get to the agenda of government. What the precise effect is in each case is unsettled—that is the reason for research and study. But I maintain that the special purview of the political scientist is the political process and how it works. His or her interest in the substance of problems and policies, therefore, is in how it interacts with process, not necessarily in the substance itself. For example, it is not in how solar energy research and development relieves the pressure on other energy sources that is of primary interest to the political scientist but in how that result in turn influences how future decisions are made. I realize that there is a bit of the "chicken-and-egg" dilemma in all of this. All I am saying is that as a matter of emphasis, I favor concentrating on process.

Second, serious reflection on how I personally react to public problems and solutions has made me realize that I also favor process-type solutions. Rather than stressing this or that substantive proposal—e.g., "we must raise the minimum wage by 50¢" or "we must support Senator Kennedy's national health scheme"—I tend to endorse certain methods of decision making and then abide by the results. I rely wholly on democratic criteria for determining what is the best decision making—i.e., a high degree of access for those who care to be involved, provision for bargaining and compromise, public accountability of leaders, free elections, etc. This also suggests that my remedies for the social system tend to be of the process variety—more access for more interests, providing for criticism and opposition, publicizing decisions and how they are made.

In a very large sense, these preferences can be associated with a highly traditional view of persons as too selfish and otherwise limited either to govern themselves individually in society or to trust governance in the hands of a few. As was stated so eloquently in *The Federalist* No. 51 (by either Alexander Hamilton or James Madison):

> If men were angels, no government would be necessary. If angels were to govern men, neither external nor internal controls on govern-

ment would be necessary. In framing a government which is to be administered by men over men, the great difficulty lies in this: you must first enable the government to control the governed; and in the next place oblige it to control itself. A dependence on the people is, no doubt, the primary control on the government; but experience has taught mankind the necessity of auxiliary precautions.[8]

It is in part this view of man's nature that is consistent with—perhaps makes inevitable—what Charles E. Lindblom refers to as "disjointed incrementalism."

It is decision making through small or incremental moves on particular problems rather than through a comprehensive reform program. It is also endless; it takes the form of an indefinite sequence of policy moves. Moreover, it is exploratory in that the goals of policy making continue to change as new experience with policy throws new light on what is possible and desirable. In this sense, it is also better described as moving *away* from known social ills rather than as moving *toward* a known and relatively stable goal.[9]

The advantage of incrementalism is that one never has to test the validity of a new idea or proposal. New decisions build on the base—with a bit more of this or that added to existing programs. Who can go wrong with that process? Obviously lots of things can go wrong if the base itself is misdirected. Our experience in Vietnam can be cited as a case in point. Thus, there are distinct disadvantages too that lead many policy scholars and activists to reject incrementalism in favor of more rational and systematic approaches to decision making. The problem for them comes to be whether one can maintain all of the tenets of democracy and still make rational policy. Providing for a high degree of access allows people to move in and upset the most orderly and rational plans. Conversely, left alone "the best and brightest," as David Halberstram called our Vietnam war architects, can provide and implement options that turn out to be no more than increments toward disaster.

Whether or not one supports incrementalism as the way to make decisions, it does seem descriptive of what normally happens in this political system. Certainly it occurs more often than does the so-called comprehensive-rational approach in which the dominant values are identified, all proposals are studied for their effect, and the choice is made on the most rational bases possible. This more rational approach is employed by policy proponents and decision makers at some levels of government, but their work typically is compromised as it moves through the full process.

This last point suggests an important distinction between *description* and *prescription*. What accurately describes a process may not at all be what we would personally prescribe. The fact that policy making in the United States appears to be more incremental and short-run oriented than comprehensive and visionary may be the stimulus to large-scale change. I see no particular reason why those who want change should limit their actions because the system is incremental. It may in fact come to limit what they are able to accomplish, but modifying their proposals in advance may only guarantee a smaller increment than could be achieved by "going for broke."

This discussion of preferences, theories of man's nature, and what is or is not ordinarily descriptive of decision making leads us to what I have labeled "initial realities." They provide a set of orienting propositions for much of what follows. They should reveal how it is I think the policy process works. Not everyone would agree with these, and there is no reason why you should accept them uncritically. I am simply trying to outline the basic tenets of my approach.[10] Here then are the "initial realities."

1. Events in society are interpreted in different ways by different people at different times.
2. Many problems may result from the same event.
3. People have varying degrees of access to the policy process in government.
4. Not all public problems are acted on in government.
5. Many private problems are acted on in government.
6. Many private problems are acted on in government as though they were public problems.
7. Most problems aren't solved by government though many are acted on there.
8. "Policy makers are not faced with a *given* problem."[11]
9. Most decision making is based on little information and poor communication.
10. Programs often reflect an attainable consensus rather than a substantive conviction.
11. Problems and demands are constantly being defined and redefined in the policy process.
12. Policy makers sometimes define problems for people who have not defined problems for themselves.
13. Many programs are developed and implemented without the problems ever having been clearly defined.
14. Most people do not maintain interest in other people's problems.
15. Most people do not prefer large change.
16. Most people cannot identify a public policy.
17. All policy systems have a bias.
18. No ideal policy system exists apart from the preferences of the architect of that system.

19. Most decision making is incremental in nature.

Taken together, these propositions suggest a highly relative and pluralistic decision-making system characterized by compromise, incrementalism, and continual adjustment. I hope they convey that image since that is what I have sought to achieve. I will have more to say about these characteristics in Chapter 2.

Benchmarks for Analysis

In a sense, this whole book is a framework for analysis, offering a basis for a reasonably systematic examination of policy development and implementation. That is, this discussion should enable you to unravel how the policy process works in the United States for farm problems, energy and environmental problems, defense problems, and so on. I have also tried to avoid making this framework too culture-bound. Though I have not tested it on other political systems, the presumption is that such a framework would be equally useful in analyzing policy in other nations and in international systems of action.

I can summarize the basic elements of the policy process framework in brief fashion: public problems exist in society as a result of the perception of needs by people, some people have problems in common, some of these organize and make demands or demands are made by those who seek to represent people, demands are perceived and judged by those with authority to make decisions, decisions are made and enforced, public problems are affected by these decisions, people react to the decisions, some people have common reactions, demands are made, and so forth. It is apparent that certain activities in this overall process can be identified and defined. These include:

Perception
Definition
Aggregation
Organization
Representation
Formulation
Legitimation
Appropriation
Implementation
Evaluation/Appraisal
Resolution/Termination

These constitute a sort of catalog of functional activities in the policy process—very much like that suggested by Harold D. Lasswell. The list is offered in the same spirit as Lasswell's: "Classifications are serviceable when they are tentative and undogmatic, and when they guide scholarly activity in directions that are presently accepted as valuable."[12] It attempts to identify the principal activities in the overall policy process which typically form patterns as identifiable systems and processes. That is, these several activities represent something rather consistent over time, to the point that we can identify definite patterns.

One point should be emphasized very early. Vastly oversimplifying what happens to bring man and government together helps to identify the functional activities listed above. By the time we come to analyze how policy is evaluated, however, it will be apparent that the agenda of government is not set by new problems emerging in a state of nature. Most of what government acts on results from the continuing application and evaluation of ongoing programs.

These patterned activities can be grouped by their relationship to the central concern here—what government does to act on public problems.

Problem to Government[13]

　　Perception
　　Definition
　　Aggregation
　　Organization
　　Representation

Action in Government

　　Formulation
　　Legitimation
　　Appropriation

Government to Problem

　　Implementation

Policy to Government

　　Evaluation/Appraisal

Problem Resolution or Change

　　Resolution/Termination

Some further definitions are now in order. It is important to distinguish between the terms "system" and "process." System refers to two or more persons engaged in patterned or structured interaction guided by shared values and directed toward the achievement of some goal.[14] A system is characterized by a definite, identifiable population, boundaries (defined by the shared values and goals), patterned behavior, and direction; it is essentially a static concept. Process refers to the action of the system; it is a dynamic concept and may apply to any number of patterned activities in a system.

Those are clearly quite formal definitions, but it is of some importance to be as precise as possible as an aid to understanding. An analogy may offer further assistance to this end. It is highly likely (but by no means certain) that you are part of a system of action as a student in this course. All of the components of a system may be present—population, structure, interaction, shared values and goals. You can see how expectations—yours, those of other students, those of the instructor—shape the boundaries of this system. You know that the instructor's expectations influence what you do in the course, but believe me when I say that your expectations are also very important in determining his or her behavior. While all of this identifies a system for you, however, it doesn't say much about how it works day-to-day. For that you need to identify the specific *processes* by which expectations develop and goals are achieved in this course, as compared to your other courses. I am confident that while many of your courses can be identified as systems, they will vary in terms of the processes designed to effect their specific goals.

Another way to clarify the distinction is to consider those courses which never really develop as systems. Interaction may be virtually nonexistent; conflict may be high; perhaps goals are vague, unstated, or not shared. Processes are disjointed and purposeless because no system really exists. Frustration for all abounds.

Frequent reference will be made to various sytems and processes in this analysis, guided by the categories of activities listed above. I will distinguish the following systems of action—problem identification, formulation, legitimation, implementation, and evaluation. Within each, processes can be identified which function to achieve the goals of the system. It is useful at this point to identify the outputs of these systems to assist in defining the nature of each.

System	*Output*
Problem Identification	Demand for action to resolve a problem
Formulation	Proposal to resolve a problem

Legitimation   Program (a legitimate course of action)
Implementation   Action to apply
Evaluation   Recommendation to adjust (e.g., demand for
                          new policy or different interpretations of exist-
                          ing policy)

I think that enough has been said to get us going. Table 1–1 summarizes the framework as it has been discussed thus far. As you can see from the table of contents, the book is structured to examine each of the systems in turn.

Table 1–1. The Policy Process—A Framework for Analysis

Functional Activities	Categorized in Government	and as Systems	with Output
Perception Definition Aggregation Organization Representation	Problems to Government	Problem Identification	Problem to Demand
Formulation Legitimation Appropriation	Action in Government	Program Development	Proposal to Budgeted Program
Organization Interpretation Application	Government to Problem	Program Implementa-tion	Varies (Service, payments, facili-ties, controls, etc.)
Specification Measurement Analysis	Program to Government	Program Evaluation	Varies (Justifica-tion, recommenda-tion, etc.)
Resolution/ Termination	Problem resolu-tion or change	Program Termination	Solution or change

Notes

1. These are the legislative actions reported for that week in the *Congressional Quarterly Weekly Report*, June 7, 1975.

2. S. David Freeman, *Energy: The New Era* (New York: Vintage Books, 1974), p. 4.

3. H. Hugh Heclo, "Review Article: Policy Analysis," *British Journal of Political Science*, vol. 2 (January 1972), pp. 84–85.

4. Heinz Eulau and Kenneth Prewitt provide a most intelligent discussion of this whole matter in *Labyrinths of Democracy* (Indianapolis: Bobbs-Merrill, 1973). See in particular pp. 464–88.

5. Heclo, *British Journal of Political Science*, p. 85.

6. Eulau and Prewitt, p. 465.

7. Eulau and Prewitt, p. 481.

8. *The Federalist* (New York: Modern Library, 1937), p. 337.

9. David Braybrooke and Charles E. Lindblom, *A Strategy of Decision* (New York: Free Press, 1963), p. 71.

10. I have already indicated two other approaches—i.e., the institutionalists and the comprehensive rationalists. But there are many other variations in how scholars view political access, decision making, and public policy. For a review of these theories and approaches see James E. Anderson, *Public Policy-Making* (New York: Praeger, 1975), pp. 9–25.

11. Charles E. Lindblom, *The Policy-Making Process* (Englewood Cliffs, N.J.: Prentice-Hall, 1968), p. 13.

12. Harold D. Lasswell, "The Decision Process: Seven Categories of Functional Analysis," reprinted in Nelson W. Polsby, et al., eds., *Politics and Social Life* (Boston: Houghton Mifflin, 1963), p. 93.

13. I have omitted from consideration certain important activities which fit generally into the category "man to government." These are the electoral, appointive, and professional hiring activities involved in manning political processes. This is the subject matter of several courses in political parties, elections, public opinion, and public administration.

14. See David Easton's trilogy, *The Political System* (New York: Knopf, 1953), *A Framework for Political Analysis* (Englewood Cliffs, N.J.: Prentice-Hall, 1965), and *A Systems Analysis of Political Life* (New York: Wiley, 1965). Also see William Mitchell, *The American Polity* (New York: The Free Press, 1962).

The Nature of Public Problems

One disconcerting characteristic of policy problems is that they do not exist as units. The student of policy tends to think of "the problem" such as urban mass transportation as a unitary problem. In fact, there is no unity with respect to the problems people actually have, the way in which they perceive the problem or, as has been pointed out, of their interests and their values. Furthermore, since the policy process has a time dimension, each of these elements changes over time.[1]

It is true, as Raymond A. Bauer suggests in this passage, that we use the term *problem* very loosely in political discourse. Reference is made, for example, to "the" education, defense, environmental, employment, economic, or housing problem as though a chief problem designator existed somewhere making pronouncements to be universally accepted by all. The fact is that one person's problem may be another person's profit. Problems result from events affecting people differently. Not all problems become public; not all public problems become issues; and not all issues are acted on in government.

Clarification of terms must precede a survey of the several types of events and issues so important in setting the context of politics in this country. I offer the following:

> *Events:* Human and natural acts perceived to have consequences on social life.
> *Problems:* Human needs, however identified, for which relief is sought.
> *Public Problems:* Human needs, however identified, that cannot be met privately.
> *Issues:* Controversial public problems.
> *Issue-areas:* Bundles of controversial public problems.

A few comments and illustrations will help clarify. Events naturally vary immensely in effect. Wars and natural disasters touch millions of lives. Inventions like the internal combustion engine have altered our lifestyle

15

dramatically. A new family in the neighborhood, however, normally has only limited consequences.

Events may cause problems to emerge and set the conditions for resolving them. Whether this happens depends on how those observing an event perceive it. Those directly affected by a zoning variance which permits construction of a new shopping center and apartment complex, for example, may identify specific needs created by this event—others affected may not identify any particular needs resulting for them. Still others, perhaps a group of environmentalists not directly affected, may identify a need for those living in the area and oppose the variance. Congruity in identifying and acting on needs is by no means guaranteed and therefore many problems may result from the same event. Conflict among problem definitions creates an issue.

If a problem can be resolved without making demands on others not immediately affected, then it is private in nature. John Dewey explains it thus:

> We take then our point of departure from the objective fact that human acts have consequences upon others, that some of these consequences are perceived, and that their perception leads to subsequent effort to control action so as to secure some consequences and avoid others. Following this clew, we are led to remark that the consequences are of two kinds, those which affect the persons directly engaged in a transaction, and those which affect others beyond those immediately concerned. In this distinction, we find the germ of the distinction between the private and the public.[2]

Note the coincidence with our definition of "problem." Human acts have consequences on others, and some of these are perceived to create needs to the extent that relief is sought. If the transaction to control consequences (regulating needs) is relatively restricted in effect, it is private. If the transaction has a broad effect, it is public. According to Dewey, "the public consists of all those who are affected by the indirect consequences of transactions to such an extent that it is deemed necessary to have those consequences systematically cared for."[3] People take actions or propose actions to control their environments—to meet their needs, to solve their problems. Sometimes these actions have consequences for others. When these consequences are *perceived* by others and considered to be significant enough to be controlled, a public is born. As David G. Smith explains:

> That which intervenes between the perceived problem and the governmental outcome is a *public*, a group of affected parties—aroused, engaged in conjoint activity, growing conscious of itself, organizing and seeking to influence officials.[4]

This concept of a "public" is important for these deliberations. Just as we have made a distinction between public and private problems, so too we can distinguish between public problems with a public and those without. In the first the problem is characterized by a group of concerned and organized citizens who intend to get action. The second is acknowledged as a problem which cannot be solved privately but which lacks that supportive element a public can bring. This distinction is critical for understanding the complex processes by which some problems get to government and others do not. As will be pointed out in Chapter 3, the objective verification that a public problem exists (e.g., the many problems of the poor in this nation) is no guarantee that a public will emerge to press for relief.

Some examples may help to clarify these several concepts. A dispute between neighbors over planting a hedge might well be settled peaceably without involving others. Or if a farmer solves the problems created by a drought by pulling in his belt and praying, again he has needs but he does not make demands on others (at least those physically present on this sphere) in meeting them. In both cases, the matter remains essentially private. Should the injured neighbor organize his friends and demand they help rip out the bushes, and should the hedge-grower call in the police and his hedge-loving friends, we have the makings of a public problem. Or should the farmer demand government payments to tide him over the drought period, again his personal needs come to be a public problem. He is making demands on you and me, as taxpayers, for relief. We are drawn into resolving his problems.

Perhaps we are of one mind in assisting drought-stricken farmers. He identifies his problem, we agree to help out, he gets the money he needs to see him through to the next crop period. No controversy arises over these actions and therefore the public problem does not develop into an issue. Seldom are demands so easily met, however. Typically disagreements arise over priorities for allocating tax monies. There may even be conflict over the effects of drought on farmers (that is, not everyone viewing this natural act comes to the same conclusion about the needs it creates). The controversy characterizing issues varies greatly in intensity, scope, and complexity.

What often get referred to as public problems—federal aid to education, public housing, mass transportation, energy—come, by these definitions, to be "issue-areas." The so-called public housing problem is, rather, a bundle of issues—various conflicting demands for relieving several sets of needs. Complicating matters even more is the fact that needs and demands, and therefore conflicts and priorities, are constantly changing—requiring almost continual definition and redefinition of the issue.

One can distinguish among political systems by examining the characteristics of problem identification processes. In a democratic system problem identification is *intended* to be more subjective; in an authoritarian system it is *intended* to be more objective. In objectively defining problems an effort is made to employ scientific measures of the effects of events on people (this says nothing about the success of these measures, of course). There is little or no reliance on how the people interpret effects of events. Subjective processes, on the other hand, place a great deal of reliance on how those affected by an event interpret their needs. Presumably we achieve the latter through elections and other representative processes.

Both objective and subjective measures are, in fact, relied on by all political systems. Again an illustration is needed to clarify. Start with the flight to the suburbs from a neighborhood in any core city. Owner-occupied housing units become rental units and deteriorate—the classic slum. We have available objective measures of what has happened. The Bureau of the Census, or the local housing unit, can describe the "problems" of this neighborhood. Statistics are available showing the declining property values, condition of the housing, number of people occupying the units, increased crime rate, the number of units, etc. Based on available data, political decision makers may logically designate this area for urban renewal. It is a story told many times.

Forget the objective data for a moment now and consider events from the perspective of those people living in the area. The "slum" designation (based on measures relied on by housing agencies) may not summarize their interpretation of the problems at all. They see a failure to enforce housing codes on landlords; a reduction of law enforcement (perhaps an increase of police harassment); reduction of other services in the area; government loan guarantees and tax breaks for buying, not renting (thus encouraging the "white flight" and perpetuating ghettos); low quality schools; and so forth. These are, or may be, subjective analyses of the flight to the suburbs leading to a quite different set of policies than those of urban renewal. In a democracy we presumably intend to err in the direction of the subjective. As is obvious with the urban renewal example, and others to be noted later, we are not always true to our intentions.

One final point should be emphasized before closing this definitional essay. In part the distinction between public and private problems is philosophical. It rests on one's interpretation of what can and cannot be treated privately. I might judge that people should be more self-reliant, managing their own affairs without calling upon others. Others may even quote the scriptures in support of a more community-oriented approach. I have sought to provide an objective basis for determining the difference by emphasizing John Dewey's distinction between consequences affecting "the persons directly engaged in a transaction" (private) and those affecting "others beyond those immediately concerned" (public). Presumably we could develop measures of each that would lead to empirically verifiable public and private problems.

Quite definitely philosophical, however, is the judgment of whether problems, public or private, should be treated by government. I do not intend to resolve that puzzle here. Rather I will alert you to the varying forms of problems which do receive governmental attention—public problems with strong organizational support from attentive publics, public problems without publics (at least among those directly affected by an event), and private problems of various types.

A Catalogue of Major Issue-Areas

One of the many advantages of an open society is that evaluations of social progress come from a variety of sources. We do not have to await the announcement of a five-year plan to determine what should be done. We get frequent private and public assessments. The president's state of the Union message, his economic and budget messages, counter programs and messages from congressional Democrats and Republicans, counterpart messages and assessments by state and local officials—constitute official evaluations of where we are and what we must do. In addition we have available any number of critical and analytical reviews from private agencies and interest groups. The Brookings Institution, an independent organization devoted to nonpartisan research, has for the past several years offered an analysis of the president's budget which has become a justly respected document.[5] Groups like Common Cause, a citizen lobby, and the Ralph Nader Center for Study of Responsive Law are devoted to a kind of government watchdog function and their reports naturally become sources of information on public problems.[6] While admittedly not altruistic in their endeavors, many national interest groups also perform similar functions as they search for policies, problems, and events which may affect their clientele. And finally, the Gallup and Harris polls in particular provide continuing data on what problems the general public judges to be important at any one time.

Taken together these various sources suggest a number of issue-area categories, that is, broad classifications of "bundles of controversial public problems." At a minimum these would include:

Foreign

> Relations with nations (individually and in alliances)
> Economic assistance to other nations

Defense

> U.S. forces
> Security assistance to other nations

Domestic

> Human resources (includes health, education, welfare, job training)
> Physical and natural resources (includes environment, energy, trans-
> portation, housing, agriculture, science)
> Civil rights
> Social control (includes law enforcement, drug control, community
> support)
> Economic control
> Government organization
> Taxation
> Financial assistance to state-local governments

Clearly these categories will vary in significance at any one time or in any one state of the Union message. During the late 1960s and early 1970s foreign and defense issues (Vietnam in particular), campus unrest, pollution, crime, and economic problems were of central concern. In 1975, the president's message dealt primarily with the economy and energy. International problems were mentioned last, and then world economic distress was emphasized. Vietnam, that word which came to symbolize conflict and frustration in American politics for nearly a decade, was mentioned just once in passing.[7]

Another sign of the times is the extent of government involvement in each of the categories. Though a discussion of budget allocation will be reserved for a later chapter, it is notable for the present discussion that any such listing for 1960, 1940, 1920, or 1900 would show a decrease in the number of categories and the government programs associated with each. That is another way of stating the obvious fact that no other trend line is steadier than that of increasing government involvement in an expansive set of issue-areas.

Issues and Events

What events have created the needs leading to these issues? Again the discussion must be conducted at a general level and designed primarily to explain contemporary trends. I identify five broad categories of events influential in shaping issues—events of *discovery*, *development*, *communication*, *conflict*, and *control*.

Discovery

Man obviously has a very inventive mind once basic physical and social needs have been met. Scientific breakthroughs require resources, however, so social systems are not equally accommodating to discovery. Where resources are so limited that people go hungry in the streets, as in India for example, little can be allocated to science. Nations with vast resources like the United States and Soviet Union, on the other hand, have encouraged scientific discovery, particularly in the post-World War II period. Only recently have questions been raised about the benefits of science—often by those who claim to have discovered (or perhaps rediscovered) other values. The huge sums freely allocated to research and development—particularly for defense and space exploration—were, by the late 1960s, being cut back and redirected.

Development/Application

Discovery itself has less impact, of course, than application of findings. It is in the development and application of an idea, experiment, or finding that issues are raised. For example, packaging and marketing the internal combustion engine has had a profound effect on people and government in this nation. In fact, the automobile has become such a part of our daily lives it is hard to believe it is such a recent phenomenon. In 1900 there were 8,000 automobiles registered in the United States—fewer than were registered in Aberdeen, South Dakota, in 1970.[8] This national total has increased 11,250 times to well over 100 million cars registered in the 1970s. Two-thirds of this increase has occurred since World War II and one-third in the last decade! Over 10 million motor vehicles of all types were produced in the United States in 1974. Total motor vehicle factory sales in this century have been approximately 280 million (through 1974)—nearly 40 percent of which have been produced in the last decade, 1965-1975.

Comparative figures on population during this century further dramatize the impact of the automobile on our lives. The population of the United States in 1900 was, needless to say, considerably greater than that of Aberdeen, South Dakota. There were 76 million people in this country in 1900—how do you suppose they survived with only 8,000 cars? The total population had not quite tripled by 1970; and yet whereas the ratio of cars to people in 1900 was about 1:10,000, in 1970 the ratio was almost 1:2. Automobile production now is actually two and one-half times the annual number of births.

The effects of this eventful discovery are staggering. We must build roads (over three million miles exclusive of city and town streets), repair the automobiles (over 400,000 business establishments employing two million people), take care of the residue (seven million cars junked each year), feed the creatures (approximately 90 to 100 *billion* gallons of gasoline each year), treat the polluted air, control the traffic, bury the dead (50,000 each year), pave the central business districts for parking, spread seven million tons of rock salt on highways in the winter, watch public transportation systems go bankrupt, etc., etc. With this enormous public investment of time, energy, and resources, one can come to appreciate why the energy shortage of the mid-1970s came to have dramatic effect on the whole social system. Without our cars, we not only cannot get around, but the shape, form, dispersion, and other physical characteristics of our cities are nonfunctional.

Communication

A revolution has been wrought in communication just in my lifetime. Radio was in its infancy when I was born. Now practically every home has two or three. Most children own a radio—can hold within the palm of their hand a device which will give them instant reports on what is going on in the rest of the world. Ninety-five percent of American households have television sets (30 percent have two or more). Over 80 percent of American households have telephones. There are, on the average, nearly 500 million telephone conversations *daily* in this country. The typical home is, in fact, a small communications center, potentially providing more information, entertainment, and contact with the outside than was available to whole communities in the last century.

The total impact of these communication "events" is inestimable. Rather than attempting to assess it, one is advised to weigh the effect on the development of specific issues. Consider, for example, the role of television in the urban and campus disorders of the 1960s. "The whole world is watching" was an appropriate chant by street demonstrators during the Democratic Convention in Chicago, 1968. Americans get daily news accounts of injustices, conflicts, discoveries, and decisions that were formerly directed to a privileged few. If information is power, then we have had tremendous dispersal of power in the past three decades. It seemed apparent that national policy in Vietnam in the late 1960s came to be very much influenced by media coverage of the war. On-the-spot coverage of battles, interviews with villagers, demonstrated inconsistencies (if not falsehoods) in discussing policies, soldier complaints about the conduct of the war—all combined with apparent affect on organization, policy, publicity, and, ultimately, strategy. Imagine the effect alone of hearing "our boys" criticize the war; or that the revered American soldier committed the atrocities at My Lai; or that U.S. planes bombed hospitals, schools, and our own troops.

Conflicts

The fantastic events of discovery, development, and communication in my lifetime have certainly not ridded us of conflict. Indeed, many break-through events in these other categories can be traced to conflict—particularly in meeting the needs of war. One can never know how it might have turned out had events been different, but major domestic and international conflict has become an accepted part of life. The total impact of war on a society is obvious; the effects of specific commitments, strategies, expenditures, are less clear. The sharp contrast between resource commitments to the declared "war on poverty" and the undeclared war in Vietnam was sufficient to activate normally quiescent citizens.

It is probably too early to determine whether campus conflict was beneficial or not—and even long-term appraisal depends on one's goals for a university. But the effects can hardly be denied. Whatever happens in the future, the curriculum, faculty-student-administration relationships, funding processes, priority setting, and university relations with the outside community are unlikely to return to the *status quo ante bellum*.

Control

By "control events" I refer to those private and public (with emphasis on the latter) sets of controls on social behavior. Since much of this book seeks to describe and analyze the American national government—a major control mechanism—it is not necessary to engage in a lengthy discussion at this point. It is sufficient here to offer illustrations of major control events (or sets of events): the military draft, the income tax amendment, expanding the meaning of the commerce clause in the Constitution, accepting Keynesian economics, passage of welfare programs (1930s, 1960s). Since most of these are properly considered in common parlance as "policies," we will return to discuss them specifically in later chapters.

Notes

1. Raymond A. Bauer and Kenneth J. Gergen, *The Study of Policy Formation* (New York: Free Press, 1968), p. 15.

2. John Dewey, *The Public and Its Problems* (Denver: Alan Swallow, 1927), p. 12.

3. Dewey, *The Public and Its Problems*, pp. 15-16.

4. David G. Smith, "Pragmatism and the Group Theory of Politics," *American Political Science Review*, vol. 58 (September 1964), p. 602.

5. The most recent at this writing is Henry Owen and Charles L. Schultze, eds., *Setting National Priorities: The Next Ten Years* (Washington, D.C.: The Brookings Institution, 1976).

6. In addition to publications by these organizations, see the National Urban Coalition, *Counterbudget: A Blueprint for Changing National Priorities*, 1971–1976 (New York: Praeger, 1971) and the Report of the President's Commission on National Goals, *Goals for Americans* (Englewood Cliffs, N.J.: Prentice-Hall, 1960).

7. The message is most accessible in *The Congressional Quarterly Weekly Report*, January 18, 1975, pp. 140–143.

8. Statistics used throughout this brief section are drawn primarily from U.S. Bureau of the Census data in various volumes of the *Statistical Abstract of the United States*, (Washington, D.C.: U.S. Government Printing Office); *County and City Data Book* (Washington, D.C.: U.S. Government Printing Office); and David Ash, *Automobile Almanac* (New York: Essandess, 1967).

3

The Politics of Getting Problems to Government

Functional Activities	Categorized in Government	and as Systems	with Output
Perception Definition Aggregation Organization Representation	Problem to Government	Problem Identi- fication	Problem to Demand

T he number of public problems is so great as to be incalculable, particularly when defined in terms of how various people view the effects of events in society. Clearly, not all of these get on the agenda of government. The process by which some get there and others do not is extremely important because the specific demands resulting from awareness of problems become the "stuff" of government in a democratic society.

I have identified a number of functional activities associated with getting problems to government (see above). It is important to emphasize that these activities represent *potential* developments when events occur in society. There is no guarantee that they will occur in this sequence, or at all. Sometimes groups organize and seek representation for general purposes, without having specifically defined particular problems. Indeed, they may be successful in getting policy programs enacted despite the fact that no one is quite sure what the problem is. Nor is there a definite set of limits or standards by which one can say "this problem has been completely defined by all those affected by this event." It is essential that the reader be reminded throughout that we are seeking to provide the basis for analyzing process here—recall my biases outlined in Chapter 1—and not set down hard-and-fast rules as to what must happen within any one issue-area. The purpose is to encourage study of public problems and how they are acted on in government.

The Functional Activities—
Problem to Government

Perception/Definition

Perception obviously is important at all stages of policy development and implementation. Everyone along the line has perceptions about the many elements involved in policy. For now, however, we will concentrate on the early stages in which events themselves are perceived.

When something happens in society, those who perceive it at all will more than likely give different accounts of what happened. Sometimes these accounts differ so much that it is inconceivable everyone is perceiving the same event. And the individual who, by some objective method, has misperceived what has happened may well consider that the event has created "a human need for which relief is sought" (the definition of a problem). Of high relevance in relieving the need is that someone (perhaps the individual himself) determine how the event was perceived. That is no simple matter, but, in most cases, it doesn't make all that much difference because we put up with lots of discomfort and compromise and half measures everyday to solve our problems. The crucial point is when it does matter—when those affected decide that enough is enough. Policy actors must be sensitive to such stress points if they want continuing support.

Perception is important in the policy process, therefore, because it conditions definitions of problems. "Definition" is a second significant functional activity. As used here, "perception" simply means to receive and register an event—to be aware of or conscious of something happening—through sight, sound, touch, smell. Involved in that comprehension, that registration, is an interpretation. The event is viewed in a particular way. Thus, *perception will refer to the event. Definition refers to problems.* Something happens; someone perceives it in a particular way and defines it as a problem.

The second definition of "definition" in *Webster's New Collegiate Dictionary*—the "act or power of making definite and clear or of bringing into sharp relief"—is serviceable for present purposes if we add the phrase "the effect of an event." Again, people "define" for themselves and for others. That is, they bring into "sharp relief" the effects of events in society—frequently with the result that a problem is defined. Our interest picks up, of course, when the effects of events are defined as problems and efforts are made to resolve them.

Of course, many of the problems that eventually get to government were first created by the implementation of policy. That is, government causes the event perceived and defined as a problem for an individual or group.

Let's try to be somewhat more concrete. Take the case of urban renewal. The steady deterioration of the central business district of a large city is perceived by a variety of individuals and groups. This deterioration is defined as a whole series of problems and relief is sought. Government is involved—courses of action are developed, legitimized, and implemented. Let's assume that the government authorizes clearing an area—removal of substandard (by someone's definition) dwellings and buildings—for subsequent redevelopment by private developers. The program is initiated in a large city. You are a private citizen living in the area and operating a small drug store which serves a clientele in the area to be cleared. The event of immediate relevance to you is the impending destruction of your home and business. Problems as defined by others cannot be solved without affecting you. What is your response? You may simply accept the circumstances and move away. You may have made an effort earlier to prevent the implementation of the policy decision. Or perhaps someone else is concerned about your plight and your relative lack of access to decision makers and decides to represent you in the political process. Your efforts, or others' efforts in your behalf, may constitute an event that others perceive and define as a problem for them. So it goes—or so it may go in the process of problems getting to government. How it goes should be the subject of your analysis.

Aggregation/Organization

Implicit in the discussion of "public problems" is the notion of aggregation. Dewey talks about "those who are affected ... to such an extent that it is deemed necessary to have ... consequences systematically cared for." Thus publics are aggregates. Also implied is a degree of organization. That is, if aggregates are going to have "consequences sytematically cared for," they are going to have to organize for action. Immediately one can see some important factors which may determine what happens in policy making. For example, the number of people affected, the extent to which they aggregate, and the degree and type of organization all may influence the policy process and the particular outcome in regard to the problems being acted on. Let me reemphasize that these functional activities do not necessarily occur with all public problems. And when they do occur, it is not always in the same manner. In fact, one principal concern in policy study is the extent to which they do occur and the particular pattern which is involved.[1]

In his treatment of interest groups, David B. Truman makes a strong case that study of a group's formal organization will reveal important features of relevance for policy making. One can determine the degree of cohesion, expectations of permanence, internal division of labor, and formalized values—all of which can "intimately affect the survival and influence of the group."[2] The particular form of the structure (federated or unitary) depends on the problems which unite members in the first place, the scope of these problems, the resources of the group, its leadership, and its belief in democratic values. Not infrequently, of course, an "active minority" emerges to interpret the needs and wants of members.[3] Again, the possibility of incongruity between the perceptions of those affected and the perceptions of their representatives develops.

Representation

With the fascinating concept of representation, we begin to work our way from the events in society to the actions designed to relieve the tensions perceived to exist. Many books have been written on the subject of representation. About the best we can do here is acknowledge the almost limitless dimensions of the term. For example, representation is used to describe participation in the Miss America contest, an American Legionnaire's antics at his annual convention, the lawyer-client relationship, a national nominating convention, and the variety of relationships between legislators and constituents. It can be interpreted in terms of a "mirror reflection" or a trusteeship or a mandate to act as the represented would act if they could be there.[4]

Fortunately we don't have to solve all of the dilemmas raised by a full inquiry into the dimensions of representation. Our interest in it is primarily as a means of access to government for publics with problems. Representation can be the link between people, their problems, and government. We don't expect that it works in a particular way for everyone who has a need—some people get represented, others don't. What does interest us in this inquiry is the particular manner in which representation occurs in regard to a specific public problem (and, for purposes of generalization, the similarities and differences among representational patterns). Involved are such considerations as the event and how it is perceived by the represented and the representative; the effects of the event and whether (and how) these are defined as problems by the represented and the representative; the extent to which those affected are represented at all; and the impact of the process.

Though this discussion is not confined to representation in any one institution, legislative representation illustrates the complexity of the process. One may be represented at many points and in various ways by legislator-representatives because they get involved in many of the functional activities of the policy process. Thus, as you examine specific issue-areas and public problems, consider that representation by and access to legislators may vary from issue to issue (the issue dimension), among the activities involved in the formulation of a course of action (formulation dimension), among the stages in the legislative process (legislative process dimension), among the actions in administering policy to the problem (administration dimension), or among the many service activities of legislative offices (constituency service dimension).[5]

The relationship among the several functional activities is important to consider. Thus, for example, if representation is a linkage between the problem and action, it is critical to consider which perceptions, definitions, and aggregations get represented. If events can result in various problems (depending as they do upon definition), and some publics have more access than others to decision making, then obviously policy output is affected accordingly. Consider our friend living in the ghetto, the one whose home and business are being demolished for urban renewal. Let's assume that he has some awareness of the deterioration of the area—he could hardly escape perceiving it. Yet he defines a different set of problems resulting from the deterioration than does the department store owner in the nearby central business district or the commuter who speeds past the area on the freeway. He may see zoning violations, lack of police protection, inadequate lighting, lack of recreation facilities. Yet the area has been designated for urban renewal; other definitions of the problems of the area are being represented. As the bulldozer knocks his house down, can't you hear our friend saying, "Very interesting, but that is not exactly what I had in mind as a solution." For various reasons, his perceptions and definitions— even if aggregated with others in the same position (or perhaps because they are not aggregated)—are not reflected in the policy-making process.[6]

This case brings us to some intriguing elements of representation. How is it possible for a group of affluent representatives (whether they be legislators or bureaucrats) to know enough about poverty publics to represent their perceptions of events and definitions of problems? How can they identify with them? Isn't it highly probable that they will tend to represent those who are more like themselves? Is it possible for affluent representatives to empathize with poverty publics? A nice word—empathy—and it appears to be a significant element of representation as an activity. Professor Henry Clay Smith defines empathy as "the tendency of a perceiver to assume that another person's feelings, thoughts, and behavior are similar to his own."[7] It seems that if a representative is to act for another person, or for a constituency, on the specific consequences of events in society, he must try to act in such a way that he is led to make the underlying assumptions of "empathy." By the nature of the representative process, he tries to create conditions whereby he can assume that others' "feelings, thoughts, and behavior are similar to his own," given the case at hand. Can this be done with the problems of the poor? No doubt some representatives are successful in attaining a high measure of empathic accuracy in such circumstances, but there are many obstacles to success.

Housing for the poor provides a good illustration of what I am talking about. For the most part, federal public housing policy is based on very little information about either the problem as defined by ghetto residents or about the priorities of problems in the ghetto.[8] Professor Nathan Glazer notes we have only limited information about the effects of poor housing (thus raising the question as to what the real problems of the ghetto are).

> What is the effect of substandard and crowded housing on the families that live in it? Here we reach into the murkiest of sociological depths. I have indicated how culture-bound are our definitions of "the standard" and "the crowded." We can find examples of entire societies living in housing that by our measures are substandard and crowded, and yet these conditions seem not to create a serious problem for family living.[9]

For the most part federal housing policy has concentrated on the problems with which the policy makers were familiar. We work with what we know. Glazer speaks of "the consistent bias in this country in favor of the owner-occupied, single-family, free-standing house, with a bit of land around it." Slums get the attention of "reformers, writers, analysts"; but

> ... it is the single-family, owner-occupied home—getting it built, getting it financed, saving it from banks, reducing its cost, increasing its amenities—that has received the chief attention of elected officials, administrators, and the majority of the American people, perhaps even the poor among them.[10]

The principal effort to aid the poor—public housing—has been a pitiful effort indeed. The number of units authorized to be built by the Housing Act of 1949 (810,000 units over a six-year period) still had not been built in the 1970s. So, too few units have been provided, they have been located in the most undesirable areas, the architecture is frequently unpleasant and sets off public housing as different, it has been limited to the poorest, it breaks up communities. As Professor Glazer notes, not even the poor much like it. "... While poor families on urban renewal sites have priority in entering public housing projects, only a minority do so."[11]

This dismal record was not established purposely. Most representatives have wanted to do the right thing. "Public housing is a graveyard of good intentions," concludes Glazer.[12] The difficulty lies in part with the extent to which it is possible to know what the problems are as defined by those experiencing them.

Interestingly, a related point can be made regarding many problems for affluent publics—though for quite different reasons. As described in Chapter 2, the increasing use in society of the gasoline engine has had considerable impact. One effect which can readily be perceived by commuters is that of air pollution. This effect is defined as a problem by many—a problem of smell, sight, perhaps of physical well-being. Typically, the commuter identifies the source of the problem as the bus, truck, or car emitting oil smoke.[13] Less likely is the conclusion that his or her own new car is also polluting the air, as approximately one gallon of gasoline in ten goes into the atmosphere through the crankcase and tailpipe. Here are consequences which potentially affect the physical well-being of affluent publics.[14] Yet the precise effects of the consequences will have to be defined by technicians, since the ordinary citizen does not have the knowledge necessary to identify these effects. How can representatives know what do do? They are presumably able to achieve a higher degree of empathic accuracy with affluent publics, but what difference does it make if both lack the technical knowledge to determine effects? The result is that policy is developed based on technical information, modified to the extent that affluent publics make demands which are perceived by representatives.

Thus, in the first case—that of public housing—one can legitimately raise the question of whether representatives can achieve empathic accuracy because of the marked differences between those who experience substandard housing and those who represent them. In the second case—that of air pollution—empathic accuracy is more likely but possibly irrelevant to the hazards involved. The point of all of this is simply to alert you to complications inherent in these early stages and to illustrate the fascinating dimensions of one of the most fundamental of democratic concepts—representation.

Conditions for Getting Problems
to Government

It is becoming evident that problems can get to government in various ways. Perhaps candidates learn about certain problems on the campaign trail, or an enterprising journalist writes a series of articles on a local issue, or Ralph Nader issues another of his now-famous reports, or a constituent complains to his congressman, or a bureaucrat encounters unexpected difficulties in administering a program. There is no way to catalogue all of these routes to government. What can be done, however, is to provide a list of some of the factors to look for in analyzing why and how this or that problem got the attention of decision makers. At minimum these factors would include:

The Events Themselves

   Scope—How many people are affected?

Perception—Who perceives what? How many people perceive consequences? What are the results of perception?

Definition—Are the perceived consequences defined as a problem? If so, by whom? Are different problems defined by different people?

Intensity—How intense are those who are affected? Does intensity vary among those affected?

Organization of Groups

Extent—How many members in the groups affected? What is their commitment to the group?

Structure—What is the relationship between members and leaders—hierarchical? democratic? Is professional staff available?

Leadership—How are leaders selected? How much authority do they have? How aggressive are they?

Access

Representation—Are those affected by consequences represented by those in policy-making positions?

Empathy—Are those in policy-making positions likely to empathize with those affected?

Support—Can support be marshaled by those affected?

Policy Process

Structure—What are the relationships between policy actors and those affected—hierarchical? democratic? bargaining? What are the formal requirements of policymaking?

Responsiveness—How responsive are policy actors to those affected? What have been the traditions regarding responsiveness?

Leadership—How are leaders selected? How much authority do they have? How aggressive are they?

Of course these conditions merely guide one's research and study efforts. They do not suggest any one formula for getting problems to government. Analyzing these factors by answering the questions listed assists in identifying how it is that the problem under study came to be acted on. The list also performs the service of illustrating the complex combinations of variables that are instrumental in agenda setting.

Theories of Agenda Setting

Democracy is a system of government based on wide public participation. Since the satisfactory resolution of public problems is one major function of any government, we may expect democracies to be characterized by a high degree of public involvement in agenda setting—i.e., in that important process by which problems deserving action are identified. At the same time, most theorists acknowledge that classical or pure democracy is unachievable in modern society. In fact, massive public participation in the detailed affairs of government can create chaos.

It is with this acknowledgement of a democracy based on limited or specialized participation that the works of David B. Truman and Robert A. Dahl have been an important contribution to our understanding of agenda setting. Truman conceptualized the governmental process as a mosaic of interacting groups—both in and out of government itself. Problem identification occurs within the context of group life. With the effort of groups to solve their problems, Truman identifies an "inevitable gravitation toward government."

> Herein lies the clue to the universal tendency of interest groups to resort to government action in the present day. Such groups will supplement their own resources by operating upon or through that institutionalized group whose powers are most inclusive in that time and place. . . . That institution today is government. . . .
>
> The effects of such reliance upon government are cumulative. Just as the direct and indirect effects of an interest group may disturb the equilibriums of related groups, so its operations through and upon government are likely to force the related groups also to assert their claims upon governmental institutions in order to achieve some measure of adjustment.[15]

Dahl posits "a preface to democratic theory" which incorporates much of the group approach but addresses the matter of how public policy is made. Selected quotes from this important work reveal his conceptualization of what he terms "the American hybrid" of democratic decision making.

> . . . on matters of specific policy the majority rarely rules. . . . elections are a crucial device for controlling leaders. . . . specific policies tend to be products of "minorities rule."[16]

Dahl argues in summary that:

> A central guiding thread to American constitutional development has been the evolution of a political system in which all the active and legitimate groups in the population can make themselves heard at some crucial stage in the process of decision.[17]

Here then is an image of a working democracy as an interlacement of "active and legitimate groups" identifying problems and bargaining for solutions. Roger W. Cobb and Charles D. Elder summarize the tenets of this revised democratic theory as including:

> (1) social pluralism, (2) diverse and competing elites that are circulating and accessible, (3) a basic consensus at least among the elites on the rules of democratic competition, and (4) elections that provide regular opportunities for citizens to participate in the selection of public officials.

Cobb and Elder correctly refer to this as a system of *limited participation* and add that "there can be no doubt [it] is empirically more viable as a descriptive statement of functioning democracies than is classical theory."[18]

While it may be descriptively accurate, some political scientists have rejected the revised theory as prescriptively desirable. For the fact is that limiting participation to the "active and legitimate groups" in society is by definition going to result in a biased agenda of public problems. "Active" implies organization, structure, leadership, support, and available resources. Not everyone in the society who is experiencing problems has these advantages. "Legitimate" implies having met some standard of social acceptability. Whatever those standards are, certain groups are excluded. Perhaps we should be more blunt. It is, or should be, no news to you that the American system has been biased toward the affluent. In fact, judged solely by what gets on the agenda of government it is fair to say that the affluent have more problems than the poor. That is, those with the resources to organize and communicate have an advantage in a system designed to respond to "active and legitimate groups." Indeed, even the problems of the poor frequently get represented by the affluent in our society. This is, after all, a highly opulent society with a large middle class and a store of material goods so enormous as to be incomprehensible.

While many scholars have challenged the acceptability of "the American hybrid," E. E. Schattschneider, Peter Bachrach, and Morton S. Baratz have proposed particularly interesting and relevant analyses. In his book, *The Semisovereign People*, Schattschneider clearly illustrates "the scope and bias of the pressure system." He challenges the notion that politically active group life is common in the United States. "The range of organized, identifiable, known groups is amazingly narrow; there is nothing remotely universal about it."[19] That which does exist, according to Schattschneider, "has an upper-class bias." The importance of this observation is not only in what any one group gets from government but also in the control of what becomes the proper business of government. For Schattschneider, competition is the essence of democracy and he is distressed to find that it exists only to the extent of producing a "semisovereign people."[20]

Bachrach and Baratz posit "two faces of power"—one in which decisions are made to favor one group or set of groups and a second in which conditions are created for excluding certain issues from being considered in government. They explain it thus:

> Of course power is exercised when A participates in the making of decisions that affect B. Power is also exercised when A devotes his energies to creating or reinforcing social and political values and institutional practices that limit the scope of the political process to public consideration of only those issues which are comparatively innocuous to A. To the extent that A succeeds in doing this, B is prevented . . . from bringing to the fore any issues that might in their resolution be seriously detrimental to A's set of preferences.[21]

Following Schattschneider, Bachrach and Baratz specify a "mobilization of bias" in the political system—i.e., "a set of predominant values, beliefs, rituals, and institutional procedures . . . that operate systematically and consistently to the benefit of certain persons and groups at the expense of others."[22] The means for sustaining this mobilization of bias is something called "nondecision making."

> A nondecision, as we define it, is a decision that results in suppression or thwarting of a latent or manifest challenge to the values or interests of the decision maker. To be more nearly explicit, nondecision making is a means by which demands for change in the existing allocation of benefits and privileges in the community can be suffocated before they are even voiced; or kept covert; or killed before they gain access to the relevant decision-making arena; or, failing all these things, maimed or destroyed in the decision-implementing stage of the policy process.[23]

It is not necessary for our purposes to employ the rather awkward and inapt term of "nondecision." We can simply record that governmental agenda-setting processes may well favor some groups and their problem definitions over others, or even actively prevent access for certain interests. Actually there is not very much new about the idea. It is a rather common theme throughout much of American history—"the rich get richer" and all that. What is common knowledge often is not incorporated into intellectual discourse and theorizing, however. Thus, whole books get written about the American political system without so much as a mention of what and how problems get to government, or the importance of finding out.

Having acknowledged the bias of a system which provides open access for "active and legitimate groups," the social architect is faced with the difficult problem of what should be done. Schattschneider was satisfied to provide for competition. "Democracy is a competitive political system in which competing leaders and organizations define the alternatives of public policy in such a way that the public can participate in the decision-making process."[24] Presumably for him there are ways to define alternatives (including how problems are to be defined and priorities set) so that the public can participate. Once that is done, it is up to the public to get cracking and involve themselves. What if they don't? Schattschneider doesn't say, but the definition suggests that the job is done if competing leaders do what he proposes.

What becomes very evident in this review of theories is that agenda setting is a complex and tricky business in a democracy. Simply maintaining an open process favors the strong; doing anything else creates other biases. It is appropriate here to reiterate one of the initial realities: "All policy systems have a bias." At minimum there appear to be the following agenda-setting options—each considered here with the problems it creates.

1. Let it happen. In this first, highly pluralistic option, government takes a relatively passive role in agenda setting. It maintains channels of access and communication so that those affected can be heard, but it does not reach out either to assist individuals and groups to define problems and organize or to assume the task of problem definition and priority setting. This option is pluralistic in the sense that its success depends on many of the tenets of the group theory of politics—that people will define their own interests, organize, seek access, involve others in support of their cause, influence decision making, monitor implementation, etc.

While "letting it happen" is attractive in concept, as Schattschneider and others point out, it also may be highly preferential. It simply ignores the fact that resources are unevenly distributed in the society. Nor are all groups of equal stature in the community. The fact is that a free system of this type favors those who have over those who don't—and that edge may well extend to how the process works as well as to what it produces.

2. Encourage it to happen. In this second option, the government reaches out to assist people in defining and articulating their problems. The bias of a totally free system toward the strong over the weak is acknowledged and an effort is made to equalize resources so that the process of agenda setting does not favor one group or set of interests over another. Note that the emphasis here is in equipping people to participate—not in assuming the tasks of identifying and defining problems for them. Thus, for example, the poor are, by some means, provided with resources to get involved in politics and policy making—to make themselves heard, in Dahl's terms. The Economic Opportunity Act of 1964 (the War on Poverty) did provide means to this end by supporting community action agencies in poverty areas.

This option, too, has problems associated with it. Those in government are put in the position of determining who needs assistance. Bias may just as easily result—as the rural poor might well have argued in regard to the poverty program. Equally troublesome is the question of whether democratic government should be in the business of building up its own agenda by providing support for certain groups. Then there is the matter of whether government is equipped to solve or even relieve the problems identified. Again the poverty program of the 1960s demonstrated some of the risks in raising the hopes, but not necessarily the income level, of the poor.

3. Make it happen. In this third option, government plays an active role in defining problems and setting goals. Policy makers do not wait for the system to work; they direct its operations by establishing problem-defining and priority-setting mechanisms within government. Government must define problems, set priorities, and establish goals with the two other options as well. But in those cases, these activities follow the signals and demands of the public. That is, political decision makers are faced with the task of giving weight to this or that pressure which has either been expressed freely or been encouraged by government. In the third case, however, decision makers do not await the emergence of demands. They systematically review societal events for their effects and set an agenda of government action.

The problems with this approach are, or should be, obvious. It places an enormous burden on government. Surveying events, judging the consequences, and setting priorities in a complex society are difficult and demanding responsibilities. Few governments have been able to accomplish these tasks successfully. And there is the further question of whether *democratic* government can achieve these ends and remain true to its principles.

Here then are three modes of government agenda setting in a democracy—from the more traditional case in which decision makers await pressures to act, to the more activist role of encouraging pressures from certain groups (essentially providing support for the process) and actually monitoring events so as to determine effects and judge where action is needed. I have identified the first method as more traditional because even now it seems to predominate in this country. We still tend to "let it happen," even when preferential treatment and deliberateness (if not downright sluggishness) invite legitimate criticism and/or social, economic, or political disaster (as with much of the debate and policy action on energy problems.) I have a label for this dominant mode. I call it *preferential pluralism* and we will have frequent opportunity to illustrate how it works throughout the book.

The other options are based on the assumption that public problems deserving government action are either not being represented in the system or are actively excluded by the "mobilization of bias" that leads to non-decision making. This conclusion has been gaining support in recent decades, particularly in reference to various socially and economically disadvantaged groups. I have already mentioned the development of community action agencies under the poverty program. Civil rights and consumer-oriented agencies would be other examples, as would various shifts to affirmative action within established agencies. We have no examples as yet of a *comprehensive* effort to "make it happen," at least to my knowledge. The five-year plans so popular at one time in Communist countries have not been developed in the United States. Still, given the predominance of middle- and upper-class representation in government, plans to relieve the problems of the poor are typically designed by those with limited subjective evidence on the topic. Put another way, the practice of middle-class decision makers of "making it happen" for lower-class publics may satisfy the demands of the third option, but it also illustrates some of the serious pitfalls.

One final point must be emphasized in this discussion of agenda-setting theories. Conclusions about the predominant mode are based primarily on domestic problems and policies. Government decision makers try to "make it happen" in foreign and defense issue-areas. They make a much more comprehensive effort to define the problems, set the priorities, and establish goals than is ever the case in the domestic arena. At the same time, many critics of the defense establishment point out that decisions are heavily influenced by certain basic industries and therefore decision makers are in fact "letting it happen"—that is, permitting industry to define the problems and set the priorities.

Types of Agendas

In his study of agenda-setting strategies for pollution policies, Layne D. Hoppe makes a fundamental point of interest to students of public policy.

> "Agenda" [comes] to have meaning in terms of specific patterns of action in government—particularly those in the early stages of policy development. An analysis of agenda-setting processes [becomes] an analysis of how problems developed, how they were defined, the courses of action formulated to act on these problems, the legitimation of one course of action over another, the emergence of policy systems designed to act on such problems on a continuing basis. The result [is] that it [is] most difficult to isolate an agenda-setting process as an identifiable, one-time, discrete process.[25]

This advisory serves to warn the student not to conceptualize the policy process as too segmented, with each activity cleanly isolable from the others. It also suggests the pitfalls in any effort at identifying various types of agendas as though each were a definite "thing" existing in some governmental office as a kind of schedule of events.

Still the term "agenda" is commonly used and does convey definite meaning as a listing of items for action. Use of the term varies considerably in the specificity of its reference point. For example, it might refer to items to be taken up at a township meeting next Wednesday evening, proposals made in the president's state of the Union message, or the general condition of the policy. Cobb and Elder have sought to clarify the usage by distinguishing between the *systemic agenda* and the *institutional agenda*. The first is defined as "all issues that are commonly perceived by members of the political community as meriting public attention and as involving matters within the legitimate jurisdiction of existing governmental authority."[26] While each of us can, no doubt, nominate issues which meet these criteria (at least, in our individual judgment), the concept itself is difficult to operationalize. Essentially it comes down to personal assessments of what ought to be acted on in government because of the scope of the problem, public concern, and the jurisdiction of government. We all have our lists. Presumably the systemic agenda would be the composite of these lists. If such an agenda were compiled on a regular basis, it might well serve to direct the third agenda-setting option above—i.e., "making it happen." That is, one could compare the institutional and systemic agendas and direct attention to those issues currently being ignored. Unfortunately the systemic agenda is not so readily compilable and we are, therefore, left with individual and group assessments as to what ought to be treated.

Cobb and Elder define the institutional agenda as "that set of items explicitly up for the active and serious consideration of authoritative decision makers."[27] They make a distinction between serious and "pseudo-agenda items" to account fot those issues which may get only vocal attention from decision makers. Once again the precise identification of the agenda is no simple matter since one must establish criteria for determining what constitutes "active and serious consideration." Further, it is essential that one specify the functional object of the consideration—for example, is it to define the problem? develop a solution? form a majority? In other words, why and how is an item being worked on at all? That question takes us back to the functional activities of policy making and suggests several institutional agendas.

> *Problem definition agenda:* Those items receiving "active and serious" research and definition.
> *Proposal agenda:* Those items which have reached the proposal stage—where the shift has been made from defining the problem to finding a solution.

Bargaining agenda: Those proposals for which support is "actively and seriously" developed.

Continuing agenda: Those items receiving continuous examination. Cobb and Elder refer to "habitual items . . . that come up for regular review."[28]

This breakdown should assist in studying government action on individual public problems, both aiding the analysis of what happens within a single issue and facilitating comparisons between issues. As with the set of functional activities identified in Chapter 1, there is no necessary or inevitable agenda sequence for any one public problem. Thus, for example, an item may never proceed beyond the problem definition agenda, or proposals may be developed over a long period of time—as with a national health plan. Having arrived on one agenda is no guarantee of a ticket to the next.

Finally, note should be taken of the formal expressions of agenda items. The more obvious ones were mentioned earlier—the state of the Union message, budget messages, specific policy messages by the president, counter assessments by congressional party leaders. These normally contain items from all of the functional agendas cited above. The president may, in the same message, request research monies to define, say, the problems of rail passenger service (problem definition agenda); make a definite proposal for manpower retraining (proposal agenda); make a plea for public support of an anticrime program (bargaining agenda); and request a reauthorization of a wheat subsidy program (continuing agenda).

In addition, however, one must look for formal expressions of agenda items within the agencies and congressional committees for indications of whether public problems are receiving "active and serious consideration" by decision makers. Not all institutional agenda items reach the White House. Much research, definition, planning, and building support occurs within the labyrinthian structure of government. In fact, the really crucial agenda-setting processes for certain problems may occur deep within a department or congressional committee where specialists determine priorities and negotiate solutions. So—while determining what reaches the high levels of government is, in itself, an important task for studying agenda setting, analysis of what happens with regard to particular public problems and issues may well require extensive probing of the work plans and schedules of governmental subunits.

Agenda-Setting Strategies

I have already emphasized that there is no one single route to government. Some problems are treated because they are immediate and of enormous scope (as with those following a natural disaster); others may require continuous strategic planning in order to get the government's attention. It is this second type which I wish to discuss briefly now.

Of the several conditions important for getting problems to government, organization and access in particular are important for determining group strategies. Consider the following variations (four among scores of possible combinations):

1. A well-organized group with established access (e.g., the American Medical Association).
2. A well-organized group without established access (e.g., any group which, though well organized for other purposes, has never found it necessary to go to government).
3. A poorly organized group with established access (e.g., farmers or others with definite advantages in access but limited capacity for defining their interests).
4. A poorly organized group without established access (e.g., many of the socially and economically disadvantaged groups in the society).

Presumably the first group will simply employ its advantages in getting problems attended to in government. Its strategic planning is greatly simplified by its unity of purpose and political contacts. In fact, much of its effort may go toward containing the issue so as not to incite others who might complicate matters by their reactions.

The second group will probably capitalize on its organizational advantages to gain access to decision makers. Assuming here that strong organization means effective leadership, unity of purpose, and available resources, any group in this second category has obvious potential political punch. Elected decision makers, in particular, can be expected to understand this fact and pay close attention to the group's demands. What I am really saying is that a strong organization can normally depend on having access when it deems it necessary to go to government.

The third type of group has the advantage of access but is incapable of exercising it effectively. In this case strategic planning must be directed toward the group itself—seeking to develop the capacity to identify problems and set priorities. Unless they are able to accomplish this goal, the group may find that problems are consistently defined for them by public decision makers and policies therefore are often inadequate.

Cobb and Elder contribute much to our understanding of the fourth group—essentially the outsiders in the political system, those with few resources to organize or gain access. They argue that agenda setting is facilitated through issue expansion—by involving other individual groups. They list four general types of groups: identification groups (those who identify with another group's interests), attention groups (those aware of the issue at hand), the attentive public ("a generally informed and interested stratum of the population"), and the general public ("less active, less interested, and less informed"). Their underlying proposition is that "the greater the size of the audience to which an issue can be enlarged, the greater the likelihood that it will attain systemic agenda standing and thus access to a formal agenda."[29]

I have already noted that issues of great scope will likely be on governmental agendas. But I was speaking of those issues which result from large-scale, dramatic events with immediate impact (natural disasters, war, the oil embargo). Cobb and Elder are speaking of expanding the scope of an issue as a conscious agenda-setting strategy. Though they do not intend to limit this approach to the poorly organized group without established access, I would argue that they have well described the only strategy available to such groups. The fact is that most policy making is limited to a relatively small number of active participants precisely because it is conducted by and for groups in the first three categories. In other words, issue expansion as an agenda-setting strategy is the exception, not the rule, in American politics. And it is most characteristic of those without the advantages of organization and access. During the 1960s in particular, we witnessed extreme forms of this strategy—including violent protest. It was an era which Amitai Etzioni appropriately dubbed "demonstration democracy."[30]

E. E. Schattschneider's analysis of this whole matter is particularly insightful. On the one hand he notes that "democratic government is the greatest single instrument for the socialization of conflict [read: expansion of the issue] in the American community."[31] On the other hand, he introduces considerable evidence to show the "scope and bias" of the decision-making apparatus. While observing that "nationalization of politics inevitably breaks up old local power monopolies . . .,"[32] he also notes that "a tremendous amount of conflict is controlled by keeping it so private that it is almost completely invisible."[33] And further: "It is the *loser* who calls in outside help."[34] Thus, we must acknowledge that whereas expanding the issue may be a beneficial agenda-setting strategy under certain circumstances, it often represents a last resort for those with established access and/or strong organization.

I can do no more here than emphasize that whatever is done depends very much on the political access and organizational resources of those perceiving a problem. The precise manner in which a group capitalizes on its access, develops greater organizational strength, or seeks to increase public awareness in order to influence agenda setting remains a matter to examine for each problem studied.

Notes

1. Gabriel A. Almond and others use the term "aggregation" quite differently. They use it to refer to the conversion of demands into policy alternatives—our formulation and legitimation functions. See Gabriel A. Almond and G. Bingham Powell, Jr., *Comparative Politics: A Developmental Approach* (Boston: Little, Brown, 1966), Ch. 5.

2. David B. Truman, *The Governmental Process* (New York: Knopf, 1951), p. 113.

3. Truman, pp. 139–155.

4. For a superb summary of the dimensions of representation, see Hanna F. Pitkin, *The Concept of Representation* (Berkeley: University of California Press, 1967).

5. I once discussed these dimensions in a seminar attended by a state legislator. He acknowledged the various dimensions of representation but provided an illustration which did not fit the categories very well. He had prepared an amendment and had lined up the support necessary for passage. When the time came to introduce the amendment, however, he couldn't find it on his desk; the bill passed without amendment while he continued to rummage through his papers. I resisted his suggestion for a sixth category—the "Stupidity Dimension."

6. For such examples, see Herbert Gans. *The Urban Villagers* (New York: The Free Press, 1962).

7. Henry Clay Smith, "Empathy," in Charles Press and Alan Arian, eds., *Empathy and Ideology* (Chicago: Rand McNally, 1966), p. 111.

8. The literature on public housing is much too abundant to list here. For a sampling, however, read Lawrence M. Friedman, *Government and Slum Housing* (Chicago: Rand McNally, 1968); Scott Greer, *Urban Renewal and American Cities* (New York: Bobbs-Merrill, 1965); Robert Taggart III, *Low-Income Housing: A Critique of Federal Aid* (Baltimore: Johns Hopkins Press, 1970); and the many books by Charles Abrams, Daniel Wilner, Jane Jacobs, and Catherine Bauer.

9. Nathan Glazer, "Housing Problems and Housing Policies," *The Public Interest* (Spring 1967), p. 22.

10. Glazer, p. 29.

11. Glazer, p. 35.

12. Glazer, p. 38.

13. See, for example, the survey results in St. Louis on the awareness of pollution: U.S. Department of Health, Education, and Welfare, Public Health Service, *Public Awareness and Concern with Air Pollution in the St. Louis Metropolitan Area* (Washington, D.C., May 1965). In answer to the question of what air pollution meant to them, respondents most frequently mentioned odor (56 percent). Only 15.6 percent mentioned motor vehicle exhausts.

14. Of course, the poor are affected as well, but air pollution is often the least of their concerns in the priorities of needs.

15. Truman, pp. 105–106.

16. Robert A. Dahl, *A Preface to Democratic Theory* (Chicago: University of Chicago Press, 1956), pp. 124, 131, 133.

17. Dahl, p. 137.

18. Robert W. Cobb and Charles D. Elder, "The Politics of Agenda-Building: An Alternative Perspective for Modern Democratic Theory," *Journal of Politics*, vol. 33 (November 1971), p. 895.

19. E. E. Schattschneider, *The Semisovereign People* (New York: Holt, Rinehart and Winston, 1960), p. 30.

20. See Schattschneider, pp. 140–141.

21. Peter Bachrach and Morton S. Baratz, *Power and Poverty: Theory and Practice* (New York: Oxford University Press, 1970), p. 7.

22. Bachrach and Baratz, p. 43.

23. Bachrach and Baratz, p. 44.

24. Schattschneider, p. 141.

25. Layne D. Hoppe, "Agenda-Setting Strategies: Pollution Policy," unpublished Ph.D. dissertation, University of Arizona, 1969, p. 2.

26. Roger W. Cobb and Charles D. Elder, *Participation in American Politics: The Dynamics of Agenda-Building* (Boston: Allyn and Bacon, 1972), p. 85.

27. Cobb and Elder, p. 86.

28. Cobb and Elder, p. 88.

29. Cobb and Elder, p. 110.

30. Amitai Etzioni, *Demonstration Democracy* (New York: Gordon and Breach, 1970).

31. Schattschneider, p. 13.

32. Schattschneider, p. 11.

33. Schattschneider, p. 7.

34. Schattschneider, p. 16.

4

Formulating Policy Proposals

Functional Activities	Categorized in Government	and as Systems	with Output
Formulation	Action in Government	Program Development	Proposal

Charles E. Lindblom, one of the leading students of the policy process in this country, makes a simple but profound statement: "Policy makers are not faced with a *given* problem."[1] That summarizes a lot of what has been said so far in this book. Problems result from any major event—some are perceived and acted on by policy makers, many others are not. Again quoting Lindblom:

> [Policy makers] have to identify and formulate their problem. Rioting breaks out in dozens of American cities. What is the problem? Maintaining law and order? Racial discrimination? Impatience of the Negroes with the pace of reform now that reform has gone far enough to give them hope? Incipient revolution? Black power? Low income? Lawlessness at the fringe of an otherwise relatively peaceful reform movement? Urban disorganization? Alienation?[2]

What Lindblom is describing in essence is a sort of second-level process of problem definition—one engaged in by elected representatives and various other public officials. At this second level, officials are seeking to comprehend the significant effects of social events by receiving and processing subjective and objective data prior to developing proposals for action. How they manage these tasks is of central concern to the student of public policy.

In this chapter we take a turn toward policy action in government. Perceptions, definitions, interpretations of events in society have reached government. What has happened has happened, and various people are aware of it. Now what takes place? People in government discuss what has happened, they do research, they interpret the available data, they prepare proposals, they meet and discuss some more, they check with people outside government, they determine what is possible, they make more proposals, they develop strategies, they coordinate, they refine proposals, they seek support. What comes of all of this activity? Maybe nothing at all concrete. Perhaps the problem has been solved outside government in the meantime. Perhaps the conflicts between the various definitions and interpretations of the problem are too great to resolve—and perhaps these too pass in time.

On the other hand, a definite course of action may be the result of all this activity. Typically, an attempt is then made to legitimate this course of action so that it can be applied to the problem. Another round of activities ensues—involving more discussion, research, meetings, planning, testing, coordination. Strategies are developed, compromise points identified, concessions made, costs analyzed. Again, there may not be any concrete program authorized for the same reasons noted above. I consistently stress this theme to drive home a point seldom appreciated or understood—that much of what happens in government is without immediate programmatic result, though it may well be the groundwork for subsequent policy development.

What Is Formulation and Who Is Involved?

Formulation is a derivative of "formula" and means simply to develop a plan, a method, a prescription—in this case for alleviating some need, for acting on a problem. It is the first of the policy development phases or activities and there is no set method by which it must proceed. That is to say, its distinguishing characteristic is simply that means are proposed by one or more persons to resolve somebody's perception of the needs that exist in society. How well all of that is done, who participates, and who gains an advantage normally will vary from one issue or problem to the next. Here are a few guidelines to assist in analysis of this important activity:

1. Formulation need not be limited to one set of actors. Thus, there may well be two or more formulation groups producing competing (or complementary) proposals.
2. Formulation may proceed without the problem ever being very clearly defined, or without formulators ever having much contact with the affected groups.
3. There is no necessary coincidence between formulation and particular institutions, though it is a frequent activity of executive agencies.

4. Formulation and reformulation may occur over a long period of time without ever building sufficient support for any one proposal.
5. There are often several appeal points for those who lose in the formulation process at any one level.
6. The process itself is never neutral.

These guidelines for study also become advisories for those wishing to influence decision making. Suppose, for example, you were opposed to military training at your university or college and wished to have it removed from the curriculum altogether. Your initial task is to organize others with similar views and make certain that university administrators understand that a problem exists. Once those in authority begin to formulate proposals, you want to ensure that they are doing so in the direction of your interpretation of the problem rather than that of ROTC officials or the local American Legion post. You may wish to formulate your own proposal and build support for it among various university clientele, or you may want to convince others to do so. If you lose the struggle within your university, you may wish to carry the battle to another decision-making point—perhaps challenging the system for the whole state or nation. All of this suggests one central point—*formulation like the other functions discussed here is very much a political, though not necessarily a partisan, activity*. Not even calling it the more neutral term "planning" can change that.

None of this is staggeringly profound—naturally you would want to influence policy makers so that they are sympathetic to your view. Wanting sympathy and actually developing strategies to affect the perceptions of policy actors are quite different, however. The first may only require publicity; the second requires a knowledge and understanding of the intricate realities of decision making in government—perhaps even engaging in a little empathy to measure how it is public officials look at problems.

What is involved in formulation? What has been said so far suggests that there is no single answer to that question. Rather this question becomes a guide for the study of any one problem or issue. Who is involved in formulating a course of action to deal with drought conditions in southeastern Colorado? or floods in the Red River Valley of North Dakota? or welfare cheating in New York City? or mistreatment of nursing home residents? These are empirical questions for which data can be collected once the activity of formulation itself is defined.

Though one cannot generalize about who will be involved in formulation across all issue-areas, it is quite possible to identify the places one might look for participants. At the national level of decision making, the principal focus of discussion in this book, one would normally begin the search in the executive branch—among both the bureaucrats and the political appointees. Typically we think of the executive as the source of planning. The president and his close associates in the White House and cabinet establish the goals and set the priorities which set boundaries for formulation of proposals. The actual development of plans and proposals normally occurs within the bureaucracy, with formal clearance of their actions by the upper echelons of political decision making. In some cases the president may judge that the departments and agencies are either incapable or unlikely to develop suitable recommendations. This conclusion may be a result of his assessment of their institutional bias or because no single agency has responsibility for the problem or problems identified. Thus, he may rely on agencies outside government or appoint a special commission to develop proposals. It should also be noted that agencies, too, often rely on outside assistance—including state and local governments, universities, professional and other interest groups, congressional committee staff, and private research organizations.

Congressmen are also frequently involved in formulation. In fact, it is quite conceivable that a particular formulation network is drawn entirely from legislative actors, to include staff persons, other legislative support units (e.g., the Congressional Research Service, Office of Technology Assessment, and General Accounting Office—all congressional agencies), and those groups outside government whose primary access is within the Congress. A sample of important issue-areas in which members of Congress have played major roles in formulating proposals in recent years would include medical care for the aged, comprehensive health care, mass transit, air and water pollution control, environmental planning, and energy conservation. It should be pointed out that the voluminous congressional committee hearings and staff reports are perhaps the most available documentary sources for determining who is engaged in formulation within an issue-area. These documents may reveal specific persons who have developed plans, what those plans include, how the members of Congress react, and what they propose either as modifications or substitutions. In fact, students of public policy are well advised to begin their analysis of problems on the national agenda by reading the relevant congressional hearings, reports, and debates. No other legislature, indeed, no other political institution, in the world provides such extensive public documentation of its policy actions.

I have already suggested that our political system permits enormous input from sources outside government. Private interests and public institutions and agencies from other governmental levels may develop proposals for consideration within national policy-making units and/or, as indicated above, Washington-based government formulators may seek advice, information, and recommendations from these other sources. Certain of these close connections between interest groups and agencies and congressional committees are obvious. For example:

Group	Executive Department or Agency	Congressional Committees
National Education Association	Office of Education (Department of HEW)	House Education and Labor Senate Labor and Public Welfare
AFL-CIO	Department of Labor	House Education and Labor Senate Labor and Public Welfare
American Farm Bureau Federation	Department of Agriculture	House Committee on Agriculture Senate Committee on Agriculture and Forestry
American Bankers Association	Federal Reserve Board Department of the Treasury	House Committee on Banking, Currency and Housing Senate Committee on Banking, Housing, and Urban Affairs
American Postal Workers Union	U.S. Postal Service	House and Senate Committees on Post Office and Civil Service
American Trucking Associations	Interstate Commerce Commission	House Committee on Interstate and Foreign Commerce Senate Committee on Commerce

These groups know where to go and whom to talk with when it comes to formulating proposals which affect their interests. But they are also sources of information for public policy makers—information about the problems being acted on as well as the probable effect of one or another policy proposal. Lobbying has always been a two-way flow of information resulting in a high degree of mutual reliance between interest groups and government.[3]

Other nongovernmental sources of formulators include the many organizations and institutions in this country that provide public services of various kinds. For example, the private foundations sponsor research and support public institutions (including governments) in various ways. The work of such national foundations as Ford, Rockefeller, Carnegie, and Mellon is familiar. These organizations produce ideas, recommendations, data, analyses, and even personnel to assist those formulating proposals. Two of the cases described at the end of this chapter—those concerning the poverty program and energy conservation—show the direct contribution of the Ford Foundation in policy formulation.

Equally significant in producing material of use in policy formulation are the nation's private or nonprofit research organizations (e.g., the Brookings Institution, American Enterprise Institute, the Urban Institute, the RAND Corporation). Often there are close ties between these organizations and the foundations which support them. Further, as with the RAND Corporation and others, some such operations are little more than extensions of government itself. Don K. Price explains:

> We have seen the creation, under government auspices, of new private corporations to do government business. Most of them have been not-for-profit corporations, chartered under the law of some state—for example, the RAND Corporation, which makes technical and strategic studies for the Air Force; the Aerospace Corporation, which is the Air Force's systems engineer for the development of ballistic missiles; and the Institute for Defense Analyses, which evaluates weapons systems in relation to strategy for the Joint Chiefs of Staff and the Secretary of Defense.[4]

University research, too, has been heavily supported both by the foundations and the national government. In some cases this support is for specific projects, perhaps under contract arrangements with government agencies; in other circumstances support is provided for basic research with no specific product requested. The result has been a close working relationship between the academic community and government in policy formulation—particularly in the post-World War II period. As Charles V. Kidd concludes in his careful study of *American Universities and Federal Research*: "Universities need support for science from government and government needs knowledge obtainable only by university research. As a result, the two have been placed in a state of unprecedented mutual dependence."[5]

Finally, brief mention must be made of the increasing number of citizen organizations which have become active in national policy making. Perhaps most active on a wide range of issues is Common Cause—the citizen's lobby group organized by John Gardner (former secretary of Health, Education, and Welfare). But a large number of environmental and consumer protection groups have joined Ralph Nader's effort to investigate the public effects of government programs and develop counter proposals to those produced by government and special interests.

Here then are a few of the sources of policy formulation—of the information and recommendations that feed into decision making. The student of policy formulation must trace these developments for the issue or problem being examined and identify who is involved, how they interact, and what they produce.

Institutional Limits on Formulation

Though a major purpose of this text is to encourage students to discover cross-institutional and interlevel policy-related networks, still it is essential that institutional limits be acknowledged and assessed for their effect on policy formulation. For however individual decision makers may communicate and otherwise interact with those outside their agency or committee, they are circumscribed by certain features of the constitutional order and existing policy authority. We need do no more than mention the constitutional features of separation of powers, federalism, bicameralism, and checks and balances. They are described and analyzed in countless texts on American government. Suffice it to say here that these principles do establish a decision-making context that cannot be ignored in the study of public policy. At minimum, as structural features these characteristics segment the policy process—thus creating a requirement for cross-institutional contact if the work of government is to be done.

Less well described is the growth of peculiar policy relationships within agencies and committees that come to influence whether and how problems are defined and proposals developed. The incrementalism described by Lindblom comes about in part because institutional characteristics limit what can or will be done. More bluntly, don't expect an agency accustomed to doing things in a particular way to innovate very often. Rather look for an effort to integrate new demands into an existing pattern of doing business.

Why is this so? Why should existing units either resist new demands or integrate them into familiar approaches? At the most simplified level of analysis, people are most satisfied when tomorrow brings the same expectations and responsibilities as today. This is not only because they are comfortable with the familiar, however. Equally important are the networks of contacts and interactions which emerge over time as an institutional unit fulfills its conception of its responsibilities. For example:

1. Clientele or constituency relationships are established and protected.
2. All agencies (and committees) require support and have typically found means for gaining this support.
3. Definite patterns of communication exist—within, between, and outside of existing units.

4. Means are developed for defining problems and formulating proposals—means highly accommodative to the interests presently served.

These interlacements are not easily broken, nor should they be if governmental stability is valued.

This is not to say that institutions are totally impervious to change or are incapable of doing things differently. Rather it is meant to suggest that change will occur within a context of how things have been done in the past. In a sense, therefore, formulation in an issue-area will have a definite pattern. To upset this pattern requires a rather dramatic event—an economic collapse, a war, riots in the streets. The most spectacular case of this type in this century occurred during the Great Depression when the Roosevelt administration acted swiftly to attack the many problems which had developed. Another case might be the general attack on poverty launched by the Johnson administration in 1964. More about that later.

Those who want change, therefore, must ordinarily think in terms of strategies which accommodate the realities of institutionalism. This means that they must take account of certain facts of life—that agents (whether they be bureaucrats, congressmen, presidents, or appointed officials) require support, that procedures exist, that people get used to doing things in a certain way. It is not unnatural for most people to resist large change in their lives. Consider your own reaction if the professor in this course insisted that you meet at 4:00 A.M. instead of the present hour. It's not that you wouldn't be able to adjust, but you probably would rather not have to make that adjustment if something more accommodating to your lifestyle could be worked out.

Types of Formulation

Many types of formulation can be identified, depending on the criteria for classification. For example, one can imagine any number of categories by subject matter—formulation of courses of action for economic problems, education problems, military problems, and so on. Each has a different set of institutional units from which formulators are drawn. Different patterns of formulation develop because of the nature of the problems and the groups affected. Or one can classify formulation by the source of what we might call the "formulation population." That is, are the formulators drawn primarily from inside or outside government or both? Again, processes and behavior would probably differ. If drawn from both inside and outside, does there appear to be one primary institutional base for formulation? As noted earlier, the executive is typically the major source of formulators inside government, but many notable cases of formulation in Congress can be cited. A case illustrating each situation is described below.

But the most interesting and useful basis for classifying formulation is that which identifies the nature of decision making. Three types are offered here:

1. *Routine formulation.* A repetitive and essentially changeless process of reformulating similar proposals within an issue-area that has a well-established place on the agenda of government.
2. *Analogous formulation.* Treating a new problem by relying on what was done in developing proposals for similar problems in the past— i. e., searching for analogies.
3. *Creative formulation.* Treating any problem with an essentially unprecedented proposal, one which represents a break with past practice.

From what has been said so far, we do not expect to see creative formulation very often in government. Even where it occurs as a limited process— say within a particular bureau or subcommittee—the proposal which results will normally be modified along the way. And if it survives to become a government program, look for adjustments toward past practices during the implementation stage. Again, sometimes truly creative programs emerge in government. The poverty program, placing a man on the moon, and the creation of the Tennessee Valley Authority come to mind, as do many of the weapons programs of the Department of Defense. Daniel P. Moynihan describes a case of creative formulation in his account of how the Family Assistance Plan (a proposal to guarantee a minimum income for every family with children) was developed during the Nixon administration. As he points out:

> One of the primary contentions of political science is that things don't change very much, or, rather, very fast. . . . The experience of Family Assistance, however, suggests that . . . an extraordinary, discontinuous, forward movement in social policy *did* occur, and in the very least promising of circumstances. Those who call for "fundamental social change" could . . . point to the events leading up to the proposal and near enactment of the Family Assistance Plan as evidence that "fundamental," rather than merely "incremental," social change *is* a realistic option for American society at this time.[6]

The Family Assistance Plan may also be used to illustrate the point that the product of creative formulation faces enormous difficulties in the legitimation process. Building support for the ordinary is demanding— building support for the unusual is downright taxing. Despite the early success of the plan (being passed in the House of Representatives), the guaranteed income was not enacted into law.

Mention should also be made of "formulation packages." The principal example is the president's program as proposed in the state of the Union and subsequent messages. Many major interest groups, for example, the AFL–CIO, U.S. Chamber of Commerce, American Farm Bureau Federation, also develop broad-scale programs on various issues. The reason for mentioning these packages here is simply to point out that they represent a second formulation process. Proposals are developed for specific issues or problems—whether to treat continuing or new agenda items—and then priorities are set. It is this priority setting that constitutes a subsequent formulation. Decisions must be made as to what proposals are absolutely necessary and which can be sacrificed. Compromise points for each individual item are also identified.

Building support for the package is quite different from gathering it for individual items. Clearly much more effort must be directed toward justifying the relatedness of specific programs and identifying the more marginal items. The enormous complexity of this task frequently drives formulators to a salvaging operation for individual proposals. In other words, the comprehensive support-building effort may be short-lived. And yet there are instances when the president and others produce an integrated package—as with a set of economic proposals—which should, by their analysis, be enacted as a whole. Seldom do elaborate proposals of this type survive the legitimation process intact.

Strategic Considerations in Formulation

I have already begun to ease into a discussion of the legitimation process—that is, having a particular proposal authorized. Not all of the attention of formulators is focused on the problem and how to solve it. They must also think ahead to what is feasible in terms of getting a course of action legitimated. And the closer formulators get to agreement among themselves about a suitable course of action, the more they must consider the requirements and conditions for legitimation. That is, in the early stages of formulation all alternatives are welcome. As discussion and evaluation pare down the alternatives and formulators prepare to offer a definite proposal, however, thought must be given to the attitudes, rules, and demands which circumscribe the behavior of legitimators. So strategic considerations are directed toward the legitimation process—building support for a proposed course of action, maintaining support held previously, deciding where compromises can be made, calculating when and where to make the strongest play and when and where to retreat, and controlling information flow to advantage.

I have not discussed legitimation in any great detail as yet—and it is a marvelously complex concept. I think it is enough now to offer one form of legitimation that will at least allow us to proceed with the present discussion. Let's limit the concept, for the time being, to the notion of majority building in a legislature. In other words, a course of action is legitimate when a majority in both houses of a legislature approve and the chief executive affixes his signature to the measure.

Given the necessity of building a majority coalition of legislators for a particular course of action, formulators must consider all of the factors involved in what sometimes is a complicated operation. Again, conditions may vary greatly. For example, the differences in majority building between the 73rd and 89th Congresses, on the one hand, and the 72nd, 86th, 93rd, and 94th on the other, were very great. In the 73rd (1933-1934) and the 89th (1965-1966), Presidents Franklin D. Roosevelt and Lyndon B. Johnson had huge majorities in the House (196 and 155 seats respectively) and the Senate (23 and 36 seats respectively). Each man had won an overwhelming victory in the popular and electoral votes and could rely on this apparent popular appeal in building majorities in Congress. Under these circumstances, "what the president has formulated, the Congress legitimates." In both Congresses, the first session in particular resulted in a flood of legislation on social and economic problems—the greatest domestic policy output in our history.

In the 72nd (1931-1932), 86th (1959-1960), and 91st (1969-1970) Congresses, however, majority building was not quite so simple. Of the three, President Herbert Hoover had the most frustrating conditions under which to operate. During the 72nd Congress, the Democrats had taken control of the House of Representatives, while the Republicans maintained control of the Senate by only *one* seat. Since the Twentieth Amendment had not yet been passed, the second session of the 72nd Congress took place *after* the 1932 elections. Both the House and Senate were full of "lame ducks," members defeated in the 1932 election but continuing to serve until the new Congress met in 1933. With all of the pressures of virtual economic chaos in the nation, President Hoover, also defeated for reelection, faced insuperable odds in trying to build majorities for courses of action.

During the 86th Congress, a consistently popular president, Dwight D. Eisenhower, was serving his last two years in office. The Democrats controlled the Congress by the enormous margin of 129 seats in the House and 32 seats in the Senate. With the end of the Eisenhower administration in sight, they were intent on recapturing the White House in 1960. Again, the conditions called for very special strategies in building majorities, regardless of whether these were formulated primarily in the executive or elsewhere.

The 93rd and 94th Congresses witnessed some of the weirdest political conditions of our history. In the 93rd, President Richard M. Nixon was buoyed by an incredible landslide victory in the 1972 presidential elections only to be toppled by the Watergate crisis. The full effect of this matter on domestic policy making has yet to be studied, and understandably so since most analysts had their hands full unraveling the unusual and unprecedented constitutional complexities of presidential impeachment and resignation. With the downfall of President Nixon, and as a result of the earlier resignation of Vice President Spiro T. Agnew, a congressionally approved vice president assumed the presidency. Gerald R. Ford was the first vice president to be selected by procedures outlined in the Twenty-fifth Amendment. With huge Democratic majorities being elected to Congress in 1974, an unelected President Ford had to work with an initially confident, though essentially unled, opposition party.

Here then are dramatic cases of presidential-congressional conditions for policy making. Each requires special strategies to supplement the ordinary efforts at majority building. I can do no more here than alert you to this fact and encourage analysis of such conditions as important to understanding policy development and implementation within a particular issue-area at any one point in time.

A subject I have been avoiding so far is that of where formulation ends and legitimation begins. For the purposes of this discussion, let's continue to define legitimation in just one way—the process of building majorities in legislatures. At what point do formulators cease performing that function and begin to perform the function of legitimators? Certainly there is overlap—both functions are part of the overall policy process. One could also say that it is a matter of degree, like everything else. *More important, however, is to establish the point that we don't really care where one ends and the other begins.* These are functional activities which may occur in regard to action on public problems. They do not have to be performed by separate individuals at different times in different institutions. To the extent that persons involved in formulating courses of action for public problems take into account the requirements for building a majority in a legislature, they are actors in the process of legitimation. Simple as that! Well, nothing is as "simple as that," but at least we don't have to get all tied up in calculating where the finish line is for each activity, as though the whole process were some kind of relay race with the baton being passed from one teammate to the next.

Any number of possibilities can be envisaged for combining these two important activities. I suggest three for purposes of discussion:

1. A perfect plan with an imperfect strategy.
2. A perfect strategy with an imperfect plan.
3. A perfect blend.

In the first, the planners propose a course of action that is "perfect" in the sense of dealing with the problem as they define it (and with all the values and preferences implicit in that definition). They are poor strategists, however, and do not take into account the essential conditions for building a majority in favor of their ideal plan, e.g., the political conditions noted above with different Congresses. Perhaps the plan will win approval on its own merits; more likely, however, it will fail. Professors Martin Meyerson and Edward C. Banfield have provided a superb case study of this situation in *Politics, Planning, and the Public Interest*, a book all students of public policy should read. In this instance, the Chicago Housing Authority—the planners—had formulated a site-selection plan for public housing in Chicago in line with their definition of the problems to be attacked. Relatively little attention was paid to the hard realities of majority building in the Chicago City Council (whose approval was necessary). The results were disastrous. The Council shredded the CHA's plan, and a long and bitter struggle ensued between the planners and the politicians—between rather pure formulators and pure legitimators. As Meyerson and Banfield note:

> The question . . . arises why the Council and the Authority engaged in a long struggle rather than in cooperation. . . .
> The strategy of the Authority was to struggle rather than to bargain. Indeed, the Authority went somewhat out of its way to provoke the leaders of the Council; it did this by refusing to enter into even a *pro forma* discussion with the housing committee of the Council before the sites were formally submitted, by locating a large project in [Councilman] Duffy's ward without giving him any advance notice of it, and by taking a hostile tone in its public appearances before the Council.[7]

One can note any number of examples of the second situation—in which a proposal gains acceptance, almost without opposition, and yet is totally inadequate to deal with the problem or problems to which it is directed. I discuss such an example below in the poverty program. For various reasons the Economic Opportunity Act of 1964 was an imperfect plan. Yet the political planning in getting a majority in Congress was almost faultless. Of course, in all cases, judgments about what is or is not "perfect" depend on one's preferences and the conditions at the time.

The third combination is intriguing—the perfect blend between plan and politics, between formulation and legitimation. In this case, all known factors are presumably taken into account. With the exception of the actual ratification of a proposal, which the law may require to occur within a legislature, formulation and legitimation are coincident functions. When one is completed, the other is as well. That is, policy actors have so thoroughly accounted for the conditions under which a majority must be constructed in a legislature that the task is completed along with the development of a course of action to solve a public problem. Surely this is the goal of many policy planners and strategists, but plans and politics are not always so compatible. I do not mean to imply that the perfect "blend" is the combining of perfect plans and perfect strategies. Rather it is a process of getting the best of both, given the circumstances at hand.

One particularly interesting development in formulation is the use of the Planning-Programming-Budgeting System (PPBS) in the executive branch of the federal government. PPBS represents an effort to be supremely efficient in planning. As the name suggests, the system relates goals to specific programs and costs. When President Johnson ordered the system to be used throughout the federal government, he claimed that it would enable us to:

1. Identify our national goals with precision and on a continuing basis.
2. Choose among those goals the ones that are most urgent.
3. Search for alternative means of reaching those goals most effectively at the least cost.
4. Inform ourselves not merely on next year's costs, but on the second, and third, and subsequent years' costs of our programs.
5. Measure the performance of our programs to insure a dollar's worth of service for each dollar spent.[8]

In short, PPBS was designed to reduce uncertainty, waste of resources, and misdirection in policy making through systematic analysis of the basic elements of that process—problems, goals, costs, allocations, appraisals. As one reviews PPBS in its pure form, it becomes evident that it is a *total policy process*. In theory, if everyone involved in policy making accepts the outcomes, then all functional activities take place within PPBS. In fact, of course, not everyone does accept the outcomes, and we can all agree that what comes out depends very much on what goes in. Given limited resources, people will debate what the goals are and where the resources ought to be allocated. In this situation, a PPBS becomes one more strategy in what Professor Aaron Wildavsky refers to as "policy politics." It can be an impressive strategy. That is, equipped with extensive computer-derived cost-benefit analyses of priorities among programs, a planner may overwhelm those who have the authority to legitimate one course of action over another. Former Secretary of Defense Robert McNamara was impressive in his performances before congressional committees, virtually inundating the members with quantitative data. But, as Professor Wildavsky warns, "... *a (if not the) distinguishing characteristic of systems analysis is that the objectives either are not known or are subject to change.*"[9] So, he concludes, a "perfect plan" becomes highly political because perfection is ultimately related to someone's analysis of goals to be achieved, priorities to be set, allocations to be made. While an effort like PPBS may increase efficiency by some measures of what that is, it is unlikely to do away with the policy process as we know it at the federal level.

> A major task of the political system is to specify goals or objectives. It is impermissible to treat goals as if they were known in advance. "Goals" may well be the product of interaction among key participants rather than some *deus ex machina* or (to use Bentley's term) some "spook" that posits values in advance of our knowledge of them.[10]

I am moved to reiterate another of the "initial realities" at this point: "No ideal policy system exists apart from the preferences of the architect of that system."

Three Cases of Formulation

I thought it would be useful to discuss three cases of formulation—cases which are strikingly different. In the case of the "war on poverty," the formulators for the principal course of action were drawn primarily from the executive and from universities and private foundations. In the case of air pollution, considerable initiative came from the legislature. With energy conservation and supply, both the president and Congress formulated comprehensive packages. Thus, both the problem to be solved and the institutional base for formulation differed in each case.

The War on Poverty—1964[11]

> . . . we have never lost sight of our goal: an America in which every citizen shares all the opportunities of his society . . .
> We have come a long way toward this goal.
> We still have a long way to go.
> The distance which remains is the measure of the great unfinished work of our society.
> To finish that work I have called for *a national war on poverty. Our objective: total victory.*
>
> President Lyndon B. Johnson
> Message on Poverty, March 16, 1964

This dramatic declaration signaled one of the most innovative and controversial policies in decades. The beneficiaries would be the poor of this nation. A first order of business was to determine who and where they were. To do that somebody had to say what poverty was. The Council of Economic Advisers set an arbitrary standard of $3,000 for a family of four and declared that 20 percent of families were poor. That measure became controversial, and Mollie Orshansky of the Social Security Administration developed other measures—establishing several categories of poor and setting a "poverty threshold" for each.[12] Gradually we had some rather sophisticated statistics on the poor of this nation.[13] But statistics are only one small part of defining the problems of poverty. By our definition of public problem, the people themselves are involved and the actual problems are many. As Anthony Downs observes, "Whether people *feel* poor or not depends to some extent on how their incomes compare with the incomes of other people around them."[14] He might have added, "Whether problems exist for them or not depends to a large extent on how they view the effects of low income."

The launching of a full-scale war on poverty had been preceded by skirmishes for several hundred years. There have always been poor people, and governments have long had some policy to treat them. Unfortunately, only very recently has that policy been in the least humane. A dominant theme in the United States has been, and still is to a large extent, that the poor are poor because of some flaw in their character. In the twentieth century, governments began to aid certain categories of poor—the aged, the blind, the retarded, dependent children.[15] And then all of a sudden even those with flawless characters were poor. The depression had the effect of extending the perception of poverty and giving policy makers some experience with the problems of the poor. A revolution in social welfare occurred in the United States with the passage of social security, housing, employment, and economic legislation. With the righting of the economy, those to whom the depression was no new experience continued to suffer the indignities of poverty. The rest of the nation prospered.

Ultimately it was this contrast—the poverty amid affluence—that brought this issue-area to the agenda of government. Despite the postwar economic success, a large group remained poor. By 1963 a large number of people in government and in the private sphere were occupied with treating symptoms. As James L. Sundquist describes it, programs in mental health, urban renewal, public welfare, and manpower retraining all pointed the way to a broad-scale effort to eliminate poverty.[16] The principal formulators included Presidents Kennedy and Johnson and persons drawn from these organizations:

> Council of Economic Advisers
> Bureau of the Budget
> Ford Foundation
> President's Committee on Juvenile Delinquency and Youth Crimes
> White House Staff
> Departments of Labor; Health, Education, and Welfare; Agriculture; Commerce; Interior
> Peace Corps
> Small Business Administration

Housing and Home Finance Agency (now the Department of Housing and Urban Development)

In view of the enormity of what was being attempted in 1963 and 1964 and the number of people involved, it is absolutely incredible that a course of action could be formulated with such speed. At first, those involved in several programs treating the symptoms of poverty found themselves communicating frequently. President Kennedy's concern about Appalachia and other "pockets of poverty" made him receptive to a broad-scale program. The Council of Economic Advisers, staffed largely by academicians, was free to devote research time to the development of proposals, and Professor Robert J. Lampman of the University of Wisconsin began to assemble data in early 1963. After the enactment of the tax cut in 1963, designed to stimulate the economy, all of the conscious and unconscious efforts in behalf of a poverty program began to take on unity and direction. By October President Kennedy had become convinced that antipoverty measures should be included in the 1964 legislative program. The CEA proceeded full-steam to assemble proposals, contacting many of the people who had unwittingly been policy formulators to that time.

On November 19, Kennedy asked Walter Heller, chairman of the Council of Economic Advisers, to have measures prepared for his review in a couple of weeks. The president then boarded the plane for Texas.

> Budget Bureau, CEA, and White House staff were in the midst of a review of the departmental responses [to their request for proposals] when they were interrupted by the news from Dallas.
> President Johnson lost no time in restoring their momentum. At his first meeting with Heller, on November 23, Johnson said, "That's my kind of program. . . . Move full speed ahead."[17]

At this point, the "idea" unit, CEA, stepped back to let the Bureau of the Budget take the leadership in formulating definite proposals. After considerable frustration in discovering "a theme or rationale that would distinguish the new legislation,"[18] the framers found the notion of community organizations, proposed by David Hackett and Richard W. Boone of the Juvenile Delinquency Committee. As Daniel P. Moynihan describes it:

> In a subtle, not entirely clear process, the coordinated community approach to problems of the poor attracted great interest and ultimately powerful and crucial support in that nerve center, indeed superego, of the federal establishment [the Bureau of the Budget].[19]

The community approach, eventually to be called "community action programs," had been tried, but not thoroughly tested, by the Juvenile Delinquency Committee and the Ford Foundation in their various projects. Despite lack of information about how it might work, "aid to community organizations was transformed from an incidental weapon in the war on poverty into the entire arsenal."[20]

Thus, by bits-and-pieces progress, the program was developing definite thrust by January 1964. The question of where to locate the problem was resolved in favor of establishing an independent agency. Many formulators were concerned that no department could provide the imagination needed for the poverty effort. Unless an independent agency were created, it was feared, funds would be used simply to bolster existing programs—all of which were inadequate.

Since a new agency was to be created, no unit existed to take the lead in developing a substantive program. The Bureau of the Budget performed its expected role of coordinating the early efforts, since it is charged with overseeing the development of the president's legislative program. But an idea of this magnitude needed somebody who was committed to it for its own sake—not because of a general responsibility for coordinating all proposals. Sargent Shriver, brother-in-law of the late president and director of the Peace Corps, was selected as that "somebody." With his appointment, the poverty program had an energetic and influential advocate—one who had experience with local aid programs overseas through the Peace Corps.

Shriver took charge of the formulation system, establishing a task force to refine the proposals which would be submitted to Congress. All ideas were reviewed again; government, foundation, academic, and state and local officials were all consulted. Interestingly, *neither the poor nor the blacks had any role in the development of the program which was to affect them.*

> ... it is worth noting now that the American poor themselves did *not* participate in the process which led to the creation of the act.[21]

> At no time did any Negro have any role of any consequence in the drafting of the poverty program. Nor did any Negro have any role of any consequence in the drafting of the CAP guidelines.[22]

So it went. The formulation process was now in high gear. Shriver was appointed on February 1; by mid-March the legislation was ready for Congress. The community action idea was expanded beyond the initial experimental program; other programs, primarily directed toward job training, were added. Then, with virtually no consultation with members of Congress, the package was sent to the Hill for legitimation. Congress, controlled by large Democratic margins working in a post-assassination mood sympathetic toward Kennedy programs, passed it overwhelmingly. Republican protests and strategies were buried in the whirlwind of publicity and support for unconditional war.

That which was to become so highly controversial later—the participation of the poor in community action programs—went almost unnoticed in the legislation. Moynihan, much involved in the construction of the program, reflects on this point.

> Although memory too readily deceives, it may be of use to record here the impression that community action simply was not much on the minds of those who were most active in the Shriver task force. In retrospect, at least, it would seem to have assumed a kind of residual function. . . .
>
> . . . The community action title, which established the one portion of the program that would not be directly monitored from Washington, should provide for the "maximum feasible participation of the residents of the areas and the members of the groups" involved in the local programs. Subsequently this phrase was taken to sanction a specific theory of social change, and there were those present in Washington at the time who would have drafted just such language with precisely that object. But the record, such as can be had, and recollection indicates that it was intended to do no more than ensure that persons excluded from the political process in the South and elsewhere would nonetheless participate in the *benefits* of the community action programs of the new legislation.[23]

Congress was programmed for quick action. The hearings were stacked in favor—only nine of sixty-nine primary witnesses in the House were opposed. Chairman Adam Clayton Powell of the House Committee on Education and Labor declared in the face of Republican protests: "I am the chairman. I will run this committee as I desire."[24] The administration was successful in getting a Southern conservative as the House sponsor (Phil Landrum of Georgia), and the bill passed both houses virtually intact. The participation of the poor was not even discussed.

The poverty program is a textbook case of the executive as formulator. It also turns out to be a good case of flawless strategy in getting a course of action legitimated. Relative to other proposals, the Economic Opportunity Act of 1964 was innovative—a break with the past. One can see how events, perceptions, definitions of problems were all building toward the development of such a program. But the exceptional nature of how the course of action was formulated caused complications in applying the policy to the problems. Administrators were given broad authority in the act, in part because no one was all that sure what ought to be done. The fact is that broad legislation was passed, a new agency created, large sums appropriated, with only the vaguest definitions of the problems of poverty.

Cleaning the Air—The 1960s

Two men stop on Wall Street to look at their watches as the skies darken. One concludes, "It *can't* be sundown, so it must be air pollution." A woman sits at dinner on an apartment balcony in Manhattan. She calls through the door, "Come, Hilary, your soup is getting dirty." Cartoons on daily irritations are better than ever. In all American cities, however, air pollution remains a significant problem—it smells; causes eye, nose, and throat irritations; is associated with numerous respiratory ailments; damages property; and even pollutes the water in rain.

The statistics on pollution are ghastly. Forget the smokestacks, backyard bonfires, buses, jet planes, and cigars; let's concentrate just on the automobile—on the internal combustion engine that has caused greater change in this country than practically any other single factor.

> Ten percent of all fuel purchased, 7 billion gallons in the United States of raw gasoline, are wasted into our atmosphere, each year.
> Let this gas can represent the 1 gallon in 10 that is emitted into the air from the uncontrolled vehicle: 10 percent is lost through evaporation, 25 percent lost through the crankcase, and 65 percent lost from exhaust.[25]

The contents of this gasoline as it comes out of *all* cars—not just old ones—do not make for clean lungs.

> The innocent-looking tailpipe of an automobile spews forth about two hundred hydrocarbons, some of which have been clearly identified as cancer-causing substances. In the course of using up a thousand gallons of gasoline, motor vehicles typically discharge 17 pounds of sulfur dioxide, 18 pounds of aldehydes, 25 to 75 pounds of oxides of nitrogen, and more than 3,000 pounds of carbon monoxide.[26]

I won't bore you with all the technical details (few of which I understand anyway), but the chemistry lesson doesn't stop with these products of the tailpipe. Sunlight and air have various effects on these chemicals—not all of which have been identified.[27]

As with low income, polluted air becomes a problem by our definition when people begin to perceive that the consequences of automobile exhaust fumes (as the major source) create a need for which they want relief. Survey data suggest that, to the extent that problems are defined in this area, people are more concerned with smell than anything else. And the source they cite is factories and businesses, which 65.5 percent mentioned in the St. Louis survey, for example. Only 12.3 percent mentioned "exhaust from transport agents" (including buses, trucks, and cars).[28] Public support for air pollution policy does exist. Whether that extends to stringent controls on automobiles or to the abolition of the internal combustion engine, as one California senator has proposed, is somewhat less obvious.

Whereas the formulators for the poverty program were drawn almost entirely from the executive, during the 1960s those for a national air pollution control policy were drawn almost entirely from Congress—with support from certain urban groups. Those principally involved included members and staff from the following committees:

Senate Committee on Public Works
Senate Committee on Labor and Public Welfare
House Committee on Interstate and Foreign Commerce
House Committee on Government Operations

Several subcommittees had jurisdiction, but none was devoted specifically to pollution before 1963. Subcommittees on flood control, health and safety, and intergovernmental relations either held hearings or developed legislation on air pollution. Representatives Kenneth Roberts (D-Alabama) and Paul Schenck (R-Ohio) and Senators Thomas Kuchel (R-California) and Homer Capehart (R-Indiana) were active before 1963.

In 1963 Senator Edmund Muskie (D-Maine) assumed leadership in this area as chairman of the newly created Subcommittee on Air and Water Pollution. From that point on Muskie became the champion of stronger controls—though he received important support from Roberts, Schenck, and John Blatnik (D-Minnesota) in the House, and Kuchel, Abraham Ribicoff (D-Connecticut), and J. Caleb Boggs (R-Delaware) in the Senate. Several subcommittee staff people were also important in the formulation in 1963 and afterwards. The United States Conference of Mayors, the American Municipal Association, and the National Association of Counties all supported the efforts of this small group of formulators—indeed, contributing assistance where possible (principally in the person of the lobbyist and legislative specialist Hugh Mields). The most important figure in the executive favoring control by 1963 was Dean Coston, then deputy assistant secretary of Health, Education, and Welfare. He and staff members of the Division of Air Pollution, created in 1960 within the Public Health Service, were very much involved in the formulation of legislation before 1963.[29]

A Senate staff report on air pollution concluded that "an identifiable federal program in air pollution was not established until 1955...."[30] At that time legislation providing for research and technical assistance by the Public Health Service was enacted. Recognizing state and local responsibility for air pollution abatement and control, the act was designed primarily to assist units at this level "in the formulation and execution of their research programs...."[31] Federal enforcement was neither considered at the time nor desired by the Public Health Service as part of their responsibilities.

Between 1956 and 1963 certain members of Congress, notably Paul Schenck, became increasingly concerned about the effects of automobile exhaust as evidence mounted, particularly in Los Angeles, that it was a major cause of air pollution. In 1958 and 1959 Schenck introduced legislation prohibiting the use in interstate commerce of vehicles which emitted unburned hydrocarbons to an extent that they were "dangerous to human health." The Public Health Service opposed the bill, arguing that it lacked the "technical know-how" to administer such controls and cited the "philosophy of local responsibility" in this area.

In 1959 the Subcommittee on Health and Safety of the House Committee on Interstate and Foreign Commerce, chaired by Roberts, revised Schenck's bill by directing the surgeon general (who heads the Public Health Service) to undertake a study of automobile exhaust. The legislation passed both houses, though not until the following year in the Senate. In essence, the subcommittee said to the Public Health Service, "If you don't know enough about the problem to administer Schenck's proposal, get the necessary technical know-how and fill us in." Here was a direct request to reluctant executive policy actors to employ their vast resources in defining a problem. The initiative came from Congress, but members were hamstrung because of lack of reliable data. Thus, much of the period 1956 to 1963 was devoted to disjointed efforts by a few people to define the problems resulting from increased air pollution.

Bolstered by the Public Health Service's report (*Motor Vehicles, Air Pollution, and Health*),[32] a staff report of the Senate Subcommittee on Air and Water Pollution (*A Study of Pollution—Air*), committee hearings, and increasing "technical know-how" among staff personnel, Congress passed the Clean Air Act of 1963. This act was a major breakthrough.

> With the adoption of the Clean Air Act in December, 1963, federal policy in the field of air pollution control underwent significant evolution. Although there was no change in the view that responsibility for the control of air pollution rests primarily with state and local governments, the federal government responded to a very real need by equipping itself to aid state and local control programs more effectively and to stimulate them to the increased level of activity considered necessary.
>
> The new Clean Air Act also includes for the first time a limited legal regulatory authority on the federal level for abatement of specific air pollution problems.[33]

For our purposes, a major result of the action in 1963 was the emergence of a continuing policy system for air pollution. No longer searching for support, air pollution control policy was expanded in 1965, and again in 1967 and 1970, with increased attention to the automobile. Senator Muskie continued to lead in Congress, but formulation and evaluation increasingly shifted to the executive as the president took a direct interest. Congressmen began to assume their more typical function as legitimators of policy in this issue-area.[34]

In addition to providing an excellent example of legislators as the principal formulators, air pollution control illustrates the roadblocks for congressmen in assuming this function. Faced with incomplete technical knowledge about an issue-area, legislators find it very difficult to formulate courses of action. Testimony by the experts that they don't know very much themselves tends to dampen enthusiasm for legislation. As in this case, however, congressmen can direct the experts to get the facts. Once research has been commissioned, formulators feel free to go ahead and implement their policy preferences, confident that the findings will support them.[35]

The Public Discovers Energy—1973-1975

What makes a television set work? or the car run? or the radiators get hot? How is steel made? Where does plastic come from? How do we get California oranges in Pittsburgh? The vital role of energy in answering these questions is obvious and always has been. But until recently neither ordinary citizens nor their elected decision makers spent much time probing the complexities of the energy issue-area. What event triggered increased awareness and concern? The famous northeastern blackout, November 11, 1965, let a few million people in on the secret that we were a highly energy dependent society. Elevators and subways stopped, communications were interrupted, appliances didn't work, the lights went out, and, as a consequence, other things went on that I'll leave to your imagination. Even more dramatic and widespread, however, was the Arab oil embargo in the fall, 1973.

> October 17, 1973, was energy Pearl Harbor day. Instead of dropping bombs, a handful of oil-rich Arab nations shut off a few valves and sent shock waves through the closely linked high-energy industrial civilization in the United States, Western Europe, and Japan.[36]

The long lines at gas stations and the threat of reduced residential heating, particularly in the northeast, forced comprehension of national excesses in energy consumption. The price rises to follow taught us something else— that much of our prosperity, individually and as a nation, was based on the availability of cheap fuel. In 1973 the Arabs discovered a means for redistributing that prosperity.

> Between 1973 and 1974 the Organization of Petroleum Exporting Countries (OPEC) increased the average export price of oil from $2.75 a barrel to $10 a barrel, thereby imposing a $75 billion "excise tax" on the oil-importing countries. Unprecedented in size and suddenness, this transfer of income sent a series of depressing shocks through the world economy. . . . The rapidity of the 1974 jump in oil prices . . . caused a simultaneous acceleration of inflation and loss of employment that the industrial countries proved unable to handle with the monetary and fiscal tools at their disposal.[37]

Here then was a major crisis with immediate personal effects because Americans had gotten used to higher energy consumption and because lots of jobs were at stake. Under the circumstances, energy problems bullied their way to the top of government agendas at all levels. There was the immediate crisis to deal with—requiring the allocation of available petroleum, negotiation with the Arab states, and the lifting of certain restrictions on development of domestic resources. And then there was the planning of future energy programs. It is this second effort which will be briefly described here since it represents a case of formulating a comprehensive policy.

One must take account of the extraordinary political context in which energy proposals were formulated in 1974-1975. President Nixon was on his way out (resigning August 11, 1974), Gerald R. Ford would enter the White House with fewer political resources than almost any president in history, and the Democrats were to increase their numbers in the 1974 congressional elections to almost veto-proof proportions (i.e., nearly two-thirds in each house). Given these conditions, one could not expect a smooth and integrated formulation exercise. Rather one could look for a disjointed and partisan process with participants drawn from both Congress and the executive, and the private and public spheres.

Nor can one ignore the policy and organizational context for energy program formulation. While the federal government did not have a coordinated national energy policy in 1974, many individual public policies directly or indirectly affected energy resource development and use. In general, these various policies were directed toward maximum exploitation of available supply. David Freeman notes that "government policy was to rely on the oil companies. . . ."[38] In fact, the government *encouraged* this reliance through various leasing and taxing policies. Gerald Garvey associates our energy-related decisions with the "frontier style" of a growing and prosperous American society.

> The frontier culture helped form the American character. It still shapes his natural resource policies. The seemingly limitless bounty of the continent fostered reckless, wasteful habits, first manifested in the frontiersman's appropriation of land and forests, then carried over into the eras of coal and petroleum development. Such a tradition of wastefulness could hardly have been sustained without an overriding optimism. Continental abundance fostered the conceit that there would always be "more." Crucial to a developing American tendency to ignore harmful side-effects of resource exploitation was the elaboration of this rustic optimism into a theory of externalities which emphasized only the beneficent spillover consequences of economic growth.[39]

The realization of shortages, of finite resources, called for a quite different philosophy and obviously promoted dramatic shifts in government policies. Thus, for example, a complete energy profile for the United States showed heavy reliance on a narrow and declining resource base. A study by the Energy Research and Development Administration (ERDA) showed that over 75 percent of energy consumption is drawn from the dwindling supplies of petroleum and natural gas, while the more abundant coal resources provide only 20 percent, and the source of greatest potential, uranium, provides about 2 percent.[40] Government policies have promoted this reliance, in part through tax breaks and leasing policies for the oil industry, and in part by never having adopted an integrated national energy policy.

Energy fought valiantly for the time and attention of national decision makers in the year of Watergate, 1974. The task of formulating coherent proposals would have been difficult even without the overriding political crisis since the federal government was neither organized nor experienced in making broad-scale energy policy. There was no Department of Energy to which President Nixon could turn for a plan; nor were there Senate and House Committees on Energy to which a plan might be sent. Therefore, reorganization was required and recommended along with proposals for reshaping America's energy supply and demand profiles.

Program formulation in energy was characterized by widespread participation among many departments, agencies, and committees; inadequate and unreliable information about the problems; premature announcement of broad-scale proposals with impossible goals; and, as a consequence of the foregoing, little or no credibility for any one set of formulations. In short, the scene was one of confusion bordering on chaos. More analytically speaking, what we witnessed was not all that unfamiliar in American politics—that is, our particular brand of crisis decision making made more dramatic by a major political upheaval.

The partisan division between Congress and the White House helped to explain the broad participation in formulation. For anything a Republican president could do, a Democratic Congress could do better. Thus, one cannot describe an organizationally tight process as was possible with the poverty program and air pollution control. Rather we witnessed a continuous process of formulating from several sources.

First, let's identify the principal governmental units—executive and legislative—which could be drawn on for program formulation before and after the Arab embargo in 1973.

Executive[41]

Atomic Energy Commission
Executive Office of the President
    Domestic Council
    Office of Emergency Preparedness

Office of Management and Budget
Office of Science and Technology
Oil Policy Committee
Joint Board on Fuel Supply and Transport

Office of Energy Policy
Department of Commerce
   Bureau of Domestic Commerce
   Office of Import Programs
Department of Defense
   Army Corps of Engineers
   Office of Naval Petroleum and
   Oil Shale Reserves
Department of the Interior
   Various Power Administrations
   (Alaska, Bonneville, Defense
   Electric, Southeastern, South-
   western)
   Bureau of Land Management
   Bureau of Mines
   Bureau of Reclamation
   Geological Survey
   Office of Coal Research
   Office of Oil and Gas
   Oil Import Administration
Department of Justice
   Land and Natural Resources
   Division
   Antitrust Division
Department of State
   Office of Fuels and Energy
Department of Transportation
   Federal Highway Administration
Federal Maritime Commission
Federal Power Commission
National Science Foundation (re-
search)
Securities and Exchange Com-
mission
Small Business Administration
Tennessee Valley Authority
Water Resources Council

Congressional Committees

Senate
Appropriations (various subcom-
mittees)
Armed Services
   National Stockpile and Naval
   Petroleum Reserves

Commerce
   Aviation
   Merchant Marine
   Oceans and Atmosphere
   Surface Transportation
Interior and Insular Affairs
   Minerals, Materials, and Fuels
   Public Lands
   Water and Power Resources
Public Works
   Water Resources
House
Appropriations (various subcom-
mittees)
Banking and Currency
   Urban Mass Transportation
Government Operation
   Conservation and Natural Re-
   sources
Interior and Insular Affairs
   Mines and Mining
   Public Lands
   Water and Power Resources
Interstate and Foreign Commerce
   Communications and Power
   Transportation and Aeronautics
Merchant Marine and Fisheries
   Merchant Marine
Public Works
   Energy
   Transportation
   Water Resources
Science and Astronautics
   Aeronautics and Space Tech-
   nology
   Energy
   Science
   Research and Development
Joint
Atomic Energy
   Energy
   Licensing and Regulation
   Raw Materials
   Research, Development, and
   Radiation
   Security

Several things stand out in reviewing this list. First and most obvious is its length, even when limited to units more directly involved in energy-related policies. A comprehensive listing would be enormous. Second, the length of the list is explained in large part by the fact that we have not had a national energy policy in this country. Rather, we have had many policies with impacts on energy supply and demand. Third, strikingly absent from this list is a Department of Energy or Senate and House Committees on Energy. In fact, of the 35 executive units included, only three include "energy" in their titles; approximately the same ratio occurs on the congressional side.

President Nixon sought to change this diffuseness in policy development through a number of proposed organizational changes—in particular the creation of a Federal Energy Administration, a Department of Energy and Natural Resources, an Energy Research and Development Administration and a Nuclear Energy Commission. No action was taken in Congress on these proposals before the Arab boycott.

Following the boycott, a number of organizational changes were made. As a consequence when President Ford began to pick up the pieces after President Nixon's resignation, he had a somewhat more coherent formulation network available for developing programmatic alternatives. The effort to centralize and coordinate energy policy making in the executive was not followed in Congress, however. As indicated below, practically every committee sought to get a piece of the action. Here then were the principal units involved in program formulation in 1974 and 1975.

Executive (Though many units previously cited continued to be involved, they are not all listed here.)

Executive Office of the President

Council on Energy Resources (chaired by the secretary of the Interior and includes most of the secretaries and agency heads involved in energy-related programs)

Department of the Interior
(Many of the same units, though some transferred to ERDA and FEA under the reorganization)

Federal Energy Administration (FEA)
(New agency responsible for managing short-term fuel shortages)

Energy Research and Development Administration (ERDA)
(New agency responsible for all research and development—initially dominated by the nuclear program from the old Atomic Energy Commission)

Nuclear Regulatory Commission

(New agency composed of the safety, licensing, and regulatory powers of the old Atomic Energy Commission)

Here then was a more rationally organized structure for program development. FEA was to be concerned with short-run allocations, ERDA with longer term planning, Interior with the management of resources, and the new council to provide coordination. While miracles do not occur as a result of reorganization, still this structure offered the president a greater potential for coherent formulation. Congress was not following in this same tradition, however. To the contrary, practically every committee found that it had some claim to energy policy making. The leadership had no means for coordinating these diverse activities. As a consequence, a unified and integrated executive program was unlikely to be judged as such by any one congressional unit. But let the subcommittees speak for themselves. Whereas only three had "energy" in their titles in 1973, nine did in 1975. My recent count (in 1976) shows 23 committees and 51 subcommittees which deal directly with some aspect of energy. ERDA claims that it must answer to 33 committees, 65 subcommittees and one panel—a total of 99 units.[42] Listing these many units did not make the point any more dramatically, and no doubt many changes will be made before these words are published anyway. A reiteration is all that is needed—to wit, an executive-formulated energy program could not be treated as a whole on Capitol Hill, nor could one expect a single legislative-formulated program in response. (See a concrete illustration of this in Table 4-1.)

This political and organizational context is particularly useful for understanding the lengthy and complex formulation activities during 1973-1975. We start with the president's energy message in April, 1973, which emphasized supply (and, in many respects, was a reworking of his 1971 message that was all but ignored by Congress). The 1973 message provided a comprehensive overview of problems and offered a number of individual programs for increasing resources and fuel imports, conserving energy, encouraging research and development, and developing international cooperation. In addition the president reintroduced his reorganization proposals. Drawing on the many agencies listed earlier, the president relied heavily on Secretary of the Interior Rogers C. B. Morton and Secretary of the Treasury George P. Shultz to coordinate program development. A Special Energy Committee and National Energy Office were established in the White House to provide coordination and to monitor events and policy developments.

In July the president took further action to provide an organizational basis for formulating a national energy policy. He created an Energy Policy Office by executive order (to supersede the temporary coordinating units noted above) and again called on Congress to act on his proposals.

Table 4–1. Distributing the President's Energy Program Among the Standing Committees

Proposal	Committees
Production from Naval Petroleum Reserves	House and Senate Armed Services Senate Interior
Creation of a national petroleum reserve	House and Senate Commerce
Deregulation of natural gas	House and Senate Commerce
Environmental law modifications	House Commerce Senate Public Works
Aid to utilities	House Commerce Senate Government Operations, Commerce and Finance
Planning for energy facilities	House Commerce Senate Interior, Public Works, Commerce
Import quotas and tariffs	House Ways and Means Senate Finance; and Banking, Housing and Urban Affairs
Building energy conservation	House Banking, Currency, and Housing Senate Banking, Commerce, and Public Works
Insulation incentives	House Banking Senate Interior, Banking, and Labor and Public Welfare
Energy labeling	House and Senate Commerce
Standby powers for president	House Commerce Senate Interior, Banking, and Judiciary

Source: *Congressional Quarterly Weekly Report*, June 28, 1975, p. 1344.

John A. Love was appointed director of the new office. The energy program was given high priority in an unusual second state of the Union message and in a presidential press conference specifically on energy in early September. Self-sufficiency was emphasized as the president concluded that the United States "must be in a position and must develop the capacity so that no other nation in the world that might . . . take an unfriendly attitude toward the United States, has us frankly in a position where they can cut off our oil. . . ."[43]

The Arab embargo, then, gave new urgency to programs already formulated by the executive. Though the president asked for energy powers and took a number of actions under existing authority, basically he reiterated the need for enacting the program introduced earlier. He did attach a new name to his proposals—"Project Independence."

> Let us unite in committing the resources of this Nation to a major new endeavor, an endeavor that in this bicentennial era we can appropriately call "Project Independence." Let us set as our national goal, in the spirit of Apollo, with the determination of the

> Manhattan Project, that by the end of this decade, we will have
> developed the potential to meet our own energy needs without
> depending on any foreign energy sources.[44]

In his speech President Nixon stressed the work done on Capitol Hill in
formulating emergency powers—particularly that done in the Senate Committee on Interior and Insular Affairs. What he proposed was that the proposals he had requested earlier be combined with those formulated by
Senators Henry Jackson (D-Washington) and Paul Fannin (R-Arizona).
While some emergency legislation was enacted, the bulk of the president's
program remained in the proposal stage.

In 1974 energy policy formulation shifted to Congress. The president
had offered his proposals and it was more than mere intransigence that
kept Congress from acting. Many Democrats simply disagreed with the administration's approach. The principal source of congressional formulation
was, as expected, the Interior committees, with Senator Jackson particularly active. Congress passed an emergency energy bill in February that
was based on a quite different view of the problem—including as it did
broad authority for the president to ration gasoline, order conservation
measures, and modify environmental standards, as well as providing a
rollback on domestic crude oil prices. The bill was vetoed and thus program development was at a standstill.

Congress did take actions in 1974 that were to influence future formulation activities, however. Much of President's Nixon's energy reorganization package was enacted (see above), and funds for research and
development were increased. Thus, by 1975 the stage was set for another
variation of program development. President Ford could rely on the new
apparatus for developing a new set of energy proposals. Meanwhile congressional Democrats were buoyed by victory at the polls in the 1974
congressional elections and more determined than ever to counter with an
energy program of their own.

In part as a result of these events, policy formulation in 1975 approached
comic-opera proportions. An unelected president, serving out the term of
the first chief executive to be forced to resign in disgrace, succeeded in
taking the initiative despite his insecure political position. Any president
has the constitutional advantage of presenting new proposals in the state
of the Union message. House Democrats sought to blunt this edge by announcing their economic and energy plans two days before the president's
message on January 15. President Ford countered by revealing the general
thrust of his proposals in a television and radio address also on January 13,
thus upstaging the Democrats. As we will see, the opening act tended to
characterize the whole play.

While we can't explore the details of the proposals offered in this essentially process-oriented description, still certain actions came to have strate-

gic importance. In the case of the president's plan, he sought to spur action on his legislative requests by making decisions already within his authority which would, he thought, force congressional movement (for example, his schedule for raising import fees and decontrolling the price of domestic crude oil). Largely because the executive was developing a more integrated energy decision-making apparatus and the president himself was establishing a more personalized and reliable set of political advisers, the executive package was generally judged to be coherent and precise in comparison with that offered on January 13 by Speaker Carl Albert on behalf of the House Democrats.

But Congress was not done participating in the formulation of energy proposals. In addition to the scores of individual legislative proposals, three groups in particular offered energy packages. Two of these were quite innovative in effort, if abortive in outcome. A seven-member ad hoc committee in the Senate, led by Senator John O. Pastore (D-Rhode Island), worked on an alternative economic and energy plan to present to the Senate Democratic Policy Committee and Caucus. They were assisted by Policy Committee staff. On the House side, a task force of the House Democratic Steering and Policy Committee headed by James Wright (D-Texas) was instrumental in the initial counter-proposals offered by the House Democrats on January 13. Thus, the party structure in each house had established a mechanism for formulating an integrated set of proposals on major domestic issues. The two special committees met in February to mold their proposals and announced a joint plan on February 27—the energy proposals of which concentrated on increasing gasoline taxes and using the proceeds for research and development, taxing automobiles as a way of forcing manufacturers to get better mileage, and imposing excess profits taxes to prevent windfalls in the current crisis.

The weakness of the party leadership structure was soon apparent as committee chairmen reacted to these proposals. In the Senate, Russell Long (D-Louisiana), chairman of the Committee on Finance that would eventually act on the taxing proposals, said: "Let Pastore have his day. . . . I don't want to take issue with him. Some of these things we'll do and some we won't."[45] In the House, the Committee on Ways and Means, where all tax proposals must go first, was formulating its own set of proposals. Chairman Al Ullman (D-Oregon) had established eight task forces to review proposals he had initially developed, and on March 2 the Ways and Means Democrats offered their proposals. Earlier Ullman had characterized the Senate proposals as "a milk-toast program."[46] He judged that it was a mistake for the Wright task force to compromise with Pastore in a joint plan. Yet the Ullman plan was in turn criticized by other House and Senate Democrats. Rowland Evans and Robert Novak summarized Ullman's position as follows:

Ways and Means Democrats will tolerate tougher action than House Democrats generally, who prefer the pablum approach of the Wright-Pastore report. And the 75 freshman Democrats, having toppled venerable committee chairmen, are not retiring from center stage. Led by Rep. Andrew Maguire of New Jersey, they met with Ullman Monday to push a program eliminating any chance of compromise with Mr. Ford. . . . Even if the chairman can perform the marvelous feat of selling it to Ways and Means Democrats, he faces the wrath of the caucus, where those 75 freshmen exert critical influence. That promises a continued stalemate over energy, with the dangerous prospect that nothing at all will be done.[47]

Here then is a classic illustration of the difficulties Congress has in producing unified programmatic alternatives to those offered by the executive. Special leadership initiatives are soon thwarted by the realities of congressional committee jurisdictions and internal party politics. Many Democratic leaders in Congress—both in the party and in committees—were intent on taking the formulation initiative away from the president in this important issue-area in 1975. But the lack of coordinative mechanisms, or, put the other way, the premium placed on action by a decentralized and independent committee system, prevented any unified action. Table 4-1 illustrates how diffuse the legislative structure can be. It shows how the president's omnibus energy program was divided among congressional committees. Clearly many members were able to pull off a piece of the action, but little or no means existed for putting the pieces back together again.

There is no need to carry this story any further—that is, into the legitimation processes by which a majority was eventually constructed for a compromise proposal. It is enough to have described how it all worked in this case, producing a number of different proposals, and to note that whereas congressional leaders were initially optimistic about their ability to act quickly ("We mean business. . . . We intend to act," Speaker Albert had declared on January 13), the compromise energy bill was not passed until December 17. At one point, Barber Conable (R-New York), second ranking Republican on the Committee on Ways and Means, observed rather plaintively: "I have a feeling that we have too many proposals before us. . . ."[48] Another Ways and Means Republican, Bill Frenzel (R-Minnesota), concluded that: "We're finding that Congress is not a bad reactor, but it's very short on leadership."[49]

Summary

No set of cases can possibly illustrate all of the dynamics of formulation. Those offered here do show the variation in types of participants, political conditions, nature and scope of the issue, strategic considerations, government experience, and bases for compromise. They also illustrate points I particularly want emphasized. That is, first, formulation is not institution-bound; second, it may result in one proposal or several; and third, it may proceed with several clear definitions of the problem or none. It is also worth stressing that formulators perform important linkage functions between problems and policies. They look in both directions at once. Moved to develop courses of action on public problems, they operate with a conception (sometimes very vague) of what those problems are, while looking ahead to the hard political realities of bargaining in the legitimation and application processes. And none of it is very tidy. If you got the impression that the process is spasmodic, spread over time, with episodic participation from persons with lots of other things to do, then the cases served the purpose I intended.

Notes

1. Charles E. Lindblom, *The Policy-Making Process* (Englewood Cliffs, N.J.: Prentice-Hall, 1968), p. 13.

2. Lindblom, p. 13.

3. For the most comprehensive and systematic study of these lobbying relationships at the national level, see Lester W. Milbrath, *The Washington Lobbyists* (Chicago: Rand McNally, 1963).

4. Don K. Price, *The Scientific Estate* (Cambridge, Mass.: Harvard University Press, 1965), pp. 42–43. For greater detail on the RAND Corporation, see Bruce L. R. Smith, *The RAND Corporation* (Cambridge, Mass.: Harvard University Press, 1966).

5. Charles V. Kidd, *American Universities and Federal Research* (Cambridge, Mass.: Harvard University Press, 1959), p. 206.

6. Daniel P. Moynihan, *The Politics of a Guaranteed Income* (New York: Random House, 1973), p. 7.

7. Martin Meyerson and Edward Banfield, *Politics, Planning and the Public Interest* (New York: The Free Press, 1955), p. 256.

8. U.S. Senate, Committee on Government Operations, Subcommittee on National Security and International Operations, *Planning-Programming Budgeting—Initial Memorandum* (Washington, D.C.: U.S. Government Printing Office, 1967), pp. 2–3. See also the De-

cember 1966 and March-April 1969 issues of the *Public Administration Review* for extensive analyses of PPBS.

9. Aaron Wildavsky, "The Political Economy of Efficiency," in Austin Ranney, ed., *Political Science and Public Policy* (Chicago: Markham, 1968), p. 65. Emphasis his.

10. Wildavsky, p. 80.

11. The Economic Opportunity Act of 1964 has been analyzed more than practically any piece of legislation in the last twenty years. Fortunately, some of those who have written about it know the story first-hand—particularly James L. Sundquist and Daniel P. Moynihan. This section relies heavily on their books—Sundquist, *Politics and Policy* (Washington, D.C.: The Brookings Institution, 1968); Moynihan, *Maximum Feasible Misunderstanding* (New York: The Free Press, 1969)—and John C. Donovan, *The Politics of Poverty* (New York: Pegasus, 1967); John Bibby and Roger Davidson, *On Capitol Hill* (New York: Holt, Rinehart and Winston, 1967), Ch. 7.

12. See *Social Security Bulletin*, January, July, 1965.

13. For a review of these, see Anthony Downs, *Who Are the Urban Poor?* (New York: Committee for Economic Development, 1968).

14. Downs, p. 8.

15. See Ben B. Seligman, *Permanent Poverty: An American Syndrome* (Chicago: Quadrangle Books, 1968), Ch. 1, for a brief history of government policy on poverty.

16. Sundquist, *Politics and Policy*, pp. 115–134.

17. Sundquist, p. 137.

18. Sundquist, p. 138.

19. Moynihan, *Maximum Feasible Misunderstanding*, p. 77.

20. Sundquist, *Politics and Policy*, p. 138.

21. Donovan, *Politics of Poverty*, pp. 31–32.

22. Moynihan, *Maximum Feasible Misunderstanding*, p. 98.

23. Moynihan, pp. 86–87.

24. Bibby and Davidson, *On Capitol Hill*, p. 241.

25. U.S. Senate, Committee on Public Works, Subcommittee on Air and Water Pollution, Hearings, *Air Pollution—1967*, 90th Cong., 1st sess., February 1967, p. 118.

26. Lewis Herber, *Crisis in Our Cities* (Englewood Cliffs, N.J.: Prentice-Hall, 1965), p. 14.

27. Particularly good sources for simple descriptions of the chemistry of air pollution are Donald E. Carr, *The Breath of Life* (New York: Norton, 1965), and Louis J. Battan, *The Unclean Sky* (Garden City, N.Y.: Doubleday, 1966).

28. Public Health Service, *Public Awareness and Concern with Air Pollution in the St. Louis Metropolitan Area* (Washington, D.C., May 1965), Table 29, p. 26.

29. Much of this is taken from brief analyses of legislation in committee reports, congressional hearings, and, principally, Randall B. Ripley, "Congress and Clean Air: The Issue of Enforcement, 1963," in Frederick Cleaveland, ed., *Congress and Urban Problems* (Washington, D.C.: The Brookings Institution, 1969), pp. 224–278.

30. U.S. Senate, Committee on Public Works, *A Study of Pollution—Air*, 88th Cong., 1st sess., staff report, 1963, p. 23.

31. U.S. Senate, Committee on Public Works, *Steps Toward Clean Air*, 88th Cong., 2d sess., subcommittee report, October 1964, p. 37.

32. U.S. Department of Health, Education, and Welfare, Public Health Service, *Motor Vehicles, Air Pollution, and Health*, 87th Cong., 2d sess., House Document 489, 1962.

33. *Steps Toward Clean Air*, p. 38.

34. For an update on air pollution legislation, see Charles O. Jones, *Clean Air: The Policies and Politics of Pollution Control* (Pittsburgh: University of Pittsburgh Press, 1975). Also take note of a most interesting book by Matthew A. Crenson, *The Un-Politics of Air Pollution* (Baltimore: Johns Hopkins Press, 1971), in which he argues that air pollution is a case of nondecision making.

35. For example, the Public Health Service's report on motor vehicles was rather inconclusive, laced with all the qualifiers used by researchers, and called for more time to complete experiments. Advocates of automotive controls plunged ahead despite the report, however, relying on findings when they would support their case.

36. S. David Freeman, *Energy: The New Era* (New York: Vintage Books, 1974), p. 3.

37. "Living with High Oil Prices," *The Brookings Bulletin*, vol. 12 (Fall 1975), p. 1.

38. Freeman, p. 14.

39. Gerald Garvey, *Energy, Ecology, Economy* (New York: Norton, 1972), p. 25.

40. U.S. Energy Research and Development Administration, *A National Plan for Energy Research, Development and Demonstration: Creating Energy Choices for the Future* (Washington: U.S. Government Printing Office, 1975), p. I-1.

41. This listing is drawn from that compiled in J. Herbert Holloman and Michel Grenon, *Energy Research and Development* (Cambridge, Mass.: Ballinger, 1975), pp. 55–62.

42. Cited in Roger H. Davidson, "Breaking Up Those 'Cozy Triangles': An Impossible Dream?" (paper prepared for Symposium on Legislative Reform and Public Policy, Lincoln, Nebraska, March 11–12, 1976), p. 7.

43. *Congressional Quarterly Weekly Report*, September 15, 1973, p. 2447.

44. *Congressional Quarterly Weekly Report*, November 10, 1973, p. 2965.

45. Quoted in *Congressional Quarterly Weekly Report*, February 22, 1975, p. 353.

46. Quoted in *Congressional Quarterly Weekly Report*, March 1, 1975, p. 426.

47. *The Washington Post*, March 13, 1975.

48. Quoted in *Congressional Quarterly Weekly Report*, March 8, 1975, p. 474.

49. Quoted in *Congressional Quarterly Weekly Report*, June 28, 1975, p. 1343.

5

Legitimating Programs

Functional Activities	Categorized in Government	and as Systems	with Output
Legitimation	Action in Government	Program Development	Program

T he processes of formulation are typically directed toward those of legitimation. Though one may identify certain side benefits from the mere participation in formulation (knowledge of the process, identification of problems, sense of opposition), the major payoff comes in the legitimation of a course of action preferred by you and your colleagues. As with so many of the basic concepts of the policy process, "legitimation" is pregnant with intriguingly complex dimensions.

Legitimacy

At least two forms of legitimation can be identified for any political system. The first is that which authorizes the basic political processes—including those designed to approve specific proposals for solving public problems. The second includes those specific processes by which government programs are authorized. For purposes of clarity, the first will be referred to as *legitimacy*, the second as *legitimation*.

Legitimacy is central to the existence of a political state. It involves authority, consent, obligation, support—indeed, the spectrum of governmental relationships with people and their problems. In her brilliant essays on obligation and consent, Hanna Pitkin questions why anyone should obey anyone else—including governmental officials. Under what conditions should one obey and who says what those conditions are? Should anyone have the last word?

Who is to say? I want to answer, each person who cares to will say—

not merely the one who acts, not merely his associates, not merely those in authority over him, not merely the detached historian or observer. No one has the last word because *there is no last word*. But in order to make that clear, one would have to say a great deal more about how language functions, and why we are persistently inclined to suppose that there must be a last word.[1]

The questions raised by Pitkin are fundamental. If she is right, however, that "there is no last word," how can any system of government be legitimate? Saying that there is no last word is, in effect, saying that legitimacy is dependent on various conditions. In practice, obligation becomes a very dynamic relationship between an individual and officialdom—shaped as it is by perceptions, values, information, hunches. Those of you in this class will vary in the extent to which you consider yourself generally obliged to accept authority. And each of you will no doubt vary depending on the circumstances. For example, have any of you ever run a red light? or had marijuana in your possession? or broken dormitory regulations? or participated in a campus disturbance? Ask yourself why you made each decision—or any others of the same sort. You no doubt can rationalize each failure to obey. In so doing, however, you may or may not reject the legitimacy of the political system. That is, you may disobey for convenience, or because you can get away with it, or because you didn't know, and still accept that the rule broken is legitimate. Perhaps your actions are intended to point out that the rule in fact is not legitimate—though you do not reject the bases upon which the processes of legitimation are established. Or perhaps your actions are meant to reestablish a new order—totally rejecting the existing structure of legitimacy.

One measure of legitimacy is the support available for government and what it does. David Easton makes an important distinction between two types of support—specific and diffuse. "Specific support flows from the favorable attitudes and predisposition stimulated by outputs that are perceived by members to meet their demands as they arise or in anticipation."[2] Therefore, it is associated with what we have identified here as *legitimation* and will be treated subsequently. Diffuse support refers to "a reserve of favorable attitudes or good will that helps members to accept or tolerate outputs to which they are opposed or the effect of which they see as damaging to their wants."[3] Here then is a "reserve of support" which will carry government through good and bad times. Why should it exist? In large part because of a widespread trust in a particular government. Easton puts it this way:

> The inculcation of a sense of legitimacy is probably the single most effective device for regulating the flow of diffuse support in favor both of the authorities and of the regime. A member [of society] may be willing to obey authorities and conform to the requirements

of the regime for many different reasons. But the most stable support will derive from the conviction on the part of the member that it is right and proper for him to accept and obey the authorities and to abide by the requirements of the regime. It reflects the fact that in some vague or explicit way he sees these objects as conforming to his own moral principles, his own sense of what is right and proper in the political sphere.[4]

Legitimacy is obviously essential for a political system. It must exist before specific processes of legitimation can be effective and its particular nature in any one system may well shape those processes. As Easton describes it, legitimacy is based on attitudes that are learned. He speaks of the "inculcation of a sense of legitimacy . . ." and notes that "the most stable support will derive from the conviction . . ." that one should obey. This suggests a number of interesting conclusions—that legitimacy can be managed in society; that incongruity among attitudes can cause complicatons; that, as Pitkin implies, legitimacy may be in the eye of the beholder; that legitimacy can be measured in a political system at any one point in time.

These conclusions, in turn, suggest a dynamic relationship between legitimacy and legitimation. For ultimately one's acceptance or rejection of government actions on specific problems may come to influence how one views the system. Short-run and intermittent disappointments may well be accepted; a consistent pattern of incongruity between expectations and output over time may threaten basic support for the system. This is particularly true when government itself is trying to manipulate legitimacy through the use of symbols. That is, the public may be learning to support a government through the flow of information and use of symbols by public officials. A new government program may be announced as consistent with or supportive of some accepted principle in society—for example, air pollution control with protection of the public health, federal aid to education with equality of opportunity, drug control with law and order. As Richard M. Merelman points out, however, there are risks attendant to any such efforts.

> . . . care must be taken to maintain the association between particular symbols and the policies they legitimize. For example, policy makers can effectively associate the symbol, "rule of law," with the policy of integrating the schools, thereby instating perceptions of secondary and primary reinforcement to be gained from support of the policy. However, over time, as opposition rises or as circumstances change, "rule of law" may very well become separated in the public mind from the policy of school integration. The continuity between legitimacy symbol and its policy referent has broken down. Government must then absorb the costs of this separation.[5]

We can all think of examples of such discontinuities during the past decade or so. At one time America's wars could be supported by a veritable avalanche of symbols—American doughboys versus the despicable Hun; the righteous Marine versus the sly and treacherous "Jap"; a Kansas general leading the forces of good against Hitler's butchers. But the Korean and Vietnam struggles were not so easily characterized. We tried to identify the enemy as worldwide communism, but in Vietnam in particular the symbols never really took hold. As a result, questions about specific policies were broadened to include the whole decision-making apparatus. "Why are we there?" "Who is responsible for this mess?" "Why can't we just get the hell out?" "How can anyone be so dumb as to have gotten us in there in the first place?" Our policies and decision-making processes were affected by this fundamental questioning of the whole structure of government.

The civil rights movement of the early 1960s also represented a challenge to the basic means by which decisions are made and enforced. Blacks have known of the discontinuities between democratic principles and policies for scores of years. From their vantage point, the principles of political equality simply had a racial addendum: "If you're black, stand back." Their efforts during the 1960s were designed to make others aware of these gaps, sometimes in very dramatic fashion (as with the urban riots during that time). But black leadership was also challenging the legitimacy of a system structured to favor whites. Put another way, they were not content to accept new policies, they wanted new processes, different leaders, and greater access to decision making for themselves.

And finally there are the remarkable events of the second Nixon administration: the president and vice president forced to resign in dishonor, two attorneys general convicted of crimes (Richard G. Kliendienst pleading guilty to a misdemeanor charge for failing to testify fully before a Senate committee and John N. Mitchell for his involvement in Watergate), a secretary of Commerce pleading guilty to illegal fund raising (unwillfully failing to report contributions), a secretary of the Treasury indicted but acquitted of accepting bribes, and countless presidential aides and campaign officials convicted and sent to prison. While not all of these resignations, indictments, and convictions were a direct result of Watergate, that event came to dominate American politics for 20 months and continues to influence decision making.

The contrast between what we expect of a president and what apparently occurred in the Watergate cover-up activities was severe, with the result that an already cynical public became even more so. Arthur H. Miller offers the following evidence from the national voter surveys of the Center for Political Studies at the University of Michigan to show that public cynicism about government increased markedly between 1964 and 1974.[6] The figures represent those agreeing with the proposition (though it should be pointed out that respondents were not asked the question in this precise way).

	1964	1970	1974	Difference (1964–1974)
Trust the government in Washington to do what is right only some of the time.	22.0%	44.2%	61.0%	+39.0%
Government is pretty much run by a few big interests looking out for themselves.	29.0	49.6	65.0	+36.0
Quite a few of the people running the government are a little crooked.	28.0	31.0	45.0	+17.0

Thus, there had been a steady deterioration of public trust in government before Watergate occurred (1964–1970)—possibly as a result of Vietnam, racial upheavals, and growth of governments and their budgets during this period—and further deterioration with the advent of Watergate revelations.

Data provided by William Watts and Lloyd A. Free also show a decline in public confidence during the Watergate months between 1972 and 1974. Though based on different questions (they relied on the Gallup Organization for their data), the Watts-Free findings document what may well be a nadir in public views of governmental capacities (the poll was conducted in April, 1974).[7]

	1972	1974	Difference
Confidence in the federal government's handling of domestic matters.	61*	52	−9
Trust and confidence in:			
—the executive branch	67	45	−22
—the legislative branch	62	59	−3
—the judicial branch	60	62	+2
Ratings of:			
—honesty, fairness, and justice in government	46	43	−3
—consideration and responsiveness	41	39	−2
—efficiency	44	37	−7

*Represent composite scores devised by Watts and Free.

However distressing these data may be, it is not at all certain that they represent a serious threat to the legitimacy of government. In fact, Jack Citrin offers evidence drawn from the Michigan national voter surveys to show that a large majority of those lowest in trust have pride in government. Further, surprisingly few of those low in trust support large change in government. Here are the data:[8]

	Trust in Government			
	Low	Middle	High	Total
Proud of government	74.3	91.8	97.9	86.0
Big change needed	25.1	9.1	4.9	14.7

Similarly Watts and Free found considerable trust and confidence in the American system overall, leading them to conclude that we are "not a people ripe for violent social or political upheaval, a call to extremism, or, indeed, any great changes that would threaten what is apparently seen as a pretty decent way of life for most (although definitely not all) of us."[9]

This distinction between how people view government in particular and how they view government in general suggests that there may be several types and objects of legitimacy. David Easton argues precisely that. He points out that legitimacy may be ascribed to *political authorities*, "such as an elite, an administrative staff, or the whole undifferentiated set of persons through whom authority is exercised," or "to the norms and structure of a *regime*."[10] Clearly the two will not always enjoy equal amounts of legitimacy. Thus, for example, one can question the legitimacy of a president elected by a mere plurality of the popular vote, or even one who wins in a landslide but is guilty of nefarious campaign practices, without challenging, or even being very pessimistic about, the workings of democratic government. In fact, one of the most frequent reactions to the Nixon impeachment proceedings and eventual resignation was that it all demonstrated the strength, not the weakness, of the American political system. Easton may well be right in asserting that we come to have "a psychological need to find some leaders and structures in which to believe."[11]

This differentiation in the objects of legitimacy suggests that dips in public confidence and trust can be accommodated without resorting to major reform of political institutions. In fact, the evidence would warn against any such reaction since there remains a significant measure of support and pride even among those who demonstrate the least confidence. A change in leadership, programmatic shifts, an economic upturn, an international triumph—any one of these might reestablish confidence. It would appear that at this writing (1975) we are experiencing a strong effort by President Ford to regain presidential legitimacy by relying on programmatic and stylistic measures rather than major reform. Members of Congress, too, sought to brighten their image during the immediate postresignation period when public concern and doubt were high. They have relied more on structural and procedural changes, however. In October and December, 1974, and again in January, 1975, significant reforms were enacted to alter traditional patterns of congressional authority (for example, changes in selecting committee chairmen and committee members, bill assignments, committee jurisdiction, the Senate filibuster). It is too soon to determine the ultimate effects of the two efforts—though at this writing the president would appear to have the edge.

In summary, legitimacy is a dynamic attribute of any political system. This is particularly the case in democracies where the people presumably have it within their collective power to ascribe or withhold legitimacy. Students of public policy cannot ignore this basic form of legitimation. If they begin their analysis without establishing the nature of legitimacy for institutions, decision makers, or the regime itself, they will have committed a fundamental error in research. For to neglect this phenomenon is to fail to consider and judge the context within which decisions occur.

It should also be noted, however, that measuring the legitimacy of government is no simple task. I have discussed indicators relied on by some—trust and confidence in government, public cynicism, pride or loyalty, views toward change. But I have also warned against hasty conclusions based on such measures. There is, perhaps, no more sensitive and complex interactive relationship between the people and their government than that involved in the conferral of legitimacy. While research may lead to an understanding of the decisional context legitimacy creates, it is probably too soon for research to permit confident predictions of events following even the more obvious shifts in public mood and confidence.

The Processes of Legitimation

The second form of legitimation to consider is that which exists to approve specific proposals. The most appropriate dictionary definition is that of "conforming to recognized principles or accepted standards. . . ." This definition clearly establishes the link between legitimacy and legitimation, between what is generally accepted and how individual decisions are made. In short, processes of approval or authorization or legitimation are, by this interpretation, dependent on social variables. Further, since they depend on the traditions, rules, and cultural development of a society, the processes of legitimation may vary considerably among political systems.

Whether a full measure of legitimacy has been conferred on a regime or not, specific processes exist within which someone or some group has the last word. That is, during those periods when a group of decision makers is striving to be "legitimate," they develop means for making choices. And, generally speaking, one may expect that these means will be developed in a way which officials perceive will be acceptable to various significant publics. That is not to say that all will agree on the means to be adopted or that public officials will be right in their assessment of what is acceptable (for any number of reasons—not the least of which is that legitimacy at this broader level is dynamic and not altogether predictable). It is to say, however, that the establishment of legitimation processes does not await the achievement of a particular measure of legitimacy. Officials must plunge ahead as though they knew what they were doing.

The principal process of legitimation in American democracy is majority coalition building. Majority rule has long been a cornerstone of democratic theory. It is a practical way of getting from political equality and popular sovereignty to a working government. As Currin V. Shields observes:

> The public desire served by the community should be satisfied to the greatest possible extent. In other words, the rules of the community should assure that the common purpose of the members is promoted as well as possible in the conduct of community affairs. How can this be achieved? The doctrine of majority rule is the Democrat's answer to this question.[12]

The doctrine then becomes a standard for measuring the product of policy making.

> What is determined by a majority vote is "right" for the community. Authority exercised according to a decision arrived at by a democratic process is, then, legitimate. The legitimacy depends on how the authority is exercised. The test is, for the democrat, entirely procedural.[13]

It is true, of course, that the architects of the American constitutional system were not quite prepared to go all the way with majority rule. They developed a number of checks to curb majority tyranny, for they believed, with James Madison, that:

> The accumulation of powers, legislative, executive, and judiciary, in the same hands [including legislative hands], whether of one, a few, or many, and whether hereditary, self-appointed, or elective, may justly be pronounced the very definition of tyranny.[14]

So concerned were these men with accumulated power that they opted for checks even on unanimities in public policy. In essence they argued that the mistakes made by not permitting quick action by large majorities are not as grave as those likely to be made when power is centered in a single group or institution. So while the legislature might sit as a representative body of the majority, and therefore should be considered the primary institution of democracy, it too must be checked.

In republican government, the legislative authority necessarily predominates. The remedy for this inconveniency is to divide the legislature into different branches; and to render them, by different modes of election and different principles of action, as little connected with each other as the nature of their common functions and their common dependence on the society will admit. It may even be necessary to guard against dangerous encroachments by still further precautions. As the weight of the legislature authority requires that it should be thus divided, the weakness of the executive may require, on the other hand, that it should be fortified. An absolute negative on the legislature appears, at first view, to be the natural defense with which the executive magistrate should be armed. But perhaps it would be neither altogether safe nor alone sufficient.[15]

You get the idea. While majority coalition building in legislatures is a basic legitimating process in a democracy, the founding fathers were wary about permitting it to operate freely. Therefore we cannot ignore their structural experimentation in designing checks on majority rule. More about these in the subsequent discussion of Congress.

Robert A. Dahl argues that the founding fathers were excessively concerned with majority tyranny. For him majority rule is a myth because there really is no majority. "If majority rule is mostly a myth, then majority tyranny is mostly a myth too."[16] He offers the concept "minorities rule," in which bargaining goes on between the legitimate groups in society that have access to decision making, and concludes that "on matters of specific policy the majority rarely rules."[17] Surely one cannot deny this proposition. On the other hand, any number of procedures have been established in American government to insure that decisions can be traced to a *numerical majority*. That is not to say that a majority of the citizenry is actively involved in making policy but rather that, at several points along the way to policy, numerical majorities are formed. The result is a system of layers of numerical majorities—in elections, in referenda, in committee action, in roll-call voting, in court decisions. It is true, of course, that pluralities are sometimes accepted, but it is also true that those who rely on pluralities are likely to be limited in their exercise of authority and subject to criticism.

While majority building is the principal process of legitimation, a number of subprocesses also exist. For example, if an agency is authorized to establish standards, let contracts, grant monies, or make decisions of other kinds, it must develop legitimation processes by which choices are made. An agency may, in fact, have authority to create a complete policy process—defining the problem, formulating proposals, legitimating programs or standards, etc. In many cases the choice of one alternative over another is made after consultations with affected groups or following public hearings—much like those conducted in a legislature. The rate- and standard-setting authority of regulatory agencies, the complex contracting processes of the Department of Defense and National Aeronautics and Space Administration, the programmatic discretion of many bureaucratic agencies, even the research and training grant approval methods of the National Science Foundation, all are illustrative of these subprocesses of legitimation. In short, wherever methods have to be developed to authorize further action, legitimation is involved. Since these subprocesses of approval are also properly analyzed as implementation activities as well, we will have occasion to discuss them again in a subsequent chapter.

Who Is Involved?

Of the functional activities, that of legitimation is most closely identified in a democracy with a specific institution—the legislature. The legislature is carefully designed to represent the interests of people. It is logical, therefore, that efforts would be made to direct all policy proposals through the popularly elected institution for approval. Symbolically it is rationalized that a majority of legislator-representatives on any issue represents a majority of the citizenry. We all know that there are many problems with that as a description of reality, but it is also apparent that the political system must establish some processes of legitimation that are consistent with the symbols of democracy. So legislators will continue to be central figures in legitimation until someone can rationalize others performing that role in democracy.

At the same time they are seldom the only actors involved. Keep in mind the definition of legitimation—"conforming to recognized principles or accepted standards. . . ." As noted, a central democratic process for "conforming to recognized principles" is majority building in a legislature. So who is involved in majority building? In any one issue-area one can conceive of a set of actors who interact for the purpose of building a majority to legitimate one course of action over another. Legislators will surely be involved, but majorities may also be put together through the efforts of bureaucrats, legislative liaison personnel, lobbyists, state and local officials, the president. Thus, I cannot provide a single answer as to who is involved. It obviously depends on what you find in studying any one public problem or issue-area. Above all, do not restrict your analysis, assuming that *only* legislators participate simply because they are the ones who vote on the floor of the House and Senate.

Special consideration must be given to the role played by the president in legitimation. The Constitution, Article 1, Section 7, includes a provision for presidential approval before a bill can become law. Just as the framers intended (see above), this simple requirement can greatly complicate the process of majority building by introducing a nonmajoritarian element into legitimation. The president can thwart a majority in Congress, though he may do so because he does not consider that the majority there truly reflects a majority in the nation. Of course, it is possible to override a presidential veto by constructing a two-thirds majority—no simple task! In order to avoid this circumstance, majority builders must consider the possibility of veto. The threat of veto, then, becomes as influential in legitimation as the veto itself. In most instances, it is the president himself seeking a majority for proposals originating from his office and thus Congress need not wonder what it is he wants.

The peculiar circumstances of the Ford presidency provide an absolutely fascinating study of legitimation politics. An unelected Republican president has consistently vetoed bills passed by an overwhelmingly Democratic Congress. Despite their strong majorities, the Democrats have found it difficult to override the vetoes. At one point, a House Democrat said: "I think it could honestly be said to be a tyranny of the minority."[18] Clearly the president's authority and position have become a major part of the equation in legitimation, even when his personal sources of power are limited. Presumably this would please James Madison.

Majority Building in Congress

It is useful to examine a major legislative body like the Congress to increase one's understanding of legitimation. Two points should be emphasized in this discussion. First, the legislative process in Congress is one of the most complicated of any parliamentary body in the world.[19] The few generalizations discussed below are meant merely to suggest some of the bases for analyzing legitimation in Congress. Second, in focusing on an institution you should recall that our basic mode of analysis is *not* institutional. Keep in mind that (1) legislators are not merely legitimators but perform other policy roles as well and that (2) other policy actors from other institutions do act as legitimators.

First, distinguishing between formulation and legitimation is still not a simple task. Formulation doesn't necessarily end because legitimation has begun. Introducing an administration-sponsored bill into the House of Representatives does not represent the transition from formulation processes to legitimation processes. As I have repeatedly stressed, these functions may be performed simultaneously by the same people in different institutions—or not, as the case may be.

Next it is interesting to observe how a legislature establishes a network for tapping the interests and knowledge of those associated with or affected by a proposal. Congress relies on many different response mechanisms, presumably as a correction to any one. Thus, for example, congressional committee hearings, staff research, diversified representation on committees, continuing contact with interest groups, research by congressional agencies (Congressional Research Service, Office of Technology Assessment, General Accounting Office), requests for information from agencies and private research groups—all contribute to a knowledge flow that is sometimes overwhelming. The point is to create means by which legislators can judge where compromise is necessary—due either to the intensity of interest or to factors not fully evaluated by those involved in earlier stages of action. Compiling such a record is no guarantee that the information will be judiciously weighed by legislators or others involved in legitimation. Congressman X may still support what he guesses to be best for his district or himself. But the continuing documentation of problems, interests, reactions, and systematic research serves many purposes in public policy making. As can be illustrated over and over again (a prime case is federal aid to education—to be discussed below), the response network working effectively may only demonstrate why no majority is currently possible. Ten years later, however, a law may finally be enacted. Thus, the legitimation process of testing responses to determine where and how a majority might be built can contribute as well to defining the problem and formulating future proposals.

A third point to consider in studying majority building in Congress is that several majorities may have to be constructed. Separating the institutions, checking and balancing them to prevent tyranny, creating a specialized committee system—these and other features so characteristic of our political system provide various access points for special interests. At the same time, however, they offer appeal possibilities for those who lose along the way. It is seldom sufficient, therefore, to collect a majority at one point; it must be maintained throughout the intricacies of a bill becoming a law. Calculate the number of majorities which must be held for a *major* bill—beginning with subcommittee action in one house. I count a dozen just for authorizing a program, without counting amendments.

House:

    Subcommittee
    Committee
    House Rules Committee
    Vote on the rule
    Vote in the Committee
      of the Whole
    Vote on the bill in
      the House
    Vote on recommital

Senate:

> Subcommittee
> Committee
> Scheduling
> Vote on the bill
> Vote on reconsideration

Obviously amendments and appropriations can multiply this number considerably so that a particularly complex piece of legislation will require fifty or sixty majorities—and still not pass, or possibly be vetoed.

Of course these several majorities may overlap considerably in population. Once a majority is put together, it may be able to withstand several challenges. On the other hand, majorities for legislation may have different populations at every stage. A fourth point is that *different strategies may be needed to build majorities for the same proposal*. For example, getting a proposed course of action adopted in a standing committee may pose an entirely different problem from getting a rule from the House Committee on Rules. Or gaining approval in the populous and formal House typically requires different strategies than gaining approval in the smaller and more leisurely Senate.

In that same connection, as a fifth characteristic, different strategies may be required over time for building majorities in the process of legitimation in Congress. Most major policies are enacted over a period of years—in some cases it takes decades before the federal government enters a particular issue-area. During these periods committees change personnel and leadership, party leaders come and go, turnover occurs in the membership, procedural changes are made. For example, getting a majority in the House Committee on Rules proved very difficult for those who favored liberal proposals during the 1950s. With the important changes in the size and prerogatives of the committee during the period 1961-1965, however, the whole atmosphere changed.[20] The committee was no longer a major stumbling block for the liberals.

Sixth, a number of nonmajoritarian and extramajoritarian considerations must be taken into account in analyzing legitimation processes in Congress. I have already mentioned the president's role. For decades the standing committee chairmen had impressive power almost comparable to a presidential veto to thwart a majority by refusing to call a meeting of the committee; sending a bill to a subcommittee known to be adverse to it; delaying, denying, or obstructing hearings; managing the timing of legislation to the least advantage for its proponents. While a majority might still work its will, the fear of reprisals and concern about precedents prevented any very frequent revolts. During the 1970s, however, the House in particular made a number of changes to curb the power of committee chairmen. In addition to drastically modifying the seniority rule by having committee leaders (chairmen and ranking minority members) subject to approval by party caucuses, each committee was required to establish rules and procedures so as to curb the arbitrary power of chairmen. These reform measures had dramatic impact in 1975 when three Democratic chairmen were turned out by the party caucus. Still the chairmen and ranking minority members remain as central figures in majority building. Whether they regain their previous status or not, the fact remains that the power of certain legislators over others introduces nonmajoritarian elements into the legislative process.

Next to the two-thirds majority required to override a veto, the infamous filibuster in the Senate is the best example of an extramajoritarian requirement for certain types of issues. For a long time in this nation, the legitimation process for civil rights legislation required a two-thirds majority in the Senate. When a motion is made to consider a bill, senators may begin lengthy speeches in opposition. A senator may speak forever if he has the stamina, but he cannot "speak more than twice upon any one question in debate on the same day without leave of the Senate."[21] Once several senators begin a round of endless speechmaking, the procedure for closing debate is cumbersome. Sixteen senators must sign a motion and until 1975 two-thirds of the membership "present and voting" had to concur. In 1975 this figure was reduced slightly to three-fifths of the entire membership, except for rules changes (where two-thirds is still required). Until 1964 a minority in the Senate—the Southern Democrats—were virtually able to veto major civil rights legislation because of this procedure. Recent events have assisted in collecting the "extra" majority, however, and though the threat of filibuster is ever present, civil rights legislation is now easier to enact.

Another general point to consider in evaluating majority building in Congress is that bargaining is a central feature of all processes in that institution. That really goes without saying, but if I failed to mention it you might think I did so intentionally. Given the ubiquity of bargaining in Congress, it is almost certain that the outcome of majority building will be a program which is not absolutely satisfactory to anyone but acceptable to many. This condition further suggests that persons making up a majority have various commitments to the policy. Support for a course of action may be offered because one really feels that a particular problem needs resolving, or because one determines that support in this instance will result in a *quid pro quo*, or because one expects to reap personal benefits of various kinds (a committee appointment, leadership post, additional staff), or because of a combination of these reasons. Obviously, the ideal situation is when a majority actually is concerned about the issue-area and determined to do something about it. Even then, of course, bargaining characterizes behavior, since not everyone can be expected to view the specific problems in the same way or agree on what ought to be done to relieve needs.

Direct mention must also be made of the role of political parties in Congress. Parties function primarily to facilitate, but not guarantee, the development of majority coalitions. That is, the two parties organize the chambers, thereby establishing the machinery by which majorities can be constructed for specific policies. That machinery—the caucus, committees of various types (policy and/or steering committees, committees-on-committees, research groups), a whip system, leaders of various types—can be used for legitimating a course of action, but traditionally it has not been well designed for formulating courses of action. The activities of the House Republicans between 1959 and 1969 stand as the outstanding exception to that generalization. Real efforts were made during that period to employ the caucus and committee structure of the party to propose alternative courses of action and to probe issue-areas not under study by the administration.[22] And in 1975, both the House and Senate Democrats proposed economic and energy programs counter to those offered by President Ford. Further, the House Democratic caucus showed signs of strength in policy matters during the early months of 1975. Whether these activities presage a new, more policy-oriented role for congressional parties is as yet unclear.

Given this facilitative role of parties, one would not normally expect party leaders to be oriented toward the substance of policy. Rather one would expect them to be more procedurally oriented—expert in the techniques of building majorities, possessing a fine sense of the possible in developing compromises, and aware of the intricacies of procedure on the House and Senate floors. Indeed, given expectations that party leaders will be more facilitative, one who injects himself too much in program development and presses too strongly for his preferences in the substance of policy will probably suffer heavy criticism.

The precise facilitative role of political parties differs between the majority and the minority and between the House and Senate. It is not necessary to go into detail on that point—it has been the subject of at least two books.[23] Suffice it to say that the majority party typically facilitates the construction of a majority in favor; the minority party often facilitates a majority against. Again, bargaining and compromise obviously characterize these activities. In regard to the two chambers, the need for political parties is greater in the House due to the larger size. Party is not insignificant in the Senate, but the greater informality reduces the need for elaborate organization and procedures.

Finally, it should be noted that legislative involvement in majority coalition building differs among issues. Thus, for example, Congress may only confirm a coalition built elsewhere, playing a minimal role in the creation of that support. Or the members may actively participate in developing a coalition—perhaps the more common role for legislators. An even stronger role is that of legislative leadership in building the majority—taking the initiative for getting the major interests and their representatives to compromise and coalesce. And a most interesting role—one described below—is when Congress seeks to satisfy what is assumed to be a majority among the public. Here then are four distinct institutional roles for Congress in legitimation. In each case Congress performs the legal task of authorizing the program. But, as I have stressed before, the actual participation of members in coalition building is not uniform.

Two Cases of Legitimation

To illustrate some of the points made in this chapter, I now offer two concrete illustrations of majority building. The first—federal aid to education—shows how majority support is built over a considerable period of time and with extensive involvement of many types of political actors. The second—federal air pollution control—offers a fascinating story of legitimation virtually occurring before formulation as a result of strong public concern about the environment.

Federal Aid Comes to Education—1965

By the 1960s the legitimation system for policy treating the vast numbers of problems in the education issue-area had had decades to mature. Since the first land endowments were made to the states for educational purposes nearly two hundred years ago, formulators had offered countless courses of action to provide general aid to elementary and secondary schools. These efforts intensified in the period after World War II, culminating in the passage of the Elementary and Secondary Education Act in 1965.[24]

The many problems that make up the education issue-area are some of the most intense in American domestic conflicts. The description by Frank J. Munger and Richard F. Fenno, Jr., is apt.

> Even the briefest history of federal aid legislation makes clear one important fact, that the struggle over federal aid has not been a single conflict, but rather a multiplicity of controversies only loosely related to one another. The situation might be compared to a better-than-three-ring circus, although, in view of the tactics at times employed, a multiple barroom brawl might make a more apt analogy.[25]

Just developing a course of action adequate to meet the demands for classroom construction, teachers' salaries, teacher training, and curriculum development is complicated enough. But, in addition, several publics view the consequences of education policies at all levels in ways that are incompatible and directly conflicting.

To the blacks, education policies have been important in keeping them the underclass in American social life. They will examine any course of action carefully to determine whether it provides them with opportunities for advancement. Many whites, on the other hand, continue to believe in racial segregation. They see nothing but bad effects for them resulting from equal opportunity for both races within the same school building.

Many parochial school advocates, primarily the Roman Catholics, view any effort to correct the ills of public schools from their perspective as taxpayers also supporting a private school system. "Double taxation" is the cry among those who send their children to parochial schools while paying to maintain another school for their neighbors' children. Protestant and Jewish groups can be expected to oppose any proposal that either includes Catholic schools in aid benefits or allows Catholics to opt out of paying for the public schools. To them, since the public schools are for everyone, all should pay. Any decision not to attend public schools is made freely and cannot release the individual family from its public responsibilities.[26]

Other sets of eyes are also fixed on efforts to involve the federal government in the elementary and secondary schools. The specter of federal controls in "your neighborhood school," with coincident loss of influence by the "folks at home," is used by many groups to oppose any additional aid. Their influence is so great that even those who support extensive aid preface their remarks by paying lip service to local control. Munger and Fenno cite the example of Matthew Woll of the American Federation of Labor, who, in testifying before a Senate committee in 1945, stated: "We are unalterably opposed to any federal control of education or direction over the education process." He then introduced a set of resolutions urging that any federal aid to states be contingent on a series of standards for the length of the school year, integration of schools, distribution of funds, teachers' salaries, matching state appropriations, creation of an equitable state aid system, and teacher tenure.[27]

If some of these publics had only limited access to policy systems, one might expect little difficulty in legitimation. In fact, however, all have impressive access. Few conflicting perceptions and definitions have been left out of the debate on federal aid to education in the past two decades. Consider, for example, the membership of the House Committee on Education and Labor in 1961 (a particularly intense year for education policy). Though there was only one black on the committee, he was the chairman—Adam Clayton Powell (D-New York), who had previously authored an amendment to deny federal aid to segregated schools. No legislation could expect approval without his support. Southern Democrats had unusually low representation on the committee but had strong bargaining positions in the Committee on Rules (chaired by Howard W. Smith, D-Virginia) and in the Senate (with the filibuster).

Catholics had strong representation among the Democrats of the 1961 committee—seven of nineteen members. In addition, Catholics could count on support from certain other Democratic members from urban districts with a large Catholic population. And the "antifederal controls" viewpoint had many stalwarts on the committee—at least six on the Republican side. With such impressive access for all, majority building was a particularly sticky endeavor.

Participants in legitimation during the 1960s were drawn from a large number of institutions and groups, including the following:

Congress

> House Committee on Education and Labor
> House Committee on Rules
> Senate Committee on Labor and Public Welfare
> Senate Democratic Policy Committee
> Senate and House Party Leaders

Executive

> Office of Education, Department of Health, Education, and Welfare
> Bureau of the Budget
> White House Office

Private Groups

> National Education Association
> National Catholic Welfare Conference (later called the United States Catholic Conference)
> National Association for the Advancement of Colored People
> National Council of Churches
> American Federation of Teachers
> American Jewish Congress
> National Congress of Parents and Teachers Associations
> AFL-CIO

During the period 1961-1965, persons from these units searched for a compromise which would get the support of a majority in Congress. After so many years of working and reworking every aspect of every proposal, the prospects for general federal aid to elementary and secondary schools seemed dim.

> What does appear clearly from the record is the strength of the forces holding the federal government back from a deeper commitment in elementary and secondary education. In 1937 the Senate majority leader, Joseph T. Robinson, described education as "the one last field into which federal activity is to be extended." ... Twenty-five years later, education remains the one last major governmental function assigned primarily to state and local government.[28]

Prospects appeared hopeless in 1962, partly because they had appeared so bright in 1960 and 1961. Federal aid bills actually passed both the House and Senate in 1960—unprecedented in the twentieth century. Each house passed different versions, however, and the House Committee on Rules refused by a vote of seven to five to take actions allowing a conference with the Senate to iron out the differences.[29] So, seven members of the Rules Committee presumed to override majorities in both the House and the Senate—a truly audacious action.

The near victory in 1960 was encouraging to proponents, and they expected to re-form the majorities necessary when the 87th Congress met in 1961. President Kennedy's strong support for legislation contrasted sharply with the ambiguous position of President Eisenhower on this issue. And the expansion of the Rules Committee from twelve to fifteen seemed to remove that stumbling block. Passage of a general aid bill was virtually secured, or so many advocates thought. President Kennedy was a Roman Catholic, however, and, as the first of his faith to be elected president, had to lean over backwards to avoid favoring his church.

> During the campaign he had repeatedly endorsed federal aid to education.... He had also emphasized that he favored such aid for public schools only and opposed granting funds to parochial schools. In his widely quoted speech to the Greater Houston Ministerial Association he had stated: "I believe in an America where the separation of church and state is absolute—where no church or church school is granted any public funds."[30]

Catholic leaders were disturbed by this statement. For them, 1961 was a crucial year. They, too, read all of the signs indicating passage of a general aid bill. *But if such legislation passed with no funds for parochial schools, a strong precedent would be set.* Unless they were included in this legislation, Catholics might never get government aid.

Building a majority suddenly became a much more complicated task. Many liberals who might ordinarily support an aid bill were Catholics—including the Democratic majority leaders in both the House and Senate, John W. McCormack of Massachusetts and Mike Mansfield of Montana.

Catholics held the balance of power in the newly expanded Rules Committee. So at many points where majorities had to be put together, parochial aid advocates had strength. Supporters of federal aid began the tedious process of trying to guarantee these majorities. Bargains were struck; compromises were the order of the day.

The Senate passed a bill with relatively little difficulty. In the House a delicate agreement had been worked out whereby some parochial school aid would be included in a different bill. In the end, however, the Catholics were fearful that their legislation would not survive. Two Catholics on the Rules Committee voted with the five Republicans and two Southern Democrats to delay the general aid bill until the parochial bill was reported out of the Committee on Education and Labor. Then one Catholic, James Delaney of New York, voted with the Republicans and Southern Democrats to table all education bills. The combination of Republicans and Southern Democrats had long dominated the Rules Committee and had been referred to as an "unholy alliance." "Now, one wit suggested, 'the unholy alliance has got religion.' "[31]

Pessimism reigned supreme after 1961. Practically every combination had been tried in offering courses of action. Legitimators were running out of strategies. In a sense, however, the fact that nobody got anything when all were so close to resolving age-old dilemmas spurred efforts to try again.

By 1965 the political climate had changed dramatically, with the result that conditions were even more conducive to the passage of legislation than in 1961. The tragic assassination of President Kennedy brought to the White House a Southern Protestant who was dedicated to enacting the Kennedy program. The largest Democratic majorities in nearly thirty years were elected with President Johnson in 1964, giving Northern Democrats greater force within their party. The Republican party made important leadership changes in the House (with younger, more positive members ousting conservative, old-guard leaders). Further changes were made to curb the power of the House Committee on Rules in 1963 and 1965. And the Civil Rights Act of 1964 had prohibited the use of federal funds for segregated public facilities—thus removing a major race issue from education aid.

Private groups were also making changes. After much painful reassessment, the National Education Association changed its stand against federal aid for parochial schools. Announcing its decision on December 16, 1964, the NEA, according to one spokesman, "recognized that if it took a rigid position on the church-state issue as an organization it would have been hamstrung politically."[32] The National Council of Churches joined NEA in its willingness to accept some form of support for church schools. With the American Federation of Teachers having been more flexible on this issue before, a basis for compromise was developing. For its part, the United States Catholic Conference had undergone an extensive review of its position after 1961. Some Catholics thought the organization had gone too far in 1961—indeed, not all church officials agreed that federal aid would be a good idea. In any event, the USCC was prepared to compromise in 1965.

With these important changes, passage of a federal aid bill seemed assured. Decades of experience in trying to build majorities in Congress had taught everyone extreme caution, however. The Commissioner of Education, Francis Keppel, was uniquely qualified to lead the last, careful expedition toward effective compromise. "Without exception the participants in these negotiations credit Keppel's work with producing a series of 'understandings' that developed into the basis for the church-state settlement. . . ."[33]

The formula for success in resolving the church-state issue was found in the Economic Opportunity Act of 1964. Why not aid the children instead of the schools? Specifically, aid was proposed for low-income school districts and could go for parochial as well as public school children. Aid was also provided for the purchase of books and the establishment of "supplementary educational centers" to serve both public and parochial schools. Linking aid to education with poverty was best summarized in this oft-quoted statement from the president's message: "Poverty has many roots but the tap root is ignorance."

Members of Congress prepared themselves for another round of hearings, executive sessions, rewritings, amendments. It is characteristic of Congress that fully 90 percent of its business is old business—expansion of existing programs, review of controversial proposals from the past, evaluation of ongoing policy, and so on. At least they had something new to consider in a time-worn issue-area in 1965.

> After many years of listening to essentially the same witnesses reiterating essentially the same statistics, showing either the existence of or lack of an education "crisis" revolving around enrollments, classroom shortages, teacher shortages, and state-local tax resources, congressmen certainly must have welcomed the change in presentation if for no other reason than variety.[34]

All major groups accepted the course of action proposed, though none were fully satisfied. So it is with compromises. Congress reflected this agreement by passing the bill in both houses by large margins. In fact, despite the years of bitter dispute, the legislative history of the Elementary and Secondary Education Act of 1965 was rather routine.[35]

In the argument for passage, those leading the fight for legitimation asked that Congress "strike while the iron is hot." That is, since at that moment in history the major roadblock appeared resolved, some legislation should be enacted. "We will worry about altering the program at some future date."[36] This approach offers interesting lessons for understanding legitimation. It is a process of striking the bargains necessary to collect a majority—within the limits set by the values of the society. The most satisfactory course of action from one public's point of view (or definition of its problem) may have to be sacrificed to get policy. Bargaining occurs in the legitimation processes in Congress, and it occurs later in the interpretations and applications of policy in the field. One member of Congress described very well what is involved in legitimation in discussing the 1965 Act.

> ... we just had to make the hard choice and face the reality that in 1965 the issue was not good education policy versus bad. The question Congress had to settle in 1965 was whether there was ever to be federal aid to the elementary and secondary schools of this nation. *The 1965 bill, in all candor, does not make much sense educationally; but it makes a hell of a lot of sense legally, politically, and constitutionally.*[37]

From his vantage point the bill did not solve the problems of education, but a principle was legitimized. One could expect therefore that the substance of policy would be established over the next several decades.

Policy Escalation in Air Pollution Control—1969–1970[38]

The previous case represents almost classic temporizing in which groups with strong interests are forced to compromise and settle for half a loaf or less. Now we turn to an instance where group interests are superseded by a quite extraordinary general public interest. We witnessed a virtual explosion in concern for the environment during 1969–1970. A national "Earth Day," local demonstrations, public opinion polls, recycling centers, citizen groups, and public hearings on pollution codes were instructive to legislators at all three levels of government that temporizing in this issue-area would not suffice. Politicians do not compromise just to do so—they find it an essential mode of operation in the business of representing. Where the general public forcefully demonstrates its preferences, elected decision makers are more than willing to accommodate.

Thus it did not take Washington officials long to interpret the mood of Earth Day, April 22, 1970. And they had an immediate opportunity to act since the Air Quality Act of 1967 expired in 1970. Normally one would have expected a series of incremental adjustments to that act—and, in fact, several such amendments had been introduced prior to Earth Day. No mere increment would suffice in 1970, however. Citizen groups and the media could be expected to monitor federal action, for environmental policy now had an attentive public.

With the general public as a major actor, we cannot so easily identify the participants in legitimation (as was done for education—see above). For what we have here is not so much the building of a majority for a particular policy option as the search for a policy option to suit a waiting majority. Since no one was quite certain what that unspecified majority might want, however, we witnessed an escalation of proposals toward what various public officials estimated would satisfy this emergent public mood.

Put another way, legitimation had, in one sense, already occurred. The public wanted strong environmental programs and Congress was willing to enact them. Since the majority was already there, one could not expect the usual set of compromises associated with building it. And, further, one would not expect various special interests to play as significant a role since their support was not needed.

It should also be pointed out that the exclusion of special interest groups from the process may invite the testing of proposals which would not normally receive much attention. Nowhere is this better illustrated than in the case of the so-called Farbstein amendment in 1970. Leonard Farbstein (D-New York) had conducted hearings on automotive pollution in New York City quite on his own initiative in 1969. As a result of these hearings, he introduced an amendment to the 1970 air pollution bill that would have phased out the internal combustion engine if it did not meet certain standards. While his proposal did not pass, it did get serious consideration. As he noted: "This is the same amendment I offered either last year or 2 years ago. . . . At that time it seemed as though it was an oddball amendment, but strange as it may seem, it has caught on."[39]

Though less dramatically different, the proposals offered by the president and the two major House and Senate committees represented significant increases in federal authority. More important for the point being made here, however, the proposals escalated from modest increments introduced by Senator Edmund S. Muskie (D-Maine) in late 1969 and early 1970 to those offered by President Nixon, the House Committee on Interstate and Foreign Commerce (Subcommittee on Public Health and Welfare), and the Senate Committee on Public Works (Subcommittee on Air and Water Pollution).

The increased public concern for the environment provided President Nixon with a theme for the domestic portion of his 1970 state of the Union address. Coincidentally, it also provided him with a means for taking the initiative away from a possible 1972 presidential election opponent—Edmund S. Muskie. Senator Muskie had generally been acknowledged to be the congressional leader on environmental policy. Here then was a perfect issue for the president, and he was not one to miss the opportunity.

> I now turn to a subject which, next to our desire for peace, may well become the major concern of the American people in the decade of

the seventies. . . . The great question of the seventies is, shall we sur-
render to our surroundings, or shall we make our peace with nature
and begin to make preparations for the damage we have done to our
air, to our land, and to our water? . . . Clean air, clean water, open
spaces—these should once again be the birthright of every American.
If we act now—they can be.[40]

The air pollution control proposals which followed this address were
generally acknowledged to constitute a strong program. Even Senator
Muskie had to concede that the president had seized the initiative, citing
his advantages in doing so as "the nature of the presidency and the power
of the presidency."[41]

Muskie had other challengers too. The House had for years assumed a
secondary role in air pollution control legislation (at least during the
1960s). With the growth in public concern and interest, however, one
could expect a more vigorous response in 1970. Paul G. Rogers (D-Florida),
a member of the Subcommittee on Public Health and Welfare and effectively the chairman for this issue since the senior member was not active,
was most anxious to establish his territorial rights. Rogers conducted a
set of hard-hitting hearings in December, 1969, which identified a number
of problems with existing federal law. He then shepherded a bill through
the full committee which was stronger in several respects than that requested by President Nixon (see Table 5-1). In keeping with the mood of
the time, the principal threat to the legislation on the floor came not from
those who wanted to temporize but rather from the Farbstein group which
wanted to further escalate controls. When this attack was beaten back, the
bill passed overwhelmingly—374-1—on June 10.

Table 5-1. Escalation of Air Pollution Proposals, 1970

Major Provisions	Administration Bill	House-passed Bill	Senate-passed Bill
Air quality standards	+	++	++
Control regions	–	++	+
Implementation plans	+	++	+++
Stationary-source emissions	+	++	++++
Automotive emissions	+	++	++++
Fuel standards	++	+	++
Aircraft emissions	–	++	+
Federal facilities	–	+	+
Money authorized	open	+	++
Judicial review	–	–	+
Citizen suits	–	–	+

– indicates no provision.
+ indicates provision included.
Additional +'s indicate strength of provision relative to other bills.
Source: Charles O. Jones, *Clean Air: The Politics of Pollution Control* (Pittsburgh:
University of Pittsburgh Press, 1975), p. 204.

The scene now shifted to the Senate where Senator Muskie formerly had the pollution control action all to himself. Not only were other intruding into this issue-area with bold proposals, but serious questions were being raised about Muskie's previous leadership. In particular, a Ralph Nader group study on air pollution was released in May, 1970, that was highly critical of Muskie.

> Muskie is . . . the chief architect of the disastrous Air Quality Act of 1967. That fact alone would warrant his being stripped of his title as "Mr. Pollution Control." But the senator's passivity since 1967 in the face of an ever worsening air pollution crisis compounds his earlier failure. . . .[42]

The Nader group charged that only with the president's entry into the issue-area had Muskie been revived. "In other words, the air pollution issue became vital again when it appeared that the president might steal the senator's thunder on a good political issue."[43]

These charges insured that the Senate would be urged by Muskie to go even further than the House. One reporter summarized the situation as follows:

> The Bill started out last winter in Senator Muskie's pollution sub-committee as a mild updating of the unsuccessful 1967 law.
>
> Along the way, consumer champion Ralph Nader unleashed a stinging study charging that the Senator had "failed the nation in the field of air-pollution control legislation."
>
> Then, in a feat of "one-upmanship," the House of Representatives last month passed a surprisingly strong bill. . . .
>
> Its hard line leaves little room for toughening. But Senator Muskie seems determined to do just that. As Capitol Hill's "Mr. Environment" and a leading presidential contender, he has a reputation to keep.[44]

To make a long story short, the subcommittee finally produced an even tougher bill by the end of the summer. Despite the outcries of industry, the legislation passed the Senate 73-0 on September 22. The bill which emerged from the conference committee was much closer to the tougher Senate version and it was, in turn, signed by the president at the end of December. Table 5-1 shows the specifics of the proposal escalation in 1970.

The result of this form of legitimation, where broad public demand on a highly technical issue creates a pre-formed majority, was, in this case, policy beyond capability. With automobile emissions no one would deny this conclusion. Indeed, the law was intended to stimulate the development of a technology which did not presently exist. We now know that it didn't work. The deadline for meeting the automotive emission standards set in the Clean Air Amendments of 1970 has been postponed several times. But it was certainly a bold move announced with much fanfare in

1970. All of this suggests that there are also risks attendant to meeting general public demands. Unfortunately no magic exists by which we get simple solutions to highly complex public problems. However much one may wish to ignore the so-called special interests and plunge ahead to enact "right" policies for "true" causes, the realities of knowledge requirements, technological developments, political support, and administrative capabilities eventually reassert themselves.

Summary

Legitimation produces an accepted base of action for alleviating human needs. But passing laws or creating standards does not, in itself, solve problems. Rather one has a somewhat more coherent starting point than before. These widely diverse cases illustrate a number of points about the process by which this happens. First, majority building is not accomplished by simple dictation from party leaders or the president. As we have seen here, it is itself reflective of what may be occurring within an issue-area. Complex and controversial matters do not conveniently subside in a democratic system. A second, concomitant point is simply that what goes on outside of government may be critical in determining whether, how, and when a majority can be collected in Congress. With the education controversy, practically every major public or interest had the power to veto proposals which ignored or underrepresented their views. With air pollution, the extraordinary general public concern and interest superseded the modifying effect of major industrial interests.

Third, I never fail to be impressed with the variation in time required for legitimating proposals. Federal aid to education is, perhaps, the classic case at the snail's end of the continuum. Federal air pollution control programs set a jet pace by comparison. From a fledging program of support for state and local agencies in 1963, the federal government had, by 1970, asserted a major role for itself—quite beyond its capacities to accomplish.

Finally, to reiterate, what has been adopted must itself be interpreted in the context of the interests affected, the support available, the ever-changing conditions associated with an issue-area. As government goes on to meet the problems, it has been provided with more or less specific guidelines. But no amount of research, planning, experience, or resolution among diverse interests totally prepares the administrator for what he or she finds in the field. All sorts of things turn up—more understanding of the problems, discovery of related or totally new problems, inconsistencies in standards, unexpected side effects, etc. Typically such new knowledge brings the whole assemblage of bureaucrats, executives, and group representatives right back to Congress for further authorization, clarification, and occasionally even recision.

Notes

1. Hanna Pitkin, "Obligation and Consent—II," *American Political Science Review*, vol. 60 (March 1966), p. 52. Emphasis added. See also Robert J. Pranger, "An Explanation for Why Final Political Authority Is Necessary," *American Political Science Review*, vol. 60 (December 1966), pp. 994–997. In answer to the question of why we obey, Pranger says, "One obeys because of the personal repercussions of not obeying."

2. David Easton, *A Systems Analysis of Political Life* (New York: Wiley, 1965), p. 273.

3. Easton, p. 273.

4. Easton, p. 278.

5. Richard M. Merelman, "Learning and Legitimacy," *American Political Science Review*, vol. 60 (September 1966), p. 553.

6. Taken from Arthur H. Miller, "Political Issues and Trust in Government: 1964–1970," *American Political Science Reivew*, vol. 68 (September 1974), p. 953; and Michael J. Malbin, "Political Parties and 1976," *National Journal Reprints* (Washington, D.C.: National Journal, 1976), p. 10.

7. Taken from William Watts and Lloyd A. Free, *State of the Nation, 1974* (Washington, D.C.: Potomac Associates, 1974), pp. 71–80. Interestingly, during this period of declining confidence in the federal government, the public's respect for state and local government increased (at least as measured in this one study). Perhaps this supports the Easton view that we *need* to have confidence in government—if not nationally, then we switch to state and local.

8. Taken from Jack Citrin, "Comment: The Political Relevance of Trust in Government," *American Political Science Review*," vol. 68 (September 1974), p. 975.

9. Watts and Free, p. 315.

10. Easton, p. 286.

11. Easton, p. 309.

12. Currin V. Shields, *Democracy and Catholicism in America* (New York: McGraw-Hill, 1958), p. 244.

13. Shields, pp. 245–246.

14. *The Federalist* (New York: Modern Library, 1939), p. 313.

15. *The Federalist*, p. 338.

16. Robert A. Dahl, *A Preface to Democratic Theory* (Chicago: University of Chicago Press, 1956), p. 133.

17. Dahl, p. 124.

18. Donald Riegle (D-Michigan) quoted in *The Congressional Quarterly Weekly Report*, June 28, 1975, p. 1333.

19. Rather than repeat the basic elements of that process, see a text on legislatures—William J. Keefe and Morris S. Ogul, *The American Legislative Process: Congress and the States* (Englewood Cliffs, N.J.: Prentice-Hall, 1973), or Malcolm E. Jewell and Samuel C. Patterson, *The Legislative Process in the United States* (New York: Random House, 1973). A good brief review is Charles J. Zinn, *How Our Laws Are Made* (Washington, D.C.: U.S. Government Printing Office, 1961).

20. For an analysis of these changes, see Robert L. Peabody and Nelson W. Polsby, eds., *New Perspectives on the House of Representatives* (Chicago: Rand McNally, 1963), Chs. 6, 7; and William MacKaye, *A New Coalition Takes Control: The House Rules Committee Fight, 1961* (New York: McGraw-Hill, 1963).

21. Rule XIX of the Standing Rules of the Senate.

22. For a description of these activities, see Charles O. Jones, *The Minority Party in Congress* (Boston: Little, Brown, 1970), Ch. 8.

23. In addition to Jones on the minority party, see Randall B. Ripley, *Majority Party Leadership in Congress* (Boston: Little, Brown, 1969).

24. See Frank J. Munger and Richard F. Fenno, Jr., *National Politics and Federal Aid to Education* (Syracuse, N.Y.: Syracuse University Press, 1962) for a brief review of legislation in the past one hundred years. Good literature by political scientists and journalists on the issue of federal aid to education is abundant. This case study relies heavily on Munger and Fenno; Eugene Eidenberg and Roy D. Morey, *An Act of Congress* (New York: Norton, 1969); Philip Meranto, *The Politics of Federal Aid to Education in 1965: A Study in Political Innovation* (Syracuse, N.Y.: Syracuse University Press, 1967); and Hugh D. Price, "Race, Religion, and the Rules Committee: The Kennedy Aid-to-Education Bills," in Alan F. Westin, ed., *The Uses of Power* (New York: Harcourt, Brace & World, 1962). See also Robert Bendiner, *Obstacle Course on Capitol Hill* (New York: McGraw-Hill, 1965).

25. Munger and Fenno, *National Politics and Federal Aid to Education*, p. 16.

26. The Supreme Court has been ambiguous on the question of parochial aid, never really hitting the issue head-on. The most important deci-

sion of relevance is *Everson* v. *Board of Education* 330 U.S. 1 (1947), where the Court strictly interpreted the "establishment of religion" clause of the First Amendment but then ruled that New Jersey could spend tax-raised funds to pay bus fares of parochial school pupils since this was aiding the child, not the religion. In his dissent, Justice Jackson cited the precedent of Julia, who, according to Byron, "whispering 'I will ne'er consent,'—consented." The fact that both sides cite the Everson case to support their positions is evidence of the ambiguity of this decision.

27. Munger and Fenno, *National Politics and Federal Aid to Education*, p. 49.

28. Munger and Fenno, p. 185.

29. This power was taken from the Committee on Rules in 1965.

30. Price, "Race, Religion, and the Rules Committee," p. 20.

31. Price, p. 63.

32. Quoted in Eidenberg and Morey, *Act of Congress*, p. 64.

33. Eidenberg and Morey, p. 87.

34. Meranto, *Politics of Federal Aid to Education*, p. 39.

35. See Eidenberg and Morey, *An Act of Congress*, for the most extensive description and analysis of the legislative history of this bill.

36. Quoted in Eidenberg and Morey, p. 92.

37. Quoted in Eidenberg and Morey, p. 93. Emphasis added.

38. The bulk of the material for this case comes from my book, *Clean Air: The Policies and Politics of Pollution Control* (Pittsburgh: University of Pittsburgh Press, 1975), Chapter 7.

39. *Congressional Record* (daily edition), June 10, 1970, p. H5383.

40. The message is reprinted in the *Congressional Quarterly Weekly Report*, January 23, 1970, pp. 245–248.

41. *The Christian Science Monitor*, February 13, 1970.

42. John C. Esposito, *Vanishing Air* (New York: Grossman, 1970), pp. 290–291.

43. Esposito, p. 291.

44. *The Christian Science Monitor*, July 6, 1970.

Appropriating for Programs

Functional Activities	Categorized in Government	and as Systems	with Output
Appropriation	Action in Government	Program Development	Budget

In his thorough account of the politics associated with public housing legislation, Leonard Freedman describes the cautious elation of those who had worked hard for passage of the Housing Act of 1949.

> As the public housing forces celebrated their victory in July of 1949, they could not free themselves of an undertone of anxiety, for their 810,000 units had been approved with reluctance and only by the narrowest of margins.
> Still, if some of them suspected that their victory might not be final, they could hardly have predicted the magnitude of the trouble that lay ahead. . . . Having at last attained their goal, they still would not be able to rest. On the contrary, the most arduous tribulations must yet be faced, and the battles which had been won must be re-fought under much less propitious circumstances than had prevailed in 1949.[1]

While, as Freedman notes, "the 1949 housing act did not . . . appear to place any significant power over public housing in the hands of the Appropriations Committees," the fact is that "authorization by Congress is one thing, appropriation another."[2] Thus, whereas the act authorized the construction of 810,000 public housing units over a period of six years, "two decades after the passage of the 1949 Act, only one-half of its authorized units had been built."[3] In reflecting on this record, Freedman noted:

> . . . the Taft-Ellender-Wagner Act [Housing Act of 1949] . . . had been given the most thorough scrutiny before it was accepted. Under most other systems of representative government, the public housing program would surely have been implemented in considerable measure at least, and then would have undergone an orderly process of

modification and adjustment as defects showed up. Its fate under the American system was very different.[4]

The London *Economist* illustrated the British perspective on such goings-on: "Since the programme requires an annual appropriation, its opponents have since had repeated opportunities of *replaying the match*."[5]

This British view provides an appropriate theme for this chapter. In essence I am asking you now to "replay the match." While in most political systems, approval (legitimation) of a program includes the money and resources for implementation, we require a rematch. Those who lose in law making can end up victors in the appropriations process, thus canceling their earlier defeat. Students of public policy, then, must trace two streams of decision making—one *authorizing* programs; another *appropriating* funds. While they are obviously associated, they run in distinctly separate channels with remarkably few connecting points downstream in Congress.

In fact, there are three channels. For on the money side, decisions have to be made about where it is to come from as well as how it will be allocated. Attention here will be directed to appropriation because of its more direct association with policy programs. But students should be aware of the tax policy process. As described by Lawrence C. Pierce in his book, *The Politics of Fiscal Policy Formation*, this process involves:

1. Forecasting of revenue, expenditures, and the economic conditions by the Office of Management and Budget, Council of Economic Advisers, and the Department of Treasury (research and definition).
2. Presidential decision making for preparing a fiscal tax policy proposal (formulation).
3. Congressional decision making by the House Committee on Ways and Means and Senate Committee on Finance (legitimation).[6]

This summarizes the institutional stream of policy development and legitimation in this field. As has been emphasized here, however, and suggested by the parenthetical entries of functional activities above, we would expect to find cross-institutional participation in each of these stages of decision making on tax matters.

But tax policy can be analyzed as a separate issue-area, relying on the conceptual framework introduced here. Appropriations, on the other hand, are directly associated with each program enacted—even tax programs. Therefore our work requires a return to formulation stages in order to trace budgetary allocation decisions. First, however, a brief discussion of budgets is in order.

The Budget

"In any year the budget is the single most important expression of the nation's priorities. . . ."[7] This statement, taken from the Brookings Institution's analysis of the 1976 budget, illustrates a point made earlier, i.e., that the budget represents an integrated policy package—at least as it leaves the executive. No other document so accurately reflects what we think government ought to be doing. The budget is a quantitative essay on our times since, as Aaron Wildavsky points out, it "is concerned with the translation of financial resources into human purposes."[8]

Since the budget is "basically a set of plans for future action," it serves the following purposes:

1. A proposal for allocating resources (between private and public sectors, within public sectors, and, in part, within private sectors).
2. An economic document "that reflects the taxing and spending policies of the government. . . ."
3. An outline of the president's requests for support for new and existing programs.
4. A report to Congress and the nation of how funds have been spent in the past.[9]

This list suggests that we will be concerned with only a part of the overall budget—that which requests funds for new and existing programs. It is important, however, to point out that in its formulation attention is directed to the broader economic context and impact of the budget.

Note should also be taken of the fact that there are several types of budget concepts which are more or less inclusive of government expenditures and economic impact.[10] Two concepts in particular are pertinent here. The *administrative budget concept* was relied on before 1968 at the federal level and simply included revenues and expenditures of annual federal fund transactions. It excluded the large trust fund activities (e.g., social security). In 1968 a shift was made to a *unified budget concept* which included all programs of the federal government, including the trust funds. Thus, comparative analysis of the federal budget between the early 1960s and the present must take into account the more expansive concept now relied on. The trust fund transactions have grown dramatically in the last two decades (by over tenfold), which accounts for part of the sizeable increase in the federal budget during this period.

Figure 6-1 clearly shows that neither the president nor Congress acts on all expenditures made by the federal government in any one year. As indicated, a sizeable amount of "unspent authority" exists for any fiscal year.

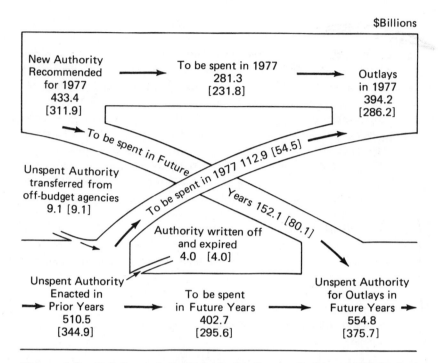

Figure 6-1. Relation of Budget Authority to Outlays—1977 Budget. Figures in brackets represent federal funds only. The difference between the total budget and federal funds shown in brackets consists of trust funds and interfund transactions between fund groups. *Source: The United States Budget in Brief: Fiscal Year 1977* (Washington, D.C.: U.S. Government Printing Office, 1976), p. 53.

Some of this money can be spent in the fiscal year being budgeted ($112.9 billion in FY 1977); other portions carry over to future years ($402.7 billion in FY 1977). Likewise, new authority requested by the president is divided between that to be spent in the next fiscal year ($281.3 billion in FY 1977) or in the future ($152.1 billion in FY 1977). And though it is not noted in the chart, much of this new authority is for existing programs whose authorizations have expired. The result is that we begin a new fiscal year with huge programmatic commitments. It is simply not possible for a new president to begin with a clean slate—no matter what he promises during a campaign. When it comes to the budget, a new broom sweeps only around a few edges.

Budget Formulation

The description and analysis provided in this chapter will appear somewhat more formal than that in other chapters for the very good reason that we are dealing with a highly formal and essentially uniform set of procedures. As Harold Wolman has correctly described it: "The appropriations subsystem is the most formalized and least open system in the policy process. Its chronological sequences have become institutionalized and most of the roles involved are clearly specified."[11] This is not to say that budgeting politics is a cut-and-dried affair—merely meeting formal conditions. Aaron Wildavsky's account of calculations and strategies involved in getting budgets approved (in *The Politics of the Budgetary Process*) should dispel that notion. Rather it is to emphasize that a routine does exist for development and approval of the budget—a routine which is followed more faithfully perhaps than that for the development and approval of other legislation. Even still, students of particular problems and programs will discover variations in the process which are frequently traceable to the nature of the program being funded.

At any one point, work proceeds on a minimum of three budgets—that being planned, that for which authorization is sought, and that which is being spent. The preparation of a new budget begins approximately 16 months before the beginning of the fiscal year to which it applies. Thus, with the present July-to-July fiscal year, work for the FY 1976 budget began in March 1974. In 1976 the fiscal year will change to an October-to-October calendar as a result of the Congressional Budget and Impoundment Control Act of 1974 (discussed below) and extend the preparation period even more.

We are saved having to describe the detailed formulation of the budget by use of a chart (Figure 6-2), prepared by the Office of Management and Budget (OMB). Several observations can be made, however, to assist in understanding the flow of action and its relationship to individual programs. First, whereas three decision-making units are identified as major participants in budget formulation—the agency, Office of Management and Budget, and the president, they only represent the tip of the iceberg. For with the agencies and the president in particular, budget decisions are normally the result of communication and consultation with other governmental units, supporting interests, agency clientele, trusted advisers, possibly members of Congress and their staff. Therefore, given the emphasis stressed here, the decisional steps noted in Figure 6-2 are but the starting points of analysis in determining who is truly involved in formulating budget requests and final proposals.

In this same connection, a quick review of the figure shows the association of all budget and programmatic decisions. While this is an obvious relationship—that is, money is normally requested for specific purposes— finding a means for coordinating the two types of decisions is anything but obvious. As a result, the balancing and maintenance of programmatic goals within the agency, between agencies, and between the agency and OMB is a continuing and complex set of operations requiring the attention of deci-

APPROXIMATE TIMING	AGENCY	OFFICE OF MANAGEMENT AND BUDGET	THE PRESIDENT
Budget Development			
MARCH (or earlier in some agencies)	Reviews current operations, program objectives, issues, and future plans in relation to upcoming annual budget. Submits projections of requirements that reflect current operations and future plans; program memoranda and related special analytic studies which identify major issues, alternatives for resolving issues, and comparisons of costs and effectiveness.	Develops* economic assumptions. Obtains forecasts of international situations. Prepares* fiscal projections.	Discusses budgetary outlook and policies with the Director of the Office of Management and Budget, and with the Cabinet as appropriate.
APRIL		Issues instructions and policy guidance on material to be developed for Spring planning review.	
MAY		Discusses program developments and management issues, and resulting budgetary effects, with agency heads. Compiles total outlay estimates for comparison with revenue estimates. Develops recommendations for President on fiscal policy*, program issues, and budget levels.	Discusses with the Director of the Office of Management and Budget and others as necessary, general budget policy, major program issues, budgetary ceilings, and projections. Establishes general guidelines and agency budgetary ceilings for annual budget.
MAY	Issues internal instructions on preparation of annual budget estimates.	Issues technical instructions for preparation of annual budget estimates.	
JUNE		Conveys President's decisions to agency heads on Government-wide policies and assumptions and the application of policies and budgetary ceilings to individual agencies.	
Compilation and Submission of Agency Estimates			

120

Figure 6-2.   Formulation of Executive Budget.   *Source:* Executive Office of the President/Office of Management and Budget.

JULY–SEPTEMBER 30	Allocates budgetary ceiling to programs. Develops and compiles detailed estimates.	Advises and assists agencies on form, language, and structure of appropriations, and on preparation of budget submissions.
Office of Management and Budget Review and Presidential Decision		
SEPTEMBER OCTOBER NOVEMBER	Submits formal estimates for annual budget including projections of requirements for future years, and completed program memoranda and special analytic studies.	Analyzes budget submissions. Holds hearings with agency representatives on program, budget, and management issues in preparation for Director's review.
		Reexamines economic assumptions and fiscal policies. Discusses program developments with agencies. In light of outlook and policy discussion with President, prepares budget recommendations for President.
		Reviews budgetary situation and decides on budget allowances for each agency.
	Revises estimates to conform to President's decisions.	Notifies agency heads of President's allowance.
DECEMBER JANUARY		Again reviews economic outlook and fiscal policy for discussion with President of tax and economic policies.*
		Drafts President's budget message, prepares budget and summary tables and appendix, special analyses, and budget-in-brief; arranges printing of budget documents.
		Revises and approves budget message. Transmits recommended budget to Congress.

*In cooperation with the Treasury Department and Council of Economic Advisers

sion makers at several levels. Things get even more difficult once the budget goes to Congress.

Another dynamic aspect of this formulation process which is suggested, but hardly made explicit, in the figure is the continuing effort by agencies to judge presidential priorities. Equally important is the effort by agencies to influence these top-level decisions. And, of course, no president can create a budget without information from bureaucrats and his own political appointees who head the departments and agencies. If one reads Figure 6-2 with this interaction in mind, the various steps come to be a gradual unfolding of decisions based on or resulting from a two-way flow of influence and communication—with OMB acting as translation and communications center.

Also less graphic in the figure is the fact that budget decisions have historical bases and, therefore, impact on the future as well. As the budget itself increases, representing as it does the growth of governmental functions in society, these historical relationships come to be more significant. This point was emphasized in the FY 1975 budget:

> In an age of increasingly complex problems requiring long-range solutions, the Nation cannot afford to look only a single year into the future when making budgetary decisions. Such decisions have longer range implications which we must try to assess before committing ourselves and our limited resources. The composition and level of the 1975 budget have been largely determined by past decisions and will, in turn, strongly affect subsequent budgets, mandating many expenditures, precluding others, and generally limiting our options in future years.[12]

Beginning with the 1971 budget, five-year projections were included in the budget analysis so that decision makers might judge the commitments involved in enacting programs.

Finally, the figure clearly indicates the critical role played by the Office of Management and Budget. Formerly called the Bureau of the Budget, this unit is located in the Executive Office of the President and performs several absolutely vital services for the president. The most obvious is well outlined in Figure 6-2. The agency serves not only to transmit and translate presidential decisions to the agencies, but to inform the president of agency programmatic goals. Inevitably OMB personnel themselves make vital decisions in performing this crucial middle-man role. They perform a similar role when the budget has been approved by controlling expenditures. When the president doesn't want to spend money, it is OMB that does the impounding.

As a logical extension of their budgetary functions, OMB also acts as a clearing house for all legislative proposals flowing from the departments and agencies to Congress. Once again, they presumably test these proposals against the programmatic priorities and interests of the president. A third function associated with their advantaged position of programmatic oversight is that of studying changes and advising agencies on organizational and management matters. This is an impressive list of functions—making service in OMB an interesting and challenging experience.

Since it too is populated with humans, not gods, OMB's actions will vary both within the agency among budget examiners and with a change in directors. Aaron Wildavsky points out that:

> There are . . . always some people in [OMB] who identify more closely with an agency or program than do others, or who develop policy preferences independent of the president. They have a creative urge. . . . They see themselves as doing the right thing by pursuing policies in the public interest and they may convince themselves that the president would support them if only he had the time and inclination to go into the matter as deeply as they had. . . .
>
> Even within the same administration, different budget directors can have an impact of their own. . . . Some directors have much better relationships with the president than others; they get in to see him more often . . .; he backs them up more frequently on appeals from the agencies.[13]

Further, OMB personnel must be sensitive to their own political position relative to those with whom they must deal—for example, the president and his staff, Congress, and the departments and agencies. They know that the wrong decisions on their part can result in loss of presidential confidence. But, as Aaron Wildavsky points out, they may face problems with Congress as well.

> The most serious obstacle to acceptance of [OMB] leadership is that Congress determines appropriations. Everyone knows that agencies make end-runs around [OMB] to gain support from Congress. If they do so too often, [OMB] finds that its currency has depreciated. Hence [OMB] frequently accepts consistent congressional action as a guide. A close eye is kept on congressional action for the preceding year before an agency's total is set for the next one. Failure to do so might leave [OMB] with a record of defeat that jeopardizes its effectiveness in other areas.[14]

In summary, whereas a routine with scheduled decision points can be identified for budget formulation, students of public policy will want to inquire beyond these points to explore the interactions among those contributing the advice, information, and conclusions that form the basis of budget construction.

Budget Legitimation

Completing his radio address to the nation on the FY 1974 budget, President Nixon said: "It is time to get big government off your back and out of your pocket. I ask your support to hold government spending down, so that we can keep your taxes and your prices from going up."[15] The new budget proposed cuts or total elimination in more than 100 programs, leading Senator Walter F. Mondale (D-Minnesota) to remark that if enacted "this nation will have effectively repealed all of the major social legislation of the last 20 years." The clash between the president and Congress was more than ordinary disagreement over this or that program. It was much more fundamental—in essence involving different philosophies of government. Speaker Carl Albert (D-Oklahoma) vowed that Congress "...will not permit the president to lay waste the great programs ... which we have developed during the decades past."[16]

And yet, whereas Congress was capable of changing individual requests, it found itself quite incapable of dealing with the budget as a whole document. In fact, the president himself spoke of the need for congressional budgetary reform:

> The cuts I have suggested in this year's budget did not come easily. Thus I can well understand that it may not be easy for the Congress to sustain them, as every special interest group lobbies with its own special congressional committees for its own special legislation. But the Congress should serve more than the special interest; its first allegiance must always be to the public interest. ...
>
> To overcome these problems, I urge prompt adoption by the Congress of an overall spending ceiling for each fiscal year. ... Beyond the adoption of an annual ceiling, I also recommend that the Congress consider internal reforms which would establish a regular mechanism for deciding how to maintain the ceiling.[17]

The president had struck a sensitive nerve since congressional Democrats were painfully aware that however much they disagreed with the Nixon budget philosophy, they essentially had none of their own—and if they did, had only limited means for implementing it. As is indicated in Figure 6-3, the formal legitimation process in Congress is in fact a whole set of processes for various programmatic areas. Once received from the president, the budget is literally torn apart and distributed to the thirteen subcommittees in each of the House and Senate Committees on Appropriations. Traditionally the document, like Humpty Dumpty, is never put back together again since subcommittees are not able, or inclined, to work at the same pace. The size of their workload, the fact that they have to wait for authorization committees to act first, and their own individual styles and procedures, combine to produce an intermittent flow of appropriations decisions. As a consequence, one doesn't know how the total

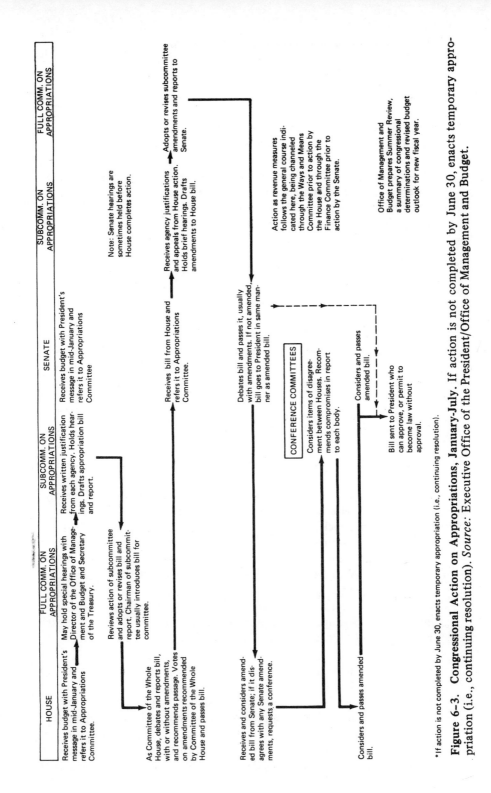

Figure 6–3. Congressional Action on Appropriations, January-July. If action is not completed by June 30, enacts temporary appropriation (i.e., continuing resolution). *Source:* Executive Office of the President/Office of Management and Budget.

*If action is not completed by June 30, enacts temporary appropriation (i.e., continuing resolution).

budget came out until the end of the year, if then. Some agencies are therefore forced to operate for several months on so-called continuing resolutions—that is, the same budget authority as for the preceding fiscal year. The last regular appropriation bill for FY 1968 was enacted on January 2—six months into the next fiscal year; for FY 1969 on October 17; FY 1970 on March 5—eight months into the next fiscal year; FY 1971 on January 11; FY 1972 on March 8; and FY 1973 on October 26. Often no single item is approved before the new fiscal year begins. And for FY 1971 and again for FY 1973 certain departmental appropriations were never enacted (Transportation for FY 1971 and Labor and Health, Education, and Welfare for FY 1973).[18] These variations in procedures emphasize that budgeting is indeed a political process in its formulation, legitimation, and implementation stages.[19]

It took the challenge of an unacceptable Nixon budget and a series of presidential vetoes to spur reform action by Congress. A Joint Study Committee on Budget Control was established to make recommendations for change. After much investigation and deliberation Congress passed the Congressional Budget and Impoundment Control Act in June, 1974, to take effect in 1976—with a test run in 1975. As a former assistant director of OMB noted: "To make it work, Congress and its individual members will have to act a hell of a lot differently than they do now."[20]

The new formal legitimation procedure is summarized in Table 6-1. Several features must be explained. First, a new budget committee has been established in each house. In the 94th Congress the Senate Committee had sixteen members (ten Democrats and six Republicans) and was chaired by Senator Edmund S. Muskie (D-Maine); the House Committee had twenty-five members (seventeen Democrats and eight Republicans) and was chaired by Rep. Brock Adams (D-Washington). Neither committee had any standing subcommittees. In addition to their own staffs, the committees receive support from a newly created Congressional Budget Office (CBO) headed by Dr. Alice Rivlin, an economist formerly with the Brookings Institution. This office plays a role roughly analogous to that of the Office of Management and Budget on the executive side. Of course, the lack of centralized leadership and hierarchical organization in Congress makes CBO's task much more difficult and its functions somewhat more ambiguous.

Second, this new set of committees has authority which inevitably clashes with that of the other committees. As suggested in Table 6-1, the budget committees become a sort of watchdog—monitoring the action of the authorization and appropriations committees. "There's a potential conflict between the budget committees and every committee on the Hill," is the way one observer put it.[21] Thus, for example, should the committees either not report legislation on time (as per the new schedule)

Table 6-1. Congressional Action on the Budget (1977 Fiscal Year)

Schedule	House				Senate			
	Budget	Committees — Authorizing	Appropriation	Floor	Budget	Committees — Authorizing	Appropriation	Floor
Nov. 10		(All receive C.S.B.)				(All receive C.S.B.)		
Mid-Jan.		(All receive budget)				(All receive budget)		
April 1	C.B.O. reports				C.B.O. reports			
April 15	Report 1st B.R.	Work on new authorization			Report 1st B.R.	Work on new authorization		
May 15		New auth. reported	Work on appropriations (See other chart)	Passes 1st B.R.		New auth. reported	Work on appropriations (See other chart)	Passes 1st B.R.
Labor Day + 7				All appro. passed				All appro. passed
Sept. 15		Reconcile all actions		Passes 2nd B.R.		Reconcile all actions		Passes 2nd B.R.
Sept. 25				Passes Reconciliation bill				Passes Reconciliation bill
Oct. 1					Fiscal Year Begins			

Key: C.S.B.—Current Services Budget; C.B.O.—Congressional Budget Office; B.R.—Budget Resolution.

or fail to meet the recommended limits, the budget committees are put in the position of having to ask for adjustments—in a sense placing themselves above the judgment of individual committees.

The schedule itself represents a virtual quantum change in congressional budget action. As noted earlier, Congress has in the past been quite leisurely in enacting appropriations. This new procedure calls for completed action on all spending bills approximately three weeks before the beginning of the new fiscal year. They hope to accomplish this goal by giving themselves more time and information on the budget. They require the executive to produce a "current services budget" on November 10 (just over a month after the beginning of the new fiscal year) which projects the costs of continuing existing services at the same level for the next fiscal year. This budget provides Congress with a baseline for analyzing the president's budget. Then the president is required to produce his requests ten months in advance of the fiscal year, compared to six months under existing procedures. This is the effect of moving the start of the fiscal year from July 1 to October 1. As a consequence, preparation of the budget is moved 20 months back from the beginning of the fiscal year.

Another important feature of the new procedure is that of enacting budget resolutions. As noted, the first resolution follows budget analysis and recommendation by CBO and the budget committees. It represents a sort of first run at establishing guidelines for the authorization and appropriations committees. A second resolution is passed in mid-September. Whereas the first is advisory, however, this second resolution becomes a directive to committees to reconcile previous actions to the levels now finally established.

It is much too early to speculate as to how this procedure will work. Everything hinges on meeting a set of interrelated deadlines. Should these be seriously violated, as they have in the past, then the whole system could become a tangled mess, perhaps even more disjointed than at present. For our purposes, the effect of the changes is to introduce a new type of majority, or another form of legitimation. Layered on the myriad majorities required for enactment of individual programs and their funding would be majorities in both houses to support an overall budgetary approach. And yet there is more implied here since such a comprehensive majority merely reflects compromises and bargaining within and between individual programs. Put another way, majority building under existing procedures (i.e., until 1975–1976) was essentially a segmented process. Once agreement was reached within an issue-area, the program was approved and funded at a particular level representing the terms of the agreement. But now these individual streams of program approval are to come together as a majority is constructed for a total legislative package—presumably representing Congress's judgment about priorities. Students of public policy will want to pay close attention to how (and whether) this rather grandiose majority building develops.

Some Institutional Constraints

No analysis of the appropriations process would be complete without some attention to the appropriations committees in each house. The leading authority on this subject, Richard F. Fenno, Jr., observes that:

> The power of the purse is the historic bulwark of legislative authority. The exercise of that power constitutes the core legislative process—underpinning all other legislative decisions and regulating the balance of influence between the legislative and executive branches of government. . . . Scarcely a political relationship exists, inside Congress or between Congress and the executive branch, for which a prototype cannot be found somewhere in the labyrinth of appropriations activity.[22]

That activity is centered in the two appropriations committees, with the House committee being, as Fenno concludes, "by a substantial margin, the single most influential . . . decision maker. . . ."[23] The House acts first on appropriations—not, as many people mistakenly believe, because of any constitutional mandate, but simply out of tradition, supported by the argument that representatives are closer to the people.[24] Let us begin with the House committee then.

In the 94th Congress (1975-1976), the House Committee on Appropriations was the largest committee in either chamber—55 members, 12 more than the next in size. Both the House and Senate committees are organized into thirteen subcommittees, many of which deal with the appropriations for specific departments:

Agriculture and Related Agencies
Defense
District of Columbia
Foreign Operations
Housing and Urban Development—Independent Agencies
Interior
Labor-Health, Education and Welfare
Legislative
Military Construction
Public Works
State, Justice, Commerce and Judiciary
Transportation
Treasury-Postal Service-General Government

Several observations can be made about this list. First, the subcommittees vary markedly in their workload, with Defense (and, more recently, Labor-Health, Education and Welfare) and District of Columbia being at opposite ends of the continuum. Second, it does not take much political savvy to judge that these units come to have immense power in relationship to the departments and agencies. Thus, one would expect an agency to develop close ties to its subcommittee—both members and staff. Third, the division of labor represented by this breakdown reflects how the members view their tasks rather than how the executive is organized. Most revealing along these lines is the Subcommittee on Public Works, which deals primarily with public power projects, dams, and other waterway construction, regardless of which agency has responsibility for the work. Military Construction is also separated from Defense. Obviously these are important matters for constituency-oriented congressmen; they want to know what is being done and where without necessarily getting involved in other agency problems.

The House Committee on Appropriations is a high prestige group and therefore membership is much sought after. Many members would prefer to be a subcommittee chairman on Appropriations to being chairman of certain other full committees. Two important results of this prestige are (1) that the committee has been able to establish a rather strong set of norms to which members are expected to conform, and (2) agencies hoping to get favorable decisions must work within the constraints created by these norms. As Fenno demonstrates, the committee norms extend to determining who gets appointed, the socialization of the members, methods of controlling behavior, reducing partisanship, and, in general, facilitating integration. These features, in turn, are apparently satisfying to the members.

> . . . it seems clear that [committee] integration helps the individual committee member to fulfill his satisfactions. He believes that a well-integrated internal structure results in committee unity before the House. And he believes that committee unity before the House is a necessary condition of committee influence (hence, his personal influence) in the chamber.[25]

For the agencies seeking money, however, these characteristics can create anxiety, primarily because the committee has traditionally viewed itself as "guardian of the federal Treasury."[26] Therefore in the complex process of majority building for program funding, the agencies must first seek to develop strong and stable access within what they accurately perceive to be the most influential group on appropriations decisions.

The Senate committee is not nearly so large (26 members) and therefore individual members have several more subcommittee assignments than on the House side (an average of five assignments each compared to just over two in the House committee). This identifies the Senate committee as less specialized and therefore less of an independent decision-making unit as compared to the House committee. It does serve a very important appeals function for those seeking program support, however. Professor Fenno describes this function:

> The Senate committee prescribes for itself the tasks of an appellate court, which makes decisions on the basis of agency appeals for the restoration of the incremental reductions made by the House committee. This goal expectation . . . is primarily a result of the fixed appropriations sequence, in which the Senate invariably acts after the House decisions have been made. And, since the House usually acts to reduce budgets, the Senate will inevitably be subjected to one-sided and intensified appeals for increases. . . . In addition, the Senate committee lacks the time to investigate agency budgets de novo.[27]

One can imagine how the House members view this process—as one once remarked to me: "That's why it's called the upper chamber; it always 'ups' the appropriations." Stephen Horn, in his book on the Senate committee, notes that senators have become sensitive to this charge and "members of Senate Appropriations began trying to undercut the House figures in some areas."[28]

When differences exist, as they do in the large majority of appropriations measures, representatives of the two committees must meet in conference to work out a compromise. Since these meetings are among the least visible and accessible deliberations in Congress, those supporting an appropriations measure must establish their views with the conferees beforehand. Conference decisions illustrate yet another variation in majority building since each group, representatives and senators, has but one vote. Therefore, the two majorities must be in agreement to approve a final figure.[29]

Here then is a highly intricate institutional network with traditions, norms, procedures, and rivalries that act as constraints or context within which those seeking program funding must work. Whether one likes how these committees operate or not, their peculiarities must be accommodated in developing appropriations strategies. Thus, for example, Stephen Horn's description of institutional rivalry may dismay the political purist, but it is part of the reality which must be taken into account by actors in this complex network of decision making.

> . . . each committee suspects the motives underlying the other's approach to spending. Senators think the House members act irresponsibly in cutting essential appropriations. . . . They suspect that the cynical view of House motives is correct: the House members

only want to look like good economizers to their constituents, and expect the Senate to restore the cuts. On the other hand, those on House Appropriations, having spent months in studying an appropriations bill, view their Senate counterparts as irresponsible when they add millions of dollars after a few days of testimony. They view members of Senate Appropriations as lackeys of the executive branch and look with disdain on their tendency to give administration officials much of what they ask for in the public hearings.[30]

The new budget committees may also be expected to develop individualized characteristics which will come to influence the appropriations process. How that will develop can only be the subject of speculation at this time, though the traditional appropriations process may be expected to influence those developments. If the committees survive to exercise the kind of authority implicit in their charge, however, the agencies, departments, and others promoting program funding will have to cope with another layer of institutional constraints.

Summary

Analyzing the appropriations function in this manner in effect interrupts the flow of decision-making activities outlined in Chapter 1. Since our political system separates program legitimation from approval of funding, however, we have two, and even three, interrelated policy streams. I might have accommodated the appropriations decisions along the way, that is, by describing budget formulation and legitimation in conjunction with the development and approval of proposals. But I thought it important, and possibly less confusing, to treat them separately.

Perhaps most important for students of public policy are the reforms recently enacted in the congressional budgetary procedures. The pre-1975 decision-making processes for taxation and appropriation are among the most comprehensively and competently described and analyzed of any in Congress—a mark of their significance.[31] If they are to be affected by the changes made, then scholars and practitioners alike have a major research agenda before them. The Brookings Institution budget analysis team viewed the new procedures with favor, concluding that "the new process should enable Congress to allocate the nation's resources among competing objectives more judiciously, with a more appropriate economic impact, and with a closer eye to its sense of the nation's priorities."[32] But having a Congress actively involved in this kind of comprehensive, rational decision making will drastically alter the nature of the policy process—so much so that one must question whether it will ever come about.

Notes

1. Leonard Freedman, *Public Housing: The Politics of Poverty* (New York: Holt, Rinehart and Winston, 1969), pp. 19–20.

2. Freedman, pp. 20–21.

3. Robert Taggart III, *Low-Income Housing: A Critique of Federal Aid* (Baltimore: The Johns Hopkins Press, 1970), p. 5.

4. Freedman, p. 56.

5. As quoted in Freedman, p. 20. Emphasis added.

6. Lawrence Pierce, *The Politics of Fiscal Policy Formation* (Pacific Palisades, California: Goodyear, 1971), p. 37.

7. Barry M. Blechman, et al., *Setting National Priorities: The 1976 Budget* (Washington, D.C.: The Brookings Institution, 1975), p. 1.

8. Aaron Wildavsky, *The Politics of the Budgetary Process* (Boston: Little, Brown, 1964), p. 1.

9. This list is adapted from a discussion in George K. Brite and Harriet J. Halper, *The Federal Budget Process: Revised* (Washington, D.C.: Congressional Research Service, 1972), pp. 1–3. This document is reprinted in a highly useful compendium of materials on the budget compiled for the Senate Committee on Government Operations entitled *Improving Congressional Control Over the Budget* (Washington, D.C.: U.S. Government Printing Office, 1973).

10. For a description of other budget concepts—administrative, unified, consolidated cash, national income accounts, capital, full employment—see David J. Ott and Attiat F. Ott, *Federal Budget Policy* (Washington, D.C.: The Brookings Institution, 1969), Chapter 2; or Brite and Halper, pp. 3–11.

11. Harold Wolman, *Politics of Federal Housing* (New York: Dodd, Mead, 1971), p. 129.

12. *The Budget of the United States Government: Fiscal Year 1975* (Washington, D.C.: U.S. Government Printing Office, 1974), p. 34.

13. Wildavsky, pp. 36–37.

14. Wildavsky, p. 41.

15. *Congressional Quarterly Weekly Report*, February 3, 1973, p. 234.

16. Both the Mondale and Albert statements are cited in *Congressional Quarterly Weekly Report*, February 3, 1973, p. 175.

17. *Congressional Quarterly Weekly Report*, February 24, 1973, p. 397.

18. Figures supplied in U.S. Senate, Committee on Government Operations, *Congressional Budget Reform*, July, 1974, p. 4.

19. For a detailed discussion of these procedures, see Louis Fisher, *Presidential Spending Power* (Princeton: Princeton University Press, 1975).

20. Quoted in *Congressional Quarterly Weekly Report*, September 7, 1974, p. 2415.

21. Quoted in *Congressional Quarterly Weekly Report*, September 7, 1974, p. 2417.

22. Richard F. Fenno, Jr., *The Power of the Purse: Appropriations Politics in Congress* (Boston: Little, Brown, 1966), p. xiii.

23. Fenno, p. xv.

24. For a review of the origination of appropriations bills, see Stephen Horn, *Unused Power: The Work of the Senate Committee on Appropriations* (Washington, D.C.: The Brookings Institution, 1970), pp. 246–253. As Horn documents, the founding fathers at one point considered phrasing which would have required appropriations measures to originate in the House, but the final wording referred only to "bills for raising revenue shall originate in the House of Representatives. . . ."

25. Fenno, p. 263.

26. Fenno, p. 100. Fenno lists the jargon used by the members in discussing the budget—words like "fat," "padding," "pork," etc., to describe the requests themselves; "cut," "carve," "slice," "prune," etc., to describe their actions; and "knife," "meat axe," "scalpel," "shears," etc., to describe the tools of their trade. See p. 105.

27. Fenno, p. 562.

28. Horn, p. 143.

29. For detailed analysis of these conferences, see Fenno, Chapter 12; Horn, pp. 154–173; and Jeffrey L. Pressman, *House vs. Senate: Conflict in the Appropriations Process* (New Haven: Yale University Press, 1966), Ch. 4.

30. Horn, p. 163.

31. In addition the works previously cited here, see John F. Manley, *The Politics of Finance: The House Committee on Ways and Means* (Boston: Little, Brown, 1970); Robert Ash Wallace, *Congressional Con-*

trol of Federal Spending (Detroit: Wayne State University Press, 1960); Richard F. Fenno, Jr., *Congressmen in Committees* (Boston: Little, Brown, 1973); Charles L. Schultze, *The Politics and Economics of Public Spending* (Washington, D.C.: The Brookings Institution, 1968); U.S. House of Representatives, Committee on Government Operations, *The Budget Process in the Federal Government* (Washington, D.C.: U.S. Government Printing Office, 1969); and Arthur Smithies, *The Budgetary Process in the United States* (New York: McGraw-Hill, 1955).

32.   Blechman, et al., p. 243.

Implementing Programs

Functional Activities	Categorized in Government	and as Systems	with Output
Organization Interpretation Application	Government to Problem	Implementation	Varies (Service, payments, facilities, controls, permits, etc.)

W e now take a rather sizeable leap in analysis—from the development of programs to their implementation. While this represents a definite conceptual break from the functional activities discussed so far, it does not necessarily reflect a clear delineation in the real world of public policy. The process of approving a compromise program seldom has resolved all of the issues. Thus, once again, we are well advised not to mistake an analytical or conceptual sequence for what happens in real life. Implementing a new program may, in fact, reveal for the first time how certain key actors define problems and/or what further bargaining is necessary before a program can be applied.

In this chapter we will explore a few of the more obvious dimensions of applying government-sanctioned programs to public problems. In addition to defining implementation (and its associated activities) and identifying the actors who may be involved, considerable attention will be focused on the bureaucracy as the primary implementing institution. Special problems to be treated include administrative discretion and the increasingly significant intergovernmental aspect of program implementation.

Implementation—A New Term
for an Old Activity

In a recent book on implementation, Jeffrey L. Pressman and Aaron B. Wildavsky record that a review of traditional literature turns up very limited use of the term. "Either [the literature] does not use 'implementation' at all, or the concept is undefined, or the word is mentioned in passing."[1] This finding is not too surprising since terms other than "implementation" have typically been used to describe the administration and enforcement of laws. "What's in a name?" the bard of Avon asks us. "That which we call a rose; By any other name would smell as sweet." Whether or not scholars have defined or used the term "implementation," they have for ages been describing the "interaction between the setting of goals and actions geared to achieve them," or "the ability to forge subsequent links in the causal chain so as to obtain the desired results" (two definitions of implementation provided by Pressman and Wildavsky).[2]

The term most frequently used to encompass these activities is, of course, "administration" or "public administration." I turned to the oldest text on public administration in my personal library—that by Leonard D. White, published in 1926—and I found a definition with many of the elements mentioned above: "Public administration is the management of men and materials in the accomplishment of the purposes of the state."[3] Even more interesting, however, is that my copy of this book comes originally from the library of John M. Gaus, another of the giants in the study of administration. Gaus had written the following as a marginal note expanding White's definition: "and a reconsideration of the policy being implemented." Unquestionably Gaus viewed administration as comprehensively as Pressman and Wildavsky define implementation. And that brings us to Gaus's own catholic conception of public administration. He speaks of an "ecology of government."

> An ecological approach to public administration builds . . . quite literally from the ground up; from the elements of a place—soils, climate, location, for example—to the people who live there—their numbers and ages and knowledge, and the ways of physical and social technology by which from the place and in relationships with one another, they get their living. It is within this setting that their instruments and practices of public housekeeping should be studied so that they may better understand what they are doing, and appraise reasonably how they are doing it.[4]

The point is that we want to concentrate on a certain set of activities which carry a program to the problem. While I am persuaded that "implementation" may well convey a somewhat more comprehensive and interactive set of behaviors than "administration," or "application," we can surely use the three terms interchangeably as long as we are agreed on what it is we are talking about. So let's get that settled first.

The Pressman-Wildavsky definitions do provide precisely the interactive elements we have sought to emphasize throughout this text. That is, they speak of implementation as "a process of interaction" between what one wants and the methods for getting it. Previous actions (problem definition, formulation, legitimation) are not necessarily conclusive in this view of implementation. Rather many unresolved dilemmas frequently carry over—thus also making implementation a dynamic concept involving continuing efforts to discern what should and can be accomplished. That is the significance of Gaus's marginal addendum to White's definition: "and a reconsideration of the policy being implemented." Program goals may get drastically revised in the process of administering a program. Walter Williams puts it this way:

> The most pressing implementation problem is that of moving from a decision to operations in such a way that *what is put into place bears a reasonable resemblance to the decision and is functioning well in its institutional environment.* The past contains few clearer messages than that of the difficulty of bridging the gap between policy decisions and workable field operations.[5]

While providing the proper theoretical context, however, the Pressman-Wildavsky definitions are not sufficiently concrete for present purposes. Let us say simply that by implementation we mean *those activities directed toward putting a program into effect.* Three sets of activities, in particular, are significant: *interpretation*—the translation of program language into acceptable and feasible directives; *organization*—the establishment of units and methods for putting a program into effect; and *application*—the routine provision of services, payments, or other agreed-upon program objectives or instruments.

Defining implementation helps to sharpen our understanding of what a program is. In essence, it is a concrete proposition about solving a public problem—i.e., somebody's estimate of what will work. Implementors are then faced with the task of testing the validity of the proposition. Pressman and Wildavsky put it this way:

> A program consists of governmental action initiated in order to secure objectives whose attainment is problematical. A program exists when the initial conditions—the "if" stage of the policy hypothesis—have been met. The word "program" signifies the conversion of a hypothesis into governmental action. The initial premises of the hypothesis have been authorized. The degree to which the predicted consequences (the "then" stage) take place we will call implementation.[6]

This again is a dynamic view of what happens in the policy process. Programs are assumed merely to be *starting places* in the continuing process of making change in society. That they have the support of a majority, as one form of legitimation, means only that one more step has been taken in the direction of the public problem deemed deserving of government action. "Program implementation thus becomes a seamless web."[7]

Who Is Involved?

As with the other functional activities discussed so far, two points should be emphasized in considering who is involved in implementation activities.

1. Many others besides bureaucrats may be involved—for example, legislators, judges, private citizens.
2. Bureaucrats themselves are involved in other functional activities besides implementation.

The first point may need more clarification than the second simply because one is not used to thinking about legislators, judges, or private citizens as putting programs into effect. Representatives and senators are overloaded with "casework," however. This term refers to the activities in congressional offices that are directed toward coping with the problems of individual constituents. Frequently the "case" results from applying a federal program, and it often is resolved by a congressional staff member going to an agency to get favorable action. Legislators are frequently consulted regarding the administration of policy in their particular areas of expertise, and they are also involved in appointments and other personnel matters of administration.

Judges also deal with cases and apply policy. When thinking about the role of the court in policy making, it is typical to think about the dramatic pronouncements regarding constitutional interpretation—particularly those striking down a national statute as unconstitutional. Such cases are the exception, however. As Professor Glendon Schubert observes:

> By far the larger function of the national courts, certainly in terms of the number of decisions and perhaps in terms of impact upon the American polity as well, lies not in "constitutional interpretation" but in the judicial interpretation of national statutes, administrative regulations and decisions, judicial regulations (such as the procedural rules for the national courts), and judicial decisions.[8]

Judges may be involved in straightforward administrative tasks; for example, naturalization of aliens, approval of passport applications, bankruptcy proceedings, and parole cases constitute the largest number of items for federal courts. But judges are involved in implementation in other ways as well. Civil and criminal cases result from the application of policy. Many of these are excluded from our analysis because they primarily involve private problems. When publics are affected, however, judges perform a type of administrative function. Professor Samuel Krislov suggests that the first major function of courts is to provide "a means for securing compliance with public policies, such as those proclaimed by legislatures."[9] Much of the docket of the Supreme Court is the result of Department of Justice decisions seeking compliance with the law. In a contest between you and the government, judges may have the last word in interpreting policy for application (one of the most important aspects of administration). Of course, it is quite possible that you have challenged the constitutional basis of the policy—in which case the court is asked to perform another vital policy function—that of evaluation or appraisal.

The participation of private groups in applying policy takes many forms.[10] Groups may cooperate with government agencies in applying policy. From the first, the poverty program has relied on citizens' groups in applying the broad policy of the Economic Opportunity Act of 1964. The American Farm Bureau Federation, now the most powerful farm group, was actually created as a result of the administration of farm policy. The Smith-Lever Act of 1914 was designed to improve farm methods through the county-agent system. Essential to the success of this policy was the development of an effective means of communicating with farmers. Encouraged by the Department of Agriculture, farm bureaus were established to assist in this communication function. The national federation eventually developed as a private group, still retaining its semiofficial status in some areas.[11]

Groups may have representatives in administrative positions. A change of administrations frequently finds representatives from one set of interests leaving, another set coming in. In other instances, groups take it upon themselves to participate in applying policy to problems whether the government wants them to or not. For example, civil rights groups have not waited for an invitation to participate in seeing to it that the legislation passed during the 1960s is applied. Veterans' groups insure that their clientele is aware of the benefits that they have helped to promote in federal policy. And environmental groups have been very active in implementing the many federal, state, and local programs in the 1970s.

So, the implementation system for any one program may be populated with a number of different types of actors. I cannot generalize for all areas but can only suggest that you let the definition of the concept "system" guide your analysis—that is, those who are interacting for the purpose of putting a program into effect.

The Role of the Bureaucracy

As public problems become more complex in a highly technological society, one naturally expects government programs as well to be increasingly technical and intricate. It follows too that the organization of government will be more specialized, creating severe problems of coordination. These are sufficient conditions for justifying a brief discussion of the bureaucracy—its role, support, growth, and programmatic organization.

In the first edition of his classic work, *Constitutional Government and Politics*, Carl J. Friedrich treats the bureaucracy first among the institutions as "the core of modern government."[12] While this insight may not be extraordinary, seldom do political scholars acknowledge it in organizing their work. More often than not, institutional analyses begin with the executive, then the legislature, the courts, and finally the bureaucracy. Yet Friedrich is so right—a complex of bureaucratic mazes is what makes our modern government so vastly different from what it was 100 years ago.

Well, what is a bureaucracy? No response would be complete without reference to the writings of Max Weber, who viewed the bureaucracy as the means for accomplishing the difficult and demanding tasks of modern government. According to H. H. Gerth and C. Wright Mills, who translated the German scholar's works, bureaucracy, for Weber, established the "routines of workaday life."[13] Weber contrasted bureaucracy with charismatic leadership or personality, the former representing the everyday life of institutions and the latter representing the unusual. Gerth and Mills summarize the comparison as follows:

> . . . mass *versus* personality, the "routine" *versus* the "creative" entrepreneur, the conventions of ordinary people *versus* the inner freedom of pioneering and exceptional man, institutional rules *versus* the spontaneous individual, the drudgery and boredom of ordinary existence *versus* the imaginative flight of genius.[14]

Thus, it was in effecting the rational order of things that bureaucracy played its most important role for Weber. By this conception one would not expect great creativity or policy innovation as products of the bureaucracy. Here is the way Weber himself defined the bureaucratic role:

> There is the principle of fixed and official jurisdictional areas, which are generally ordered by rules, that is, by laws or administrative regulations.
>
> 1. The regular activities required for the purposes of the bureaucratically governed structure are distributed in a fixed way as official duties.
>
> 2. The authority to give the commands required for the discharge of these duties is distributed in a stable way and is strictly delimited

by rules concerning the coercive means, physical, sacerdotal, or otherwise, which may be placed at the disposal of officials.

3. Methodical provision is made for the regular and continuous fulfillment of these duties and for the execution of the corresponding rights; only persons who have the generally regulated qualifications to serve are employed.

In public and lawful government these three elements constitute "bureaucratic authority."[15]

Here then is modern governmental machinery, putting into effect the rules, laws, or regulations. In its ideal form, this institution offers "technical superiority" by providing "precision, speed, unambiguity, knowledge of the files, continuity, discretion, unity, strict subordination, reduction of friction and of material and personal costs. . . ."[16] Note that *these advantages accrue when bureaucracy is functioning as it should*, according to Weber. It is quite possible that the machinery will not achieve these advantages for any number of reasons. All Weber sought to do was to identify a set of functional activities and an organizational form for effecting these activities. By no means was he arguing that anything called "bureaucracy" produced the advantages noted above.

Nor was Weber insensitive to the political role of the bureaucracy. He pointed out that:

Once it is fully established, bureaucracy is among those social structures which are the hardest to destroy. Bureaucracy is *the* means of carrying "community action" over into rationally ordered "societal events." Therefore, as an instrument for "societalizing" relations of power, bureaucracy has been and is a power instrument of the first order—for the one who controls the bureaucratic apparatus.[17]

There are several clues in this important statement which suggest why it is that Weber's ideal bureaucratic system seldom is realized—particularly in democracies. First, being "fully established" presumably means meeting the criteria set down by Weber. Yet in a democracy, meeting the conditions of fixed jurisdictional areas, specialization, hierarchy, etc., is complicated by innumerable political pressures. Therefore bureaucracy is never really "fully established." Even a partially established bureaucracy is difficult to destroy, however. Second, "carrying 'community action' over into rationally ordered 'societal events'" is a highly complex and politically sensitive operation involving the sort of implementation activities identified above—interpretation, organization, and application. Each of these activities requires that bureaucrats maintain communication with those who make the laws and those who must obey them. In other words, Weber has, in this second sentence, described a process seemingly identical with what Pressman and Wildavsky identify as "implementation." As we have stressed, however, implementation is a dynamic process which may vary considerably among issues, thus raising doubts about a particular idealized version applicable everywhere under all circumstances. Third, Weber's accurate, almost axiomatic, statement that bureaucracy is "a power instrument of the first order—for the one who controls the bureaucratic apparatus" must be assessed in light of the probability that no single person or group will be in control in a pluralistic state. Indeed, there is unlikely to be a single bureaucratic apparatus.

Where does this analysis leave us in assessing the role of the bureaucracy? It suggests that while Weber may have identified certain ideal characteristics against which bureaucracies are measured, real-life government bureaus are highly dependent units which must monitor the intentions of the rule makers and the demands of their clientele. And this conclusion supports the generalization stated earlier that bureaucrats are inevitably drawn into activities beyond the simple application of rules or standards to public problems and conflicts. The role of bureaucracy then is much more politically dynamic than is that conjured up by Weber's "machine" imagery.

Viewing bureaucracy as a political institution stresses its need for support. It is not enough to promise efficiency; agencies need to nurture their constituencies every bit as much as legislators. Francis E. Rourke stresses this theme in his analysis of the bureaucratic policy system.

> The power of government agencies can be looked upon as resting essentially on political support. Agencies have power when they command the allegiance of fervent and substantial constituencies. . . .
> A first and fundamental source of power for administrative agencies in American society is their ability to attract outside support. Strength in a constituency is no less an asset for an American administrator than it is for a politician, and some agencies have succeeded in building outside support as formidable as that of any political organization. The lack of such support severely circumscribes the ability of an agency to achieve its goals, and may even threaten its survival as an organization.[18]

Some agencies are fortunate enough to have highly attractive programs to administer and can reap the benefits of broad public support. For example, if you work for the Social Security Administration, you may be assured of a job forever if you behave yourself. The program continues to be expanded and the benefits increased. Other agencies are not so fortunate. Consider the United States Information Agency or the Agency for International Development (the foreign aid agency). Both serve a clientele outside the country. Not unexpectedly, they consistently have trouble in Congress maintaining their budget authority.

One measure of the variable support for federal agencies is their growth as indicated by the number of employees and the size of budgets. Table 7–1 provides some examples.

Table 7-1. Departmental Growth in Employment and Budget Authority, 1965-1975

	Civilian Employment (000's)				Budget Authority (billions)			
Growth Departments	*1965*	*1970*	*1975*	*% Change 1965-1975*	*1965*	*1970*	*1975*	*% Change 1965-1975*
Health, Education, and Welfare	87	108	144	+66	7	58	114	+1,529
Justice	33	39	50	+52	.4	.8	2	+400
Labor	10	11	14	+40	.7	5	20	+2,757
Treasury	89	92	120	+35	13	20	40	+207
Maintaining Departments								
Agriculture	113	116	105	-7	7	9	14	+100
Commerce	34	33	36	-6	1	1	1.7	+70
Defense	1,034	1,192	1,038	-4	51	75	89	+75
Housing and Urban Development	14	15	17	+21	1	5	5.1	+410***
Interior	71	71	73	+3	1	1	3.9	+290
State	41	40	32	-20	.4	.5	.9	+125
Transportation	*	66	72	+9**	*	9	19	+111**

Source: *Statistical Abstract of the United States*, 1966, 1975.
*Did not exist as a department in 1960.
**% Change, 1970-1975
***New Department in 1965; % Change, 1970-1975, +2.

These figures produce some surprises. For example, Health, Education, and Welfare (HEW) is far and away the fastest growing department in the federal government. Justice and Treasury too show strong growth. The Department of Defense (DOD), on the other hand, has leveled off in employment and expenditures. However DOD still employs over 60 percent of the civilians employed by departments and 37 percent of the civilians employed by the federal government.

The growth of government departments and agencies is normally a direct result of the public problems we face as a nation. Since these problems vary, we may expect departments and agencies to wax and wane in readily available support. This phenomenon is most clearly illustrated among the independent agencies—those governmental units which deal with important matters but have not as yet achieved departmental status (and may never do so). Some of these agencies employ more persons and spend more money than full-fledged departments, but their existence may be relatively short-lived. The National Aeronautics and Space Administration (NASA) at one time was a rapidly growing agency, employing over 35,000 people in the late 1960s. It has declined steadily since that time, however, in employment and budget authority. The Environmental Protection Agency (EPA), on the other hand, is growing rapidly—from just over 7,000 employees when it was established in 1971 to well over 10,000 in 1975. And the newly created Energy Research and Development Administration (ERDA) [incorporating much of the dissolved Atomic Energy Commission] promises to grow even faster than EPA. Meanwhile the Veterans Administration continues its steady growth and strong support in Congress. It employs more civilians than any department except Defense and has a budget that normally exceeds that of seven of the departments.

Another statistical indicator of the role of the bureaucracy in contemporary America is the overall budget outlays in the past fifteen years. Under the unified budget concept (see Chapter 6), actual outlays amounted to $92.2 billion in 1960, and $196.6 billion in 1970 (2.13 times greater than in 1960). It is estimated that the outlays for 1976 will be $349.4 billion—3.79 times greater than in 1960 and 1.78 times greater than in 1970. While these figures are incomprehensible to the normal mind, they do, in the aggregate, project the staggering responsibilities of our depart- · ments and agencies. Consider the task of implementing various human resources programs (i.e., education, training, social services, health, income security, and veterans' benefits) which have increased from $25.5 billion in 1960 to $72.7 billion in 1970 (2.85 times greater than in 1960) and are estimated to total $177 billion in 1976 (6.94 times greater than 1960 and 2.43 times greater than in 1970).[19] These are mind-boggling statistics when conceived of in terms of actually managing the dollars involved so as to achieve the goals stated or implied in the law. Yet this is the task of bureaucracy as defined by·Weber and the nature of implementation as defined by Pressman and Wildavsky.

These comparative figures permit establishing another important point concerning the role of the bureaucracy. As fantastic as the budget increases appear to be, they tend to remain roughly proportionate to the growth of the economy as reflected in the gross national product (GNP). The figures show that federal budget outlays were 18.3 percent of GNP in 1960, 20 percent of GNP in 1970, and are estimated at 21.5 percent in 1976.[20] The point is that government programs, the budget, and the bureaucracy all reflect in fairly direct measure what is happening in the society. Therefore, an increasingly complex technological or technetronic society unquestionably will be served by an increasingly intricate bureaucratic network.

Organization of the Federal Bureaucracy

The federal bureaucracy is composed of a wide variety of organizations, as any trip through the *U.S. Government Organizational Manual* will graphically illustrate.[21] First there are the cabinet-level departments which presumably reflect and administer the most significant government functions. Since departmental secretaries are members of the president's cabinet, one might assume that they are in a favorable position for getting support. In fact, of course, presidents vary greatly in their use of the cabinet and in their relationships with individual departmental secretaries. Further, certain departments can be rather tightly organized and administered (e.g., Treasury, Labor, Commerce)—others are no more than conglomerates of individual bureaus, some of which may have independent sources of power with either the president or Congress (e.g., Defense and HEW).

Second are the myriad agencies, only a few of which either gain departmental or cabinet status (note that an agency head may be designated a member of the cabinet by the president). Here is a partial listing of such agencies as of this writing.

> Environmental Protection Agency (EPA)
> Energy Research and Development Administration (ERDA)
> General Services Administration (GSA)
> National Aeronautics and Space Administration (NASA)
> Veterans Administration (VA)
> Arms Control and Disarmament Agency
> Civil Service Commission (CSC)
> Consumer Product Safety Commission
> National Labor Relations Board (NLRB)
> National Science Foundation (NSF)

Railroad Retirement Board
Small Business Administration (SBA)
United States Information Agency (USIA)

As is indicated by the titles of these units, they vary in terms of their organizational structure (agency, administration, board, commission, foundation), leadership, and scope of responsibility. They also serve very different types of clientele and thus face enormously varying problems in building and maintaining political support. For example, GSA and CSC are essentially "in-government" service agencies—GSA for buildings, property, and supplies; CSC for personnel management; NASA works with and spawns technologically oriented industries; NSF relates to the universities and private research organizations, etc. Each has special problems in its dealings with Congress, the president, its "constituents," and the public-at-large.

Third are the regulatory commissions whose independent status derives from the long terms of the commissioners and their protection from arbitrary control of the president. These units are charged with regulating practices which Congress has determined require control, though it must be noted that regulatory authority is given as well to other agencies (e.g., EPA) or units within departments (e.g., the Food and Drug Administration in HEW). Here is the current list of regulatory agencies:

Civil Aeronautics Board
Federal Communications Commission
Federal Maritime Commission
Federal Power Commission
Federal Trade Commission
Interstate Commerce Commission
Securities and Exchange Commission

Fourth there are several government corporations established to carry out specific functions which presumably bear some relationship to ordinary business operations. The most recent example would be the Postal Service, which was reorganized from a cabinet-level department into a government corporation. Other examples would be the Tennessee Valley Authority, the Federal Deposit Insurance Corporation, the Reconstruction Finance Corporation of the 1930s, and the Overseas Private Investment Corporation.

Any number of other types of boards, commissions, councils, offices, companies, foundations, institutions, and authorities populate the executive branch of government and are involved in some manner of implementation. But special mention must be made of the units within the Executive Office of the President. Though highly engaged in formulation activities, these instrumentalities assist the president in seeking to oversee and coordinate the implementation of programs. Perhaps more than with the other agencies, their responsibilities span the functions identified here—primarily due to their location in the hierarchy. In addition to the Office of Management and Budget, discussed in Chapter 6, these units include:

Council of Economic Advisers
National Security Council (and its intelligence arm—the Central Intelligence Agency)
Domestic Council
Office of Economic Opportunity
Office of the Special Representative for Trade Negotiations
Council on Environmental Quality
Council on International Economic Policy
Office of Consumer Affairs
Council on Economic Policy

One important lesson from all of this is that where a program is located in this maze can make a great deal of difference in how it is implemented. Knowing this, promoters of a particular program may try to create a new agency, get it located in an agency or department known to be sympathetic, or perhaps seek reorganization of an existing agency bound to get a program. Victory in the legislative halls may be short-lived if the program goes to the wrong place in the bureaucracy. At any one point the following situations may exist:

1. An old-line agency continues to administer increments of policy as these are legitimated over time. No major shift in the structure or status of the agency has occurred. (Countless examples.)
2. A new agency is created within an existing parent department. The policy to be administered represents a relatively new area of concern, but the decision is made to include it within the jurisdiction of an existing department or division. (Example: Rural Development and Conservation in the Department of Agriculture.)
3. An existing agency is upgraded in status. Policy developments in an issue-area, or several related issue-areas, are interpreted to require departmental status for the administrative units. (Examples: creation of the Department of Health, Education, and Welfare and the Department of Housing and Urban Development.)
4. No agency exists. The policy to be administered represents a relatively new area of concern, and the decision is made to create a new

agency (perhaps for strategic reasons). (Examples: Office of Economic Opportunity, National Aeronautics and Space Administration, Environmental Protection Agency.)

5. An old-line agency determines, or it is determined for such an agency, that policy developments dictate a reorganization to adjust to shifts in administrative activities. (Examples: reorganization of defense-related agencies, leading to their unification in the Department of Defense; abolishment of the Atomic Energy Commission in favor of the broader Energy Research and Development Administration.)

Obviously, many other possibilities exist for creating or rearranging departments, agencies, bureaus, divisions. The point is that implementation of policy may vary, depending on the particular stage of agency development. For example, Anthony Downs suggests that "every bureau is initially dominated by either advocates or zealots."[22] The OEO experience is particularly illustrative of this generalization, but many of you will be familiar with the Peace Corps as well. With maturation comes increased efficiency, greater knowledge, more formalized procedures. Based on such observations, Downs proposes the "law of increasing conservatism": "All organizations tend to become more conservative as they get older, unless they experience periods of rapid growth [e.g., expansion of number of agencies, no. 2 above] or internal turnover [e.g., reorganization of an agency, no. 5 above]."[23] Such developments affect individual administrative actors; pressure on them to become more conservative increases as an organization ages. It is not much of a jump from such observations to those concerning such factors as the manner in which policy is applied by various agencies, the extent to which actors other than bureaucrats are involved in administration, the interpretations of policy by bureaucrats, or the perceptions of bureaucrats of public problems for which policy is intended.

Interpretation—What Does It All Mean?

During the 93rd Congress (1973-74) 26,216 bills and resolutions were introduced. Approximately 500 of these became law. Table 7-2 offers a sample of the programs authorized by Congress during this period. This list constitutes an enormous implementation agenda. And what do all these thousands of pages and millions of words mean? The implementors must make a determination. What seems obvious to some actors may not be evident to others. So processes of interpretation develop—processes by which political executives, bureaucrats, and others involved in carrying out programs seek to give real-life meaning to statutory language. The task

Table 7-2. Major Legislation, 93rd Congress

1st Session (1973)	Authorization Status	Implementing Agency
Farm Program	Amended	D/Agriculture
Law Enforcement Assistance Grants	Continuing	D/Justice
Trans-Alaska Pipeline	New	D/Interior
Mandatory Fuel Allocation	New	Federal Energy Office
Health Maintenance Organization	New	D/HEW
Omnibus Health Program Extension	Continuing	D/HEW
Manpower Training and Emergency Employment	Amended	D/Labor
Airport and Airways Aid	Continuing	D/Transportation
Federal Highway Program	Amended	D/Transportation
Social Security Benefits	Amended	D/HEW
2nd Session (1974)		
Creation of Office of Juvenile Justice	New	D/Justice
Small Business Loans	Continuing	Small Business Administration
Unemployment Compensation	Amended	D/Labor
Elementary and Secondary Education	Continuing	D/HEW
Clean Air	Amended	EPA
Nonnuclear Energy Policy	New	ERDA
National Cancer Program	Continuing	D/HEW
Veterans Benefits	Amended	VA
Mass Transit	Amended	D/Transportation
Housing and Community Development	Amended	D/HUD
Pension Reform	New	New government corporation
Minimum Wage	Amended	D/Labor
Legal Services Corporation	New	New government corporation

varies, of course. With "continuing" programs, implementors must assess whether existing interpretations still suffice. The record compiled during formulation and legitimation phases must be studied for clues as to changes in intention. Perhaps a congressional committee will have held oversight hearings and clarified the intent of the law before acting to continue the program. Congressmen instructing departmental secretaries, assistant secretaries, and various other agency personnel on what they meant is not an uncommon sight on Capitol Hill.

Where a program has been significantly amended or a new program enacted, the task of interpretation is considerable. And more often than not, whatever is decided will cause controversy. It may well be that the program was approved at all only because certain conflicts were avoided in the formulation and legitimation phases—conflicts bound to reappear in the implementation stage. How can this happen? Perhaps there is public pressure to do something, anything, about a problem (as with the development of environmental control programs in the early 1970s), or the time may be right to get a program enacted even though the problems are not well understood (as with many of the Great Society programs in the mid-1960s). Under these circumstances, interpretation becomes a highly sensitive activity which can create difficult political problems for an agency. Since program goals are often vague and subject to varying interpretations and change, the specific act of application or enforcement is bound to trigger a negative reaction from someone. For who can know for certain what is in the minds of all parties to a complex contract?

Often this matter of interpretation is discussed as "administrative discretion." I have a slight preference for the term "interpretation" simply because "discretion" is a bit too special, referring as it does to the "power of free decision; individual judgment; undirected choice." Whether or not implementors have this kind of power, they must interpret their authority. Discretion then becomes a particularly complex and comprehensive power to interpret. It may even include authority to define the problems, formulate proposals, and legitimate one proposal over another. In short, whole policy processes may be authorized to exist with little or no immediate legislative involvement. It would seem that the Central Intelligence Agency (CIA) has in the past had such power. Apparently those in charge interpreted their responsibilities as providing broad discretion in collecting and acting on intelligence. But whereas the CIA has become a celebrated case of what its supporters term "occasional excesses," other agencies too are provided with awesome tasks requiring a full complement of policy determinations that appear to make them total decision-making systems. As Lowi observes in his review of the Interstate Commerce Act: "There was delegation of the 'full ambit of authority'—executive, legislative, and judicial—in a single administrative body."[24]

The extent of discretionary authority can come to be a worrisome matter in a democracy. If the legislature, as the principal democratic institution, delegates too much responsibility to less visible and accountable units, then there is cause for concern. Theodore J. Lowi expressed these sentiments in his book, *The End of Liberalism*. He speaks of "policy without law" as "a broad delegation of power."[25] He sees a growing network of alliances between interest groups and agencies which subverts the legislature, and thus democracy. This network favors discretionary authority so it may make its accommodations as problems arise without going back to the legislature. Thus, according to Lowi, we have a new concept of representation.

Traditional, progressivistic expansions of representation are pre-

dicted on the assumption that law is authoritative and that therefore one must seek to expand participation in the making of laws.
The "new representation" extends the principle of representation
over into administration, since it is predicated on the assumption that
lawmaking bodies and conventional procedures cannot and ought
not make law.[26]

Lowi sees many evils in this development, "for it tends to derange almost
all established relations and expectations in the democratic system."[27]
Whether or not Lowi is correct in his predictions, he has identified a significant development which commands the attention of policy scholars
and emphasizes the importance of the processes of interpretation.

Application—Doing the Job

Having determined what the words mean for an agency's authority is only
the beginning. This authority then must be applied to the problems at
hand. Further adjustments may be made at this point since a politically
feasible interpretation of authority may not turn out to be practical in the
field. Application is often a dynamic process in which the implementor
or enforcer is guided generally by program directives or standards and
specifically by the circumstances of the real-life situation. For example,
meeting the national ambient air quality standards for carbon monoxide,
hydrocarbons, photochemical oxidants, and oxides of nitrogen required
that cities alter their patterns of automobile transportation. Proposals to
this end had to be submitted to the states, which in turn were required to
send plans to EPA in Washington for approval. A part of the plan for the
city of Pittsburgh included a rush-hour ban on passenger cars carrying less
than three persons from one of the busiest outbound parkway ramps in
the central city. Enforcement of the ban was announced on a Thursday (to
go into effect the following Wednesday), the Pennsylvania Department of
Transportation was swamped with complaints from the public on Friday,
and the ban was postponed for 90 days on Saturday (with EPA approval).
Adjustments to reality are not often so abrupt but they occur on a daily
basis in government.

   Murray Edelman is particularly instructive on this matter of accommodating even unambiguous laws to the circumstances at hand in his book,
The Symbolic Uses of Politics. He uses the example of speed limits, point-
ing out that since we all know "most speeders will not be caught or fined,"
behavior is adapted to this assumption.

   . . . drivers speed when the chance of being caught is slight or considered worth taking. Policemen stop some but not all violators, and
   let some of these off with a warning. As long as the game is played in
   this way, both drivers and policemen accept the order of things fairly

contentedly. . . . Similarly, employers accept health, safety, child labor, and minimum wage laws on the assumption that inspectors will appear at the plant only once in a while, and that if they are caught in violations on *these* occasions, a fine may have to be paid.[28]

Edelman further illustrates what may happen when the law is too strenuously enforced with the case of Officer Muller in Chicago who ticketed state and city officials' cars parked in a nonparking zone near city hall. "The conscientious Mr. Muller was assigned to a remote beat."[29] Clearly judgment is as much valued in applying legal remedies to the problem as is an accurate understanding of what these remedies are. While rules may not strictly be made to be broken, they are typically made to be prudently applied.

We all can cite cases similar to that of Officer Muller. Normally we use them to illustrate favoritism in the system. Edelman tells us that such adjustments are common and therefore to be expected in all administration. He describes the process of accommodation as "mutual role-taking."

> . . . so far as the great bulk of law enforcement is concerned "rules" are established through mutual role-taking; by looking at the consequences of possible acts from the point of view of the tempted individual and from the point of view of the impact of his acts upon the untempted. The result is a set of unchallenged rules implicitly permitting evasions and explicitly fixing penalties. Administrators are thereby able to avoid the sanctions of politically powerful groups by accepting their premises as valid; while at the same time they justify this behavior in the verbal formulas provided in the rules.[30]

And further:

> Politics always involve conflicts. For the individual decision maker group conflict means ambivalence, and ambivalence can be described in behavioral terms as the concomitant of taking of incompatible roles. . . . Enforcers and "enforced" alike assume both the role of the potential violator and the role of his victim. Out of their responses to such mutual role-taking come the rules as actually acted out; the specification of the loopholes, penalties, and rewards that reflect an acceptable adjustment of these incompatible roles.[31]

This analysis surely describes an active and ever-changing process and thus is well suited to the emphasis relied on throughout the book. It not only assigns a low probability to literal application or enforcement of the law but suggests that those making such an effort may well face problems within their organization. This interpretation is at variance with the more traditional concepts of public administration and scientific management which stress the establishment of policy goals to be effectively and efficiently implemented by an objective civil service.

The Intergovernmental Partnership

In his examination of intergovernmental relations during the 19th century, Daniel J. Elazar concludes that the three levels of government were partners engaged in "cooperative endeavors."

> The administrative agencies of the federal and state governments provide the setting. The political figures and public administrators of five generations serve as the cast of characters, and the action to be observed is the interaction between the two sets of agencies and their staffs.[32]

The partnership still exists today—what has changed is its magnitude. The federal government was a relatively small enterprise in the 19th century. Expenditures typically averaged between $300 and $400 million annually during the latter third of that century (after the Civil War). In 1974 federal aid to state and local governments alone was in excess of $43 billion—over 100 times greater than all federal expenditures in a typical year in the late 19th century.[33]

Much of this dramatic increase occurred as a result of the domestic programs enacted during the Great Depression of the 1930s, the readjustment period following World War II, and the Johnson administration in 1964–1968. The 1930s programs provided the breakthrough on the domestic front—the post-World War II period provided the growth of individual programs (notably social security and housing) and expansion to other issue areas (e.g., medicare, education, transportation). Federal support of state and local government (principally in the form of grants with various strings attached) rose from $894 million in 1946 to approximately $25 billion in 1970. The significance of these figures for present purposes lies in the intricate intergovernmental network of implementation required simply to spend the money. Richard H. Leach describes the situation:

> By fiscal 1970, expenditures for [state and local support] . . . involved more than 500 separate federal categorical grant-in-aid programs, which were administered by over 150 departments in Washington and over 400 federal offices in the field. . . . More new programs involving appropriations of federal aid were initiated by the 85th through the 89th Congresses [1957–1966] than by all the previous sessions of Congress since the beginning of the Republic. The 89th Congress (1965–1966) alone passed no fewer than 136 major domestic bills, including seventeen new resource development programs, seventeen new educational programs, twenty-one new health programs, fifteen new economic development programs, twelve new programs on city problems, and four for manpower training. By 1969, there were all told fifty different programs for vocational and job training, thirty-five programs for housing, sixty-two for community facilities, and twenty-eight for recreation, as well as countless others in a great variety of fields.[34]

These are all intergovernmental programs, and thus one may expect to find an implementation system populated by persons from all levels. Of course, there is no one implementation system. Rather look for what Governor Terry Sanford has described as a picket fence. "The lines of authority, the concerns and interests, the flow of the money, and the direction of the programs run straight down like a number of pickets stuck into the ground."[35] Once again we are instructed to pay attention to the issues and the programs as a way of understanding how the institutions work. That is, whether it be public housing, vocational education, agriculture, urban renewal, pollution control, welfare, highways, or whatever, we should search for the connections among federal-state-local officials (as well as the ties between them and private persons) that are important in putting the program into effect. Thus, for example, when state and local housing officials hear of a new federal program in their area, they know that their lives are about to change again. Many come to be as attentive to what goes on in Washington as to what goes on in their more immediate governments.

Morton Grodzins has described all of this as "marble-cake federalism" in which there is a high degree of mixing and sharing of governmental functions.[36] While few would disagree with Grodzins, still the nature of this intergovernmental sharing varies over time with the growth and change in programs and means for implementing them. Deil S. Wright has studied these variations and his conclusions are offered in Table 7-3. The trends identified here must be studied in conjunction with the growth of federal aid and involvement cited earlier. Note in particular the growth of various types of grants in the post-World War II period and how these grants tend to focus or channel intergovernmental relations during the concentrated phase, then proliferate with "a superficial appearance of fusion" during the creative phase, and finally result in a highly fragmented and uncertain competitive phase. Wright puts it this way:

> The proliferation of grants, the clash between professionals and participation-minded clients, the gap between program promises and proven performance, plus the intractability of domestic urban and international problems, formed a malaise in which IGR [intergovernmental relations] entered a new phase.[37]

Part of the tension in recent years is reflected in the emergence of revenue sharing. In a sense, this concept of state and local governments sharing federal revenues, with few strings attached, grows out of both the frustrations of state and local officials in working with grant programs and the realization by many that federal programs do not solve everything everywhere. The State and Local Fiscal Assistance Act of 1972 authorized payments of over $30 billion to state and local governments during a five-

Table 7-3. Phases of Intergovernmental Relations (IGR)

Phase Descriptor	Main Problems	Participants Perceptions	IGR Mechanisms	Federalism Metaphor	Approximate Climax Period
Conflict	Defining boundaries Proper spheres	Antagonistic Adversary Controversy Exclusivity	Statutes Courts Regulations	Layer-cake federalism	pre-1937
Cooperative	Economic stress International threat	Collaboration Complementary Mutuality Supportive	Policy planning Broad formula grants Open-ended grants Tax credit	Marble-cake federalism	1933–1953
Concentrated	Program needs Capital works	Professionalism Objectivity Neutrality Functionalism	Categorical grants Service standards	Focused or channelled federalism (water taps)	1945–1960
Creative	Urban-metropolitan Disadvantaged clients	National goals Great society Grantsmanship	Program planning Project grants Participation	Fused-foliated federalism (proliferated)	1958–1968
Competitive	Coordination Program effectiveness Delivery systems Citizen access	Disagreement Tension Rivalry	Revenue sharing Reorganization Regionalization Grant consolidation	Picket-fence federalism (fragmented)	1965–?

Source: Deil S. Wright, "Intergovernmental Relations: An Analytical Overview." Reproduced by permission from *The Annals* of the American Academy of Political and Social Science, Volume 416, 1974.

year period, 1972–1976. In general, these grants (going to approximately 39,000 governments) were supplemental to existing grants, which remain numerous and fragmented despite efforts to consolidate and simplify.[38]

Two Cases of Implementation

I have selected two cases which illustrate the problems of organizing while interpreting new authority. First, we take a brief look at how an existing agency is restructured to administer a quantum jump in federal responsibility for education. Second, we describe the challenge associated with creating a new agency and an elaborate intergovernmental network to rid the nation of poverty.

From Washington to the Classroom

As described in Chapter 5, Congress approved a sort of back-door approach for federal aid to education. The Elementary and Secondary Education Act of 1965 (ESEA) declared that:

> In recognition of the special educational needs of children of low-income families and the impact that concentrations of low-income families have on the ability of local educational agencies to support adequate educational programs, the Congress hereby declares it to be the policy of the United States to provide financial assistance . . . to local educational agencies serving areas with concentrations of children from low-income families to expand and improve their educational programs by various means (including preschool programs) which contribute particularly to meeting the special educational needs of educationally deprived children. (Title I, Sec. 201, Elementary and Secondary Education Act of 1965).

Here was a deceptively simple goal—aid children who need special help. But, of course, those associated with formulating and adopting this legislation understood its broader implications. With school consolidation in recent decades, few, if any, school districts in the nation would not qualify for program benefits. For the fact is that while the rich/poor distinction between school districts remains, it is considerably less sharp than it used to be. Thus, here was a program that required the development and maintenance of contact and communication between Washington, the 50 states, and nearly 25,000 school districts. Further, since the act carried only a one-year authorization, administrators had to act fast to justify an extension. "The federal aid advocates had won a stunning victory, but they knew full well that they would have to renew the battle again the following session [of Congress]."[39] And finally, there was little or no organizational memory available to direct this massive operation. The U.S. Office of Education (USOE) had been a relatively obscure unit in the Department of Health, Education, and Welfare; and many, if not most, school districts "had no previous experience in carrying out federally connected projects of any kind."[40]

Books have been written on this whole subject. Consequently the most we can do is illustrate a few of the more difficult problems of implementation. Three topics in particular will be emphasized here—the reorganization of the Office of Education, the myriad intergovernmental connections which had to be established, and the early efforts to interpret and apply the law.

"The job of administering Public Law 89-10 [ESEA] fell to an agency with a long and pedestrian past."[41] In their full treatment of ESEA, Stephen K. Bailey and Edith K. Mosher list the many problems of the Office of Education as an organizational unit before its reorganization: atomization and specialization (powerful "guilds of professionals" running the place), superannuated personnel and personnel systems (an average age of over 50 among the professional staff), archaic financial and management information systems, an unrationalized bureau and field structure (it had "'growed' like Topsy"), anomie within the executive branch, and a constant fear of the charge of federal control.[42]

Anticipating the passage of a comprehensive federal aid to education program, the commissioner of education, Francis Keppel, well understood the need to retool this clumsy and outmoded structure. Occupied himself with the legislative battles necessary to pass ESEA, Keppel obtained the services of one Henry Loomis as deputy commissioner and charged him with the responsibility of reorganizing the office. Described as a "no-non-sense type," Loomis "began what was probably one of the most extraordinary, bruising, controversial, if in some ways effective, administrative operations in the recent annals of the federal government."[43] The strategy was simple in concept, but required extraordinary skill in execution. A special task force (not drawn from HEW) was appointed to study the organizational insufficiencies of USOE, and then its recommendations were effected in a very short period of time. The theory behind this move was that outside help was necessary in rationalizing and supporting the changes, and that carefully paced implementation of reforms over time only invited resistance from the many fiefdoms in USOE. So "quick and dirty" was the chosen method. The results were stunning, if a little traumatic. Bailey and Mosher describe it as follows:

> . . . less than two weeks after submission of the report, the reorganization *was effected*. The speed of action and the fact that the plan was shattering to *all* vested interests produced a reaction of numbed, bewildered, bitter acquiescence. . . . The anguish can only be imagined. The ensuing, if temporary, administrative chaos was shattering.

> For days and weeks, people could not find each other's offices—
> sometimes not even their own. Telephone extensions connected
> appropriate parties only by coincidence. A large number of key
> positions in the new order were vacant or were occupied by acting
> directors who were frequently demoralized by status ambiguity and
> eventual status loss. . . . And all of this came at a time of maximum
> work load.[44]

It should be noted further that HEW itself was undergoing important personnel and policy shifts.

But organizational accommodation in Washington was only part of the story. Education has traditionally been a state and local concern and state departments of education, local school boards, and other local policy and administrative apparatus exist to develop and implement policy in this sphere. Now the "feds" were to be heavily involved too, with the dollar bill as their calling card. Though the national government had, in the past, provided various types of special support, here was the first attempt to fashion a federal-state-local education policy system. Title I of ESEA was the principal stimulus for this development in its provisions for aid to low-income children. The intergovernmental distribution of responsibility for this program was as follows:

The United States Office of Education

1. Develops and disseminates regulations, guidelines, and other materials regarding the approval of Title I projects.
2. Reviews and assesses the progress under Title I throughout the nation.

State Education Agencies

1. Approve proposed local projects in accordance with federal regulations and guidelines.
2. Assist local educational agencies in the development of projects.
3. Submit state evaluative report to USOE.

Local Education Agencies

1. Identify the educationally deprived children in the areas where there are high concentrations of low-income families and determine their special educational needs.
2. Develop and implement approved projects to fulfill the intent of Title I.[45]

The trained eye can spot mountains of paper with each set of responsibilities. An experienced observer would also see any number of possibilities for tension among the various levels of government in this distribution of responsibilities. An elaborate system of interdependency was created which was bound to result in conflict. As federal funding increased, it became clear that no one layer could accomplish its goals without the other. As Frederick M. Wirt and Michael W. Kirst point out, federal and state governments are dependent on local governments to run the schools, and the locals depend on federal and state financial aid.[46] Further, any number of private, citizen, and professional groups were involved in applying this policy, including groups representing low-income families.

I have stressed throughout this text that laws passed are not laws universally understood or enforced. Not surprisingly, many educators throughout the nation were ill-informed about the specifics of ESEA. After all they were engaged on a daily basis in running the schools. "Congressional consideration of ESEA had progressed so rapidly that few state and local school authorities understood the Act's specific recommendations or its thrust toward certain basic educational changes."[47] Put it all together and one finds an uncertain agency undergoing drastic reorganization administering a massive new program to a well-established clientele, some of whom were uninformed on federal policy, most of whom were wary of federal intentions. ESEA was to be accomplished in this context.

Bailey and Mosher conclude that the process of implementation:

> ... involved an administrative dialectic—a series of promulgations from USOE which were preceded, accompanied, and followed by inputs and feedbacks from affected clientele. The process was cumbersome, and involved both underprescriptions and overprescriptions from Washington.[48]

This description fits well with the generalizations set forth in this chapter which stress the interactive and dynamic qualities of implementation. It properly ignores the neat flow-chart process of administration wherein an agency simply puts into effect legislative intent. Bailey and Mosher are, in essence, describing a process of interpretation, estimation, and adjustment.

In their study of implementing economic development policy, Pressman and Wildavsky stress that many decision points are involved to implement any major program. They conclude that "the probability of agreement by every participant on each decision point must be exceedingly high for there to be any chance at all that a program will be brought to completion."[49] The many tasks associated with just getting money to school districts which qualified involved countless decision points. At the federal level, the initial tasks—those required just to get the process underway—were as follows:

1. The development of standards and procedures for the funding and control of authorizations;

2. The construction of ground rules and guidelines for educational programming and project design;
3. The preparation and analysis of reports and other informational and administrative data.[50]

Many of these actions were taken in consultation with state and local officials. "Just as the drafting of ESEA involved a delicate balance of intergovernmental interests, so the development of ground rules became a matter of vital concern to all the affected groups."[51] But though guidelines are essential, they too require interpretation and adjustment if a comprehensive federal program is to be adopted to the social, economic, and political diversity represented by the 50 states. And so the many decision points associated with preparing the basis for program implementation are multiplied many more times as local school districts actually develop plans to spend the money. All of this activity consumed several months and millions of man-hours at all levels of government. As David B. Truman correctly concludes: "The administration of a statute is, properly speaking, an extension of the legislative process."[52]

With the passage of ESEA, one of the last remaining exclusive state-local responsibilities had settled within the national decision-making orbit. Norman C. Thomas has observed: "It has often been asserted that 'education is a local responsibility, a state function, and a national concern.'"[53] After ESEA "there was no longer serious debate over the propriety of a major federal role in education."[54] Little wonder, then, that the initial stages of implementation were complex and often confused. A new intergovernmental decisional system was in the making. Bailey and Mosher cite David B. Truman's view that administrators are forced "to seek . . . a means of converting the controversial into the routine."[55] In the case of ESEA, educational officials were handed "an adjustment, among conflicting interests" (Truman's definition of a mandate in this setting) that no one knew for certain would last. That it has, and that a rather high degree of conversion of conflict into routine has occurred in this issue-area stands in marked contrast to the next case to be examined.

From Washington to the Ghettos

On January 4, 1975, President Ford signed legislation to abolish the Office of Economic Opportunity (OEO) and transfer its remaining programs to an independent Community Services Administration (later to be placed in the Department of Health, Education, and Welfare). OEO had from the first resided somewhat uncomfortably in the Executive Office of the President—a rather unusual location for a bureaucratic agency. After a decade of uncertainty, and two years of determined effort to dismantle

OEO, the deed was finally done. President Nixon had, in 1973, announced his intention to kill both the agency and its programs. He appointed an avowed opponent of the program, Howard J. Phillips, as director "with orders to shoot his own agency out from under himself" within six months. Phillips tried but failed. As one observer noted: "The war on poverty may yet be remembered as the policy that was ordered to leap off a cliff, leapt, and survived."[56]

OEO itself was living on borrowed time, however. While there was broad congressional support for the programs, having a poverty agency located within the Executive Office of the President was an organizational contretemps of the first order. Thus, the "congressional dispute [in 1974] . . . focused not on whether to continue the OEO programs, but where to house them."[57] In describing the formulation of the poverty program (see Chapter 4), I noted that administrators were bound to face difficult problems in effecting the policies. They were, in fact, so enormous that the wonder is not so much in OEO's eventual dismantlement, but rather in its continuance for ten years.

We will, of course, only sample the implementation complexities experienced by this innovative welfare and self-help program. Specifically, we will examine the initial challenge to the agency in interpreting and accomplishing a formidable set of goals and then review the myriad organizational problems associated with the agency's location and relationship to local governments.

"America's War on Poverty is a story in superlatives," according to one of its most careful students, James L. Sundquist.

> It was the boldest national objective ever declared by the Congress—
> to do what no people had ever done, what the Bible says cannot be
> done—to *eliminate* poverty from the land. . . . It granted the broadest
> of power and discretion to a single administrator—Sargent Shriver—
> to upset and remake, if he could, the institutional structure of com-
> munity after community across the land. It became . . . the most
> controversial of all the domestic programs of the Kennedy-Johnson
> era.[58]

The boldest of the programs was that directed toward community action. For not only were the goals imaginative, but the organizational mandates were extraordinary (more about that later). In essence, OEO was authorized to establish minipolicy systems throughout the nation. These systems were, in turn, directed to define the problems of poverty and plan programs which would solve those problems. Congress itself had not clearly defined the targets of its legislation, nor understood its implications. As Sundquist notes: "After Congress had acted, its members had little comprehension of what, precisely, they had done—particularly with regard to community action."[59]

The result from the point of view of the new agency was an awesome directive—i.e., eradicate poverty—and with only the most limited legislative guidelines for proceeding to do so. What occurred was almost classic buck-passing. Not able to define problems accurately in the first place, the Shriver Task Force asked for general authority to do so. Congress agreed, again not systematically examining either problems or proposals. OEO, in turn, created local units to do the job. Thus, the ambiguity characterizing the program at the top was duly transmitted down the line. John G. Wofford, who served as deputy director of the Community Action Program, questioned whether one could, in fact, even identify a program.

> To be sure, . . . (OEO) published a suggested definition of poverty. . .; it had some notions that poverty arose out of a complex relationship between the opportunity structure . . . and those who should have been seizing the opportunities . . .; and it believed that the solution lay in changing both that structure and those aspirations, abilities, and assumptions.
> But these federal definitions, notions, and beliefs did not amount to a program. The program was to be designed by each community to meet its own needs.[60]

Interpretation has been stressed as a highly important and most difficult activity associated with implementation. The poverty program is a fine illustration of how challenging this activity may become. For not only were administrators faced with making intelligent estimates as to what their own authority really meant, they had to act with incredible speed. The first year of the poverty program "was telescoped into about six and a half months of administrative action" due to delayed appropriations. This meant that OEO officials had to launch this innovative program, "find worthy projects for $800 million," and go back to Congress to justify increases, and all in a six-month period.[61] As noted earlier, Professor Lowi has expressed concern about such broad delegations of power to executive agencies which are closely allied with interest groups. In this case, the sizeable discretionary authority came to be as much a burden as a blessing. Further, there were only a few well-organized interests among the target population which might immediately benefit from this delegation. In fact, a large part of the challenge for OEO was to create organizational ties to the poor. Let us now turn to that important aspect of implementing this program.

Earlier I cited OEO as an example of the creation of an agency where none existed. That is not entirely correct. While there was no poverty agency as such, the Departments of Health, Education, and Welfare; Labor; and Housing and Urban Development might well have housed elements of the poverty program. A special agency was intentionally created, however, and strategically placed close to the president. Whatever advantage OEO might have gained by its proximity to the White House, it lost in the complexity and inherent conflicts of its assignments. Units in the Executive Office of the President are typically there to coordinate and oversee various programs that are actually administered elsewhere (e.g., the Office of Management and Budget, Council of Economic Advisers, Council of Environmental Quality, etc.). OEO was, in fact, to engage in this type of coordination since many federal agencies administered programs which impacted on the poor. In addition, however, the agency was directed to administer programs of its own. As John C. Donovan observed: "The fish or fowl dilemma . . . plagued OEO from that day forward."[62] The director, Sargent Shriver, was soon having to defend the agency against charges that the program was an "administrative shambles." Donovan doubts it could have turned out differently.

> To conceive a new multimillion-dollar national program which is to be administered in part by a White House-level coordinating agency and in part by operating departments, and which at the same time is to be coordinated by some new White House office which itself becomes part of the administrative overlap, is to postulate administrative chaos. Only a nation as gifted as we are in organizational talent would risk launching a promising new program in such a highly disadvantageous administrative setting.[63]

But this speaks only to the organizational problems faced within the Washington setting. As has been stressed before, most domestic programs conceived in Washington are administered with state and local cooperation. Often under the best of circumstances that cooperation is difficult to arrange and still guarantee effective implementation. In the case of the poverty program, however, local administration required the creation of 1,000 community action agencies. So, in addition to the challenge of working with existing state and local governments, new units had to be established, some of which were bound to conflict with and thus disturb local politics. These disturbances, as expected, were soon picked up by congressmen, many of whom came to be strong critics of the program.

Still further, the program called for "maximum feasible participation" of the poor in defining the problems and planning the solutions. Here was a bureaucratic agency seeking to maximize citizen participation while striving for a modicum of efficiency. This, according to J. David Greenstone and Paul E. Peterson, "was a naive effort to realize two mutually exclusive goals."[64] At the same time, however, it should be noted that the participation requirement had the positive side effect of generating political access for many blacks and other minorities. Further, it might be argued that this participation socialized some whites to other sets of values and needs in the society. If so, and there is some supporting evidence, then we have an illustration of how a program designed to achieve one goal may, in fact, achieve others. In this case, government support for the political organization of blacks would be an unacceptable goal on its own. It can only be realized through indirect means.[65]

Jack Conway, the first director of the Community Action Program, referred to the local agencies as "three-legged stools." That is, support for the program was derived from public officials in the community, private agencies with experience in fighting poverty, and representatives of the poor.[66] No one of these groups was supposed to dominate or dictate the programs. Rather the stress was on "community." No more serious violation of Weber's ideal-type bureaucracy has ever been formed in the mind of man. And no better illustration exists for us of the variety of persons who may become involved in implementation—in this case by legal directive. In the classical sense, there was no administration, only the authorization of program development tailored to meet the needs of individual communities.

This conclusion finds support in David E. Epperson's study of the community action program in Pittsburgh. A former director of Community Action Pittsburgh, Epperson found the traditional modes of administration of little assistance in meeting his needs. Rather he stressed that:

> The antipoverty program was . . . designed and built on speculation. A lack of policy and program definition was apparent from the beginning. It necessitated speculation on the results of many specific programs in the cities because program knowledge was not available.[67]

Epperson identified a number of strategies for maintaining support locally and from Washington—strategies at some variance with those normally associated with the administration of more traditional programs.

1. Promoting innovation in programs;
2. Insuring quick, highly visible results;
3. Quickly establishing a credible organization;
4. Encouraging participation by those unused to having a role in decision making;
5. Developing and maintaining close contact with the clientele, the media, and political decision makers;
6. Promoting "responsible" support activities acceptable to the community-at-large;
7. Anticipating adverse outcomes.[68]

In summary, the results show a new, misplaced agency with enormous discretion implementing a program through local units of mixed participation and high potential conflict. These are hardly conditions for peaceful implementation. They would make Weber turn over in his grave. On the other hand, if one views the effort as social experimentation, a quite different perspective and set of expectations follow. Under these conditions one might look for unusual arrangements, testing of various proposals, efforts to individualize solutions, the phasing in and out of organizational units, less emphasis on uniform output. One might also expect the agency itself to fade away in time, as contrasted with most bureaucracy.[69]

Because it was new, different, and experimental, OEO was never able to rise above conflict to establish firm routines. In Truman's terms it never discovered the "means of converting the controversial into the routine." Indeed, due to the nature of its work and organization, OEO was responsible for identifying and promoting conflict which had not as yet surfaced. For it to have survived would have been the ultimate evidence that agencies never die. For it to have survived for ten years was support enough for the proposition that agencies die hard.

Summary

With implementation we watch policy actors move toward the problems of society—presumably equipped to relieve certain needs of people. It is a simple matter, of course, when a hungry man asks for food and those with authority, and the resources, say: "Give the man food." We have seen that programs are seldom so unambiguous either in goals or directives. Nor are implementing organizations designed for such swift and pointed action. Rather major federal programs are multifaceted, subject to varying interpretations, competitive with other programs at various levels of government, administered by a labyrinth of organizational units throughout government, and, therefore, the object of considerable negotiation. The two cases presented here offer a limited sample of these characteristics, demonstrating in particular the organizational and interpretational problems associated with improving education and reducing poverty.

Notes

1. Jeffrey L. Pressman and Aaron B. Wildavsky, *Implementation* (Berkeley: University of California Press, 1973), p. 167.

2. Pressman and Wildavsky, p. xv.

3. Leonard D. White, *Introduction to the Study of Public Administration* (New York: Macmillan, 1926), p. 2.

4. John M. Gaus, *Reflections on Public Administration* (University, Alabama: University of Alabama Press, 1947), pp. 8–9.

5. Walter Williams, "Special Issue on Implementation: Editor's Comments," *Policy Analysis*, vol. 1 (Summer 1975), p. 451. Emphasis added.

6. Pressman and Wildavsky, pp. xiv–xv.

7. Pressman and Wildavsky, p. xv. For a useful, extended analysis of the concept, see Carl E. Van Horn and Donald S. Van Meter, "The Implementation of Intergovernmental Policy," in Charles O. Jones and Robert B. Thomas, eds., *Public Policy Making in a Federal System* (Beverly Hills, Calif.: Sage Publications, 1976), pp. 39–62.

8. Glendon Schubert, *Judicial Policy-Making* (Chicago: Scott, Foresman, 1965), p. 60.

9. Samuel Krislov, *The Supreme Court in the Political Process* (New York: Macmillan, 1965), p. 34.

10. See Harmon Zeigler, *Interest Groups in American Society* (Englewood Cliffs, N.J.: Prentice-Hall, 1964), Ch. 10.

11. David B. Truman, *The Governmental Process* (New York: Knopf, 1951), Ch. 4.

12. Carl J. Friedrich, *Constitutional Government and Politics* (New York: Harper, 1937), Ch. 2. Friedrich notes that: "The cradle of modern government has been variously recognized in the kingdoms of France and England, in the Italian city state, in the Roman Catholic Church, and even in the Sicilian realm of the brilliant Emperor Frederich II. All of these claims are based upon one aspect common to these several political bodies: the possession of a bureaucracy, a body of servants devoted to prince, civiltà or church" (p. 20).

13. H. H. Gerth and C. Wright Mills, *From Max Weber: Essays in Sociology* (London: Routledge & Kegan Paul, 1948), p. 52.

14. Gerth and Mills, p. 53.

15. Gerth and Mills, p. 196.

16. Again quoting Weber—Gerth and Mills, p. 214.

17. Gerth and Mills, p. 228.

18. Francis E. Rourke, *Bureaucracy, Politics, and Public Policy* (Boston: Little, Brown, 1969), pp. 1, 11.

19. Figures taken from Barry M. Blechman, et al., *Setting National Priorities: The 1976 Budget* (Washington, D.C.: The Brookings Institution, 1975), pp. 5–6.

20. Blechman, et al., p. 5.

21. A brief but useful review of these several types of agencies may be found in Lewis C. Mainzer, *Political Bureaucracy* (Chicago: Scott, Foresman, 1973), pp. 18–24. Also consult a recent edition of the *U.S. Government Organizational Manual*, or the *Congressional Directory*. Congressional Quarterly, Inc., has also compiled a very handy *Washington Information Directory*, 1975–1976, that includes information on agencies and their clientele groups.

22. Anthony Downs, *Inside Bureaucracy* (Boston: Little, Brown, 1967), p. 8.

23. Downs, p. 20.

24. Theodore J. Lowi, *The End of Liberalism* (New York: Norton, 1969), p. 131.

25. Lowi, p. 126.

26. Lowi, p. 96.

27. Lowi, p. 96.

28. Murray Edelman, *The Symbolic Uses of Politics* (Urbana: University of Illinois Press, 1964), p. 45.

29. Edelman, p. 45.

30. Edelman, p. 48.

31. Edelman, p. 51.

32. Daniel J. Elazar, *The American Partnership* (Chicago: University of Chicago Press, 1962), p. 1.

33. Taken from Advisory Commission on Intergovernmental Relations, *Trends in Fiscal Federalism, 1954–1974* (Washington, D.C.: U.S. Government Printing Office, 1975), pp. 26–27.

34. Richard H. Leach, *American Federalism* (New York: Norton, 1970), p. 168.

35. Terry Sanford, *Storm Over the States* (New York: McGraw-Hill, 1967), p. 80. Deil S. Wright has provided a conceptual outline of this concept of "picket-fence federalism" in "Intergovernmental Relations: An Analytical Overview," *The Annals*, vol. 416 (November 1974), see p. 15.

36. Morton Grodzins, *The American System* (Chicago: Rand-McNally, 1966).

37. Wright, p. 13.

38. The revenue-sharing program is just now receiving extensive evaluation. In particular see Richard P. Nathan, et al., *Monitoring Revenue Sharing* (Washington, D.C.: Brookings Institution, 1975); Paul Dommel, *The Politics of Revenue Sharing* (Bloomington: Indiana University Press, 1974); and Michael D. Reagan, *The New Federalism* (New York: Oxford University Press, 1972), Ch. 4.

39. Eugene Eidenberg and Roy D. Morey, *An Act of Congress* (New York: Norton, 1969), p. 176.

40. Stephen K. Bailey and Edith K. Mosher, *ESEA: The Office of Education Administers a Law* (Syracuse: Syracuse University Press, 1968), p. 101. It should be noted that this account of the implementation of ESEA draws heavily on the scholarship of Bailey and Mosher.

41. Bailey and Mosher, p. 72.

42. Bailey and Mosher, pp. 72–75.

43. Bailey and Mosher, p. 77.

44. Bailey and Mosher, p. 89.

45. As summarized in Frederick M. Wirt and Michael W. Kirst, *The Political Web of American Schools* (Boston: Little, Brown, 1972), pp. 154–155.

46. Wirt and Kirst, p. 158.

47. Bailey and Mosher, p. 99.

48. Bailey and Mosher, p. 159.

49. Jeffrey L. Pressman and Aaron B. Wildavsky, *Implementation* (Berkeley: University of California Press, 1973), p. 107.

50. As summarized in Bailey and Mosher, p. 102.

51. Bailey and Mosher, p. 109.

52. David B. Truman, *The Governmental Process* (New York: Knopf, 1951), p. 439.

53. Norman C. Thomas, *Education in National Politics* (New York: David McKay, 1975), p. 19.

54. Thomas, p. 34.

55. Truman, p. 444.

56. Both quotes from *The Christian Science Monitor*, June 23, 1973.

57. *The Congressional Quarterly Weekly Report*, January 11, 1975, p. 87.

58. James L. Sundquist, ed., *On Fighting Poverty* (New York: Basic Books, 1969), p. 3.

59. Sundquist, p. 29.

60. John G. Wofford, "The Politics of Local Responsibility: Administration of the Community Action Program—1964-1966," in Sundquist, p. 70.

61. John C. Donovan, *The Politics of Poverty* (New York: Pegasus, 1967), p. 53.

62. Donovan, p. 51.

63. Donovan, p. 52.

64. J. David Greenstone and Paul E. Peterson, *Race and Authority in Urban Politics* (New York: Russell Sage Foundation, 1973), p. 14.

65. Greenstone and Peterson are not sanguine about the wide-spread success in attacking political poverty. Still they do offer some evidence to show a redistribution of political power at the local level. See p. 5.

66. Cited in Wofford's paper in Sundquist, p. 77.

67. David E. Epperson, "Administering a Federal Policy: The Case of the Pittsburgh Poverty Program," Ph.D. dissertation, University of Pittsburgh, 1975, p. 212.

68. Epperson, p. 212.

69. Of course, it is one thing to plan a social experiment, quite another to decide along the way that that is the best one can do. If one plans it in advance, then constant evaluation and rational adjustment are consciously included so that systematic learning can take place. While evaluations of the poverty program were made, little systematic learning took place.

8

Evaluating Programs and Policy

Functional Activities	Categorized in Government	and as Systems	with Output
Specification (of criteria) Measurement Analysis Recommendation	Program to Government	Program Evaluation	Varies (justification, program change, etc.)

Properly conceived, evaluation is an activity which can contribute greatly to the understanding and improvement of policy development and implementation. That is, students of the policy process will find program evaluation a productive entry point for their analysis since it inevitably draws them into problem definition and goal setting and from there to other functional activities. Likewise, the practitioners of public policy increasingly turn to evaluation for justifying existing programs, assessing the costs and benefits, and proposing change.

However important evaluation may be, until very recently it was one of the least explored of the functional activities in the policy process. As Jerry W. Lansdowne properly observed in 1968: "There has been a propensity to think in the relatively static terms of politics and administration as the totality of the policy process."[1] Since that time, there has been growing interest in evaluation among scholars and policy makers—permitting a somewhat less speculative analysis of the topic than in the first edition of this book.

What Is Evaluation?

Our meaning of evaluation is partially revealed in how it is categorized in government—i.e., "program to government." This means simply that individual programs are, in a sense, returned to government for review. But, of course, much more is involved, as is revealed by almost any definition of evaluation. Carol H. Weiss correctly observes that: "Evaluation is an elastic word that stretches to cover judgments of many kinds." She also notes, however, that all uses of evaluation "have in common . . . the notion of judging merit."[2] Of course, the present concern is with *judging the merit of government programs*—of determining whether and how these programs have affected the public problems to which they are directed.

Evaluation will be used in two ways here—first as a functional activity which occurs in all political systems; second as a more systematic endeavor to judge the merits of specific programs. The two uses are highly related but clearly not the same. With the first, we look for those means by which government reviews, oversees, and judges its progress. With the second, we seek to identify the systematic methods by which programs are evaluated, for example, experimental design, comparative evaluation, replication, cost-benefit analysis. The results of these more systematic efforts may or may not be influential in the broader judgments about what government is doing. More about that later.

At whatever level it occurs, evaluation involves any number of differentiated activities. First is the *specification* of what is to be evaluated. The object may be precise, e.g., determining whether a housing program has resulted in more houses, or imprecise, e.g., determining whether a set of economic policies has reestablished confidence in political leadership. Specification of the object or purpose of evaluation is as important to that process as problem definition is to policy making. As with problem definition, however, there is no guarantee that specification will occur just because it is important. Evaluations are increasingly mandated by law and will occur as formal exercises whether or not they are done right.

Second, *measurement* of some type must be used to collect data on the object of evaluation. Again, the variation is considerable—from highly scientific and systematic efforts to those which are anything but. Consider the difference between a comparative traffic count to determine highway use conducted by the Federal Highway Administration and a congressman's casual visit to persons in a local nursing home to check on improvements resulting from a new federal program. The first employs exact measures and results in quantative data. The second is highly impressionistic and qualitative.

Third is *analysis* of the information made available so that a conclusion may be drawn as to the effectiveness of the program in question. Here, too, one may expect to find significant differences in method and style, ranging from powerful quantitative techniques for comparative analysis of costs and benefits to highly impressionistic and experiential methods. It should be emphasized that with each of these activities, the more scientific and systematic efforts are likely to take place at staff levels in the executive and legislature. This work is then fed into higher level decision making to compete with other less rigorous sources available to policy makers. It is not uncommon at that point for decision makers to take from the staff analyses whatever suits their preconceptions as developed from their individualized sources of information.

In summary, evaluation for our purposes is an activity designed to judge the merits of government programs which varies significantly in the specification of object, the techniques of measurement, and the methods of analysis. Above all, it must be stressed that there is no one way to do it, or that it is, in fact, done. It occurs at many levels of government by people with different training, experience, and aptitudes. And the results are frequently political.

The Politics of Evaluation

Carol Weiss asks: "Which purposes shall the evaluation serve and for whom?"[3] This question is very much in order and therefore places evaluation within the kind of politics which Harold D. Lasswell defined as "who gets what, when, how." Judging the merits of government programs is seldom a value-free endeavor. Someone must judge it important to do in the first place, resources have to be committed to accomplish it, methods for doing the work must be selected. Thus, somebody wins and somebody loses even before the results are announced.

When the results are in hand, however, politics begins in earnest. As Professor Weiss, a leading student of evaluation processes, observes:

> Evaluation has always had explicitly political overtones. It is designed to yield conclusions about the worth of programs and, in doing so, is intended to affect the allocation of resources. The rationale of evaluation research is that it provides evidence on which to base decisions about maintaining, institutionalizing, and expanding successful programs and modifying or abandoning unsuccessful ones.[4]

Knowing this, one can imagine how important it is to control the evaluation process and how motivated one would be to influence the outcome if your agency or program were being reviewed.

Another important point to consider is that the politics of evaluation is no longer small-town stuff. As the federal government continues to move

into the domestic sphere, there is a natural tendency for greater routiniza-
tion and standardization of social programs. Weiss says that:

> Programs may actually be no more standardized in form, content,
> and structure than they ever were, but they are funded from a com-
> mon pot and bear a common name: "community action program,"
> "Head Start," "model cities," "legal services," "neighborhood ser-
> vice centers," "Title I of the Elementary and Secondary Education
> Act," "maternal and child health program," and so forth.[5]

Consequently, evaluations are huge enterprises with potentially massive
effects. This very fact reinforces the importance of an agency managing
the "who, what, when, and how" of program evaluation.

Donald T. Campbell proposes another important political dimension to
evaluation. In discussing social reforms, he points out that many policy
makers become committed to such an extent that objective evaluation is
not possible. Indeed, "if the political and administrative system has committed itself in advance to the correctness and efficacy of its reforms, it
cannot tolerate learning of failure."[6] It might also be said that such
commitments also provide protective lenses through which decision
makers will view program evaluations. Those findings which are supportive
will filter through—those which are critical will not.

Motivation and Criteria for Evaluation

As we move to consider the detailed aspects of the evaluation process, it
becomes apparent that we must clarify the distinction made earlier between the broader scaled evaluations occurring within Congress and the
presidency and those more specialized program and project evaluations
conducted within agencies. The motivation for the former might be highly
political—in the partisan sense of a Democratic Congress seeking to em-
barrass a Republican administration, in a personal sense of a member of
Congress or a president seeking support for or opposition to a particular
program, or simply as a part of the policy process in which there is a
continuing review of programs for reauthorization and further appropriation. Whether strictly political in motivation or not, we have also
witnessed a growing tendency to require program evaluation and to provide funds for this purpose. While one might argue that mandatory evaluations are no more than common sense, it is also the case that they can
be justified more easily in Congress during a period in which the minority
party happens to occupy the White House.

Turning now to the more specialized evaluations, one obvious motivation
is that of the aforementioned legal requirement to do the job. Beyond
that, and possibly determining how seriously the mandatory evaluation

will be carried out, are the programmatically rational purposes of assessing whether and how to continue a particular program as well as the politically rational purposes of building support and/or protecting the agency from criticism. Weiss points out that a decision maker may be "looking for ways to delay a decision . . ." hoping to produce "dispassionate evidence that will make the decision for them . . . ," or pursuing "self-glorification."[7] Evaluation studies can provide means to these ends. Obviously it is not possible here either to survey all of the possible motivations for evaluation or to generalize about which is likely to stimulate analysis at any one point and for any one program. It is enough to emphasize and illustrate the variation as an advisory to those studying this important activity.

As a further aid to this pedagogical purpose, one might do well to assume that evaluation is primarily an exercise in justification. That is, presidents and executive agencies either evaluate their programs, or call in outside evaluators, in order to justify what they have been doing. Evaluations by this conception become an important means of support. Those which fail to justify the program are not given much, if any, publicity. Even congressional committee involvement in evaluation can be viewed in this way. Typically, the process of reauthorization and oversight is a process of justification. Members of the administration present supporting evidence drawn from their formal or informal evaluations. Members of Congress either accept the evidence, offer support of their own for programs they are committed to, or provide weak opposition by drawing on independent evaluations (e.g., their own unsystematic study, staff reports, General Accounting Office evaluations). The style may even be adversarial, but the process is one of justification.

This is not to say, of course, that evaluation may not result in strong criticism and significant change. Not all programs can be justified, even by those administering them. What I am proposing rather is that students will find it generally useful to study evaluation in this way, understanding that evaluation as justification does not inevitably mean that a program will expand or even continue (though most surely will). It might also be noted that an extensive and highly visible evaluation may result in important programmatic and organizational changes but, nevertheless, continued expansion of an agency. A case in point might well be the House and Senate investigations of federal intelligence agencies. While hardly justifying existing practices, the evaluation will not result in the disbanding of these units. To the contrary, one may expect their reorganization and expansion along more acceptable lines in the future.

This particular example of the intelligence services raises the important matter of the criteria for evaluation. Before one can judge the merits of a program, a base point must be set. What will that base be? And will all those involved in either the process of evaluation or in systematic studies agree? These are, of course, fundamental questions—the answers to which may determine the force and function of a particular evaluation.

One base for measurement is the program objectives. Are they being met? That sounds like a simple basis for assessing a program. And yet there are objectives and objectives. There are the often high-minded preambles to major domestic legislation: for example, "the goal of a decent home and suitable living environment for every American family . . ." (Housing Act of 1949); "a national war on poverty. Our objective: total victory" (President Johnson's message on poverty); "to create and maintain conditions under which man and nature can exist in productive harmony . . ." (National Environmental Policy Act of 1969). These are obviously susceptible to varying interpretations and thus require further specification. The law itself may provide detailed objectives; they may be set within the agency, by the Office of Management and Budget, or perhaps by the president; or they may never be very explicit.

Can a program be administered where the objectives are not clear? Apparently it happens all the time. In their study of federal evaluation policy the Urban Institute found that:

> Most of the programs examined lacked adequately defined criteria of program effectiveness. This lack stems partially from the fact that the typical federal program has multiple objectives and partially from difficulties in defining objectives in measurable terms, particularly when the authorizing legislation is very general.[8]

Inadequate specification of objectives has a rather fundamental effect on evaluation. As the Urban Institute report noted:

> The widespread absence of evaluation criteria stems mainly from two things—the failure of program managers to think through their objectives, and the failure by evaluators to insist on the guidance they need to define evaluation criteria.[9]

Here then is a double indictment—poorly defined objectives and little effort by evaluators to determine objectives. Despite these problems, evaluations are increasingly called for. Presumably this demand will eventually result in perfected means for determining the effectiveness of programs. In the meantime, however, many studies fail before they even begin due to insufficient specification of what one is measuring.

Peter H. Rossi argues that the task will never be simple again. During the days of the New Deal programs, he points out, estimates of progress were relatively simple. The problems were principally economic in nature. The programs were directed to getting people jobs and income.

> Given these goals, the problems of evaluation were quite simple. The programs either provided income or they did not, and the public works which they accomplished could be counted and arrayed.

The social welfare programs of the 1960s are more difficult to weigh, however, because they are "designed to bring about changes in individuals and in institutions. . . ."

> The goals set for [these] programs were difficult to state with either specificity or clarity. Thus the preambles to enabling legislation tended to refer to very broad objectives—for example, improving the quality of life in urban neighborhoods, or providing better health care for disadvantaged neighborhoods, or improving the quality of education to poor children, etc. These are objectives for which we do not yet have indicators on which there would be broad consensus.[10]

And yet they are enormously significant—representing as they do a major shift in government responsibility toward greater concern with and involvement in social life. The complexity of the task itself makes unlikely the crisp identification of objectives. Once the program is established, however, it must be administered in some fashion, whether or not its goals are articulated or well understood. The challenge for policy implementors in all of this is considerable. As Rossi wisely observes: "It is hard enough to change individuals, but it is even harder [shall we say hopeless] to change individuals to an unspecified state."[11]

The most that can be said in conclusion is that those who study evaluation in government tell us that it falters at a very basic point—the establishment of well-stated criteria. That fact does not necessarily interrupt the process of evaluation. It proceeds because there are political and other reasons for making judgments and/or because such analysis is required by law. What is recommended here is that students try to determine what criteria are involved in making judgments about programs—whether these judgments are made in the political arenas or as basic to systematic evaluation research. Edward A. Suchman concludes that: "The process of evaluating is highly complex and subjective."[12] The trick for students of the policy process is to unravel the complexities and identify the intrinsic subjectivities.

Measurement and Analysis

Since everything we have discussed so far has stressed variation in both purpose and process, it should not be surprising that we once again mark the differences among the form and methods of evaluation. One set of differences would be associated with the distinction between ongoing evaluation processes and the more systematic efforts to test individual programs and projects. By definition, the methods are more difficult to identify with the first and thus all that is done here is to identify various institutional procedures—congressional authorization and oversight, budgeting, presidential commissions—and certain nongovernmental evaluation research. The second, more systematic set of procedures can be discussed as a developing science of evaluation research. The literature in this field has grown significantly since the first edition of this book in 1970.

Institutional Evaluation Procedures

A leading student of legislative oversight, Morris S. Ogul, points out that:

> There is a large gap between the oversight the law calls for and the oversight actually performed. . . . One reason for the gap between expectations and behavior lies in the nature of the expectation. The plain but seldom acknowledged fact is that this task . . . is simply impossible to perform. No amount of congressional dedication and energy, no conceivable boost in committee budgets will enable the Congress to carry out its oversight obligations in a comprehensive and systematic manner.[13]

Here is a realistic account of what is supposed to be one of the most institutionalized evaluation processes. In essence, Professor Ogul argues that oversight proceeds as an unsystematic sampling method in which a few programs may be selected for review. Certainly this is the most that the committees with oversight responsibility can hope to accomplish. The Legislative Reorganization Act of 1946 charges the Senate and House Committees on Government Operations with the staggering tasks of:

1. Studying the operation of government activities at all levels with a view to determining its economy and efficiency.
2. Evaluating the effects of laws enacted to reorganize the legislative and executive branches of the government.
3. Studying intergovernmental relationships. . . .[14]

While the committees do conduct many investigations, they can never conduct the type of comprehensive analyses called for by this act.

Where does one look for evaluation then? Essentially institutionalized congressional evaluation is more a state of mind that leads to discontinuous surveillance as programs are developed, funded, and adjusted over time. Carol Goss wisely describes it as:

> . . . a continuous process which occurs when a committee considers new legislation concerning a program, when it is engaged in specific review activities, and when agency-relevant business is conducted at other times. The one activity blends into the other as the cumulative experience of the executive agency-congressional committee relationship bears on the policy problems at hand.[15]

Thus Ogul and others advise us to look to the full set of congressional-executive relations for a full understanding of how it is Congress "oversees" and evaluates programs and their implementation. That search takes one to authorizations, wherein programs are initially legitimated; appropriations; reauthorizations; and even to casework, where members are fed information about how well a program is accomplishing its objectives.

The annual budgeting process also provides routine opportunities for evaluation. This is not to say that any very systematic evaluation will in fact occur, but the whole theory and practice of budgeting invite "judging the merits" of programs. The agency must justify its current activities and support any new projects with the understanding that they will compete eventually with requests from elsewhere. The Office of Management and Budget must comparatively analyze agency requests and measure these by presidential priorities. And, of course, Congress has traditionally demanded justifications in its appropriations process. Its recent budgetary reform has even sought to establish priorities which may serve as a basis for assessing the executive budget.

Seldom has federal budgeting been characterized by systematic, "front-end" evaluation, however. Rather, at year's end one can observe that a sort of evaluation has occurred. The Planning-Programming-Budgeting System, on the other hand, represents an effort to establish an integrated evaluation process where goals are clearly set, cost effective means developed for their realization over time, and performance measured "to insure a dollar's worth of service for each dollar spent."

In the best of all possible worlds, PPBS is both desirable and workable. It seems quite logical that one would prefer to have mechanisms which would measure effectiveness in terms of the goals of a system and the resources available. And it would be wonderful if all of this could happen without introducing the frailities of human judgment. The design of PPBS is to do exactly that. How does it work? Though developed elsewhere, PPBS was pioneered at the federal level by the Department of Defense under Secretary Robert S. McNamara. Professor Aaron Wildavsky, a skeptical political analyst of PPBS (and very convincingly so), argues that the problems of using the system for all policy analysis are inherent in its success in the Defense Department. To operate effectively, PPBS requires very special conditions. Most of these conditions existed in the Defense Department—particularly talent, resources, planning experience, and subject matter (for example, as Wildavsky points out, "Defense policy dealing with choices among alternative weapons systems was ideally suited for policy analysis"). But when the order came to implement the system throughout the federal government, conflict between the prerequisites of PPBS and the hard realities of "muddling through" was inevitable. Not every agency was well equipped to adopt the system. Wildavsky explains why:

> All the obstacles previously mentioned, such as lack of talent, theory, and data, may be summed up in a single sentence: no one knows how to do program budgeting. Another way of putting it would be to say that many know what program budgeting should be like in general, but no one knows what it should be like in any particular case. Program budgeting cannot be stated in operational terms. There is no agreement on what the words mean, let alone an ability to show another person what should be done. The reason for the difficulty is that telling an agency to adopt program budgeting means telling it to find better policies and there is no formula for doing that. One can (and should) talk about measuring effectiveness, estimating costs, and comparing alternatives, but that is a far cry from being able to take the creative leap of formulating a better policy.[16]

Wildavsky describes a pattern of frustration in which agency personnel would seek advice from defense specialists, who knew little about the policy area in question. They would then seek advice from the Bureau of the Budget (now the Office of Management and Budget), which issued the original instructions on "how to do it." The response (according to Wildavsky): "Silence. The word from on high is that the Office of Management and Budget does not interfere with agency operations; it is the agency's task to set up its own budget. After a while, cynicism reigns supreme."[17]

The future of PPBS was always somewhat problematic since it was contextually inappropriate—at least as that political and policy context has been identified here (see the initial realities cited in Chapter 1). This really was the essence of what Wildavsky was saying—a scientific budgeting system cannot substitute for a pluralistic political order. Thus, while as Allen Schick notes, PPBS was not necessarily destined for failure, "the traditions of budgeting and the manner of implementation made its failure likely."[18]

> PPB died of multiple causes, any of which was sufficient. PPB died because of the manner in which it was introduced, across-the-board and without much preparation. PPB died because new men of power were arrogantly insensitive to budgetary traditions, institutional loyalties, and personal relationships. PPB died because of inadequate support and leadership with meager resources invested in its behalf. ... PPB failed to penetrate because the budgeters didn't let it in and the PPB'ers didn't know how to break down the resistance.[19]

The importance of these difficulties for us comes in understanding the complications of achieving comprehensive planning and evaluation in our decision-making system. It is not that systematic planning does not have a role to play in a democratic system. It is just that it is unlikely ever to constitute the whole of the democratic system. Therefore, the most comprehensive PPBS, one that even includes political considerations, is unlikely ever to substitute for other, less systematic and more intentionally subjective decision-making processes.

A third institutional evaluation technique is that of the special commission. Daniel Bell classifies government commissions as follows: advisory, evaluation, fact-finding, public relations, and policy recommendation.[20] They are both permanent and ad hoc.

Principal interest here is directed to the ad hoc evaluation and policy recommendation type of commission. These groups are typically multimember, limited to a particular issue-area, lacking in power to implement their findings or recommendations, and composed in part of persons from the private sphere.[21] Some focus more on the substance of problems, others on government organization; some seek to develop policy proposals, others seek to evaluate policy. Regardless of their specific charge, however, many of the following were drawn inexorably into evaluation of existing policy and administration.

> Commission on Organization of the Executive Branch of the Government (Hoover Commission)
> President's Water Resources Policy Commission
> President's Commission on Higher Education
> Commission on Intergovernmental Relations (Kestnbaum Commission)
> Commission on Foreign Economic Policy (Randall Commission)
> President's Committee on Government Housing Policies and Programs
> President's Commission on Law Enforcement and Administration of Justice
> National Advisory Commission on Civil Disorders (Kerner Commission)
> President's Committee on Juvenile Delinquency and Youth Crime
> National Commission on the Causes and Prevention of Violence
> President's Commission on School Finance
> President's Commission on Federal Statistics

As is obvious from this very small sample, the commission technique is used for a wide variety of issue-areas. Despite the limitations inherent in an ad hoc civilian review board that cannot enforce its decisions, presidents obviously see definite purposes for such groups. Alan L. Dean notes some of these: focusing public attention on a problem, evaluation independent of government agencies, representation of differing viewpoints, utilizing expertise from the private sphere, forestalling precipitate action (an important symbolic function for commissions), increasing public pressure for action.[22]

As with congressional oversight, but in contrast to PPBS, the idea behind an evaluation commission is that it is important to have review and analysis outside of the bureaucracy itself. The information needs for evaluation don't change, however, just because a presidential commission is appointed. Often, therefore, the commission must rely on agencies for information, or it may be dominated by the members who are public servants, or the commission staff (not infrequently drawn from the civil service) may become more influential in decisions than anyone intended.

The result is that most commissions have little immediate impact on policy. While they face many of the same problems in evaluation that congressional committees face, most are ad hoc and therefore do not have the continuing role in other functional activities of policy that legislators have. Thus, the one-shot review depends for success on career policy actors. The optimum conditions for impact by a presidential evaluation commission would appear to be:

1. A report coincident with other supporting events.
2. Commission members from public service who are in important positions of authority in government and are committed to the recommendations.
3. Commission staff who return to positions in government in which they will influence the acceptance of recommendations.
4. A report which supports the president's policy preferences in the issue-area under consideration.

This fourth condition is emphasized by Thomas R. Wolanin in his study of presidential advisory commissions. He observes that "presidents created commissions primarily to make independent policy analysis and to provide window dressing for presidential initiatives." Their work then fits within ongoing national policy making. "Most commissions are formed because the president wants to act but is not sure how, or is not sure that important segments of public support, congressional leadership, or executive branch agencies are ready to support him."[23] Wolanin also observes that so-called crisis-induced commissions (e.g., the Kerner Commission) typically receive less presidential support.

It might be worth noting that I served on a commission—the Commission on Political Activity of Government Personnel. The group (variously appointed by the president, the vice president, and the Speaker of the House) was charged to investigate the laws relating to political activity of civil servants (the Hatch Act). My experience supports the observations noted above. The commission labored hard to develop a series of recommendations following a complete evaluation of existing policy. The report received almost no attention and little action in Congress. Its usefulness will no doubt be limited to scholars unless the Supreme Court declares the Hatch Act unconstitutional as violating the rights of civil servants under the First Amendment.[24]

Nongovernmental Evaluation

Frequently the most dramatic evaluations of government policy come from outside government—from the press, television, individuals, private groups, scholars. Identification of public problems and evaluation of public policy are time-honored functions of the press. In addition to the almost daily evaluation in the nation's great newspapers, many magazines devote several articles in every issue to judging existing policy. Notable among these currently are *The Nation*, *The New Republic*, *The National Review*, *Commentary*, *The Progressive*, *Society*, and *The Public Interest*. Sometimes articles from these and weekly news magazines will trigger congressional investigations or publicize ongoing investigations.

Television journalism has had a major impact in the post-World War II period (though the precise impact has had little systematic study). The many special news programs on air and water pollution, urban crises, the poverty program, migrant workers, hunger, and the like, have publicized the inadequacies of existing domestic policies. And though the effect is difficult to measure, surely the on-the-spot coverage of the Vietnam war, the Middle East conflict, Cyprus, Angola, etc., increased criticism of American policies. The fact is that the only efficient wars where good triumphs are those fought by John Wayne in the late movies on television. The contrast between those and the daily "foul-ups," disorganization, and the inhumanity now presented at supper each evening is too great not to lead to critical evaluation on a mass scale.

Certain individuals also contribute important appraisals of existing policy—either in their role as scholars, free-lance writers, or, as in the case of Ralph Nader, as self-appointed overseers of government action. Nader emerged in the 1960s as a sort of "watchdog" for the consumer. Politicians and bureaucrats have come to know Mr. Nader and his task groups very well as he has delved into meat and fish inspection, mine safety, auto safety, regulation of trade, mental health, air and water pollution, pensions, nursing homes, and the general consumer protection policies of the federal government.[25]

Interest groups obviously remain alert to the effect of policy on problems of direct concern to them. Many maintain rather extensive research units to evaluate policy—notably the American Medical Association, the Chamber of Commerce, the AFL-CIO, the National Association of Manufacturers, the American Farm Bureau Association, the National Education Association, the NAACP, the Urban Coalition. Of the independent research organizations, the Brookings Institution and the RAND Corporation are best known. RAND, however, has been more advisory in the development of policy alternatives than evaluatory.[26] While Brookings has also played important advisory roles, in general it has remained independent of the government and has provided important evaluations of existing policies in a number of areas. The annual budget analysis by Brookings has come to be an important document suggestive both of national priorities and the status of existing programs.[27] Any citizen would do well to obtain this document along with *The U.S. Budget in Brief*, available annually at minimum cost from the Government Printing Office.

Here then is a combination of governmental and private activities which, while not all explicitly and by design evaluatory, constitute in total a discontinuous set of judgments on the merits of government programs. This is the very essence of the first use of the term "evaluation"—as a functional activity which occurs in all political systems. Whether or not one explicitly and consciously includes an evaluative component in public policy, people will make judgments in a democratic system and these tend to get collected to form a basis for further decisions.

Systematic Program Evaluation

In her provocative book, *Systematic Thinking for Social Action*, Alice M. Rivlin asks a question she does not really answer: "Can we find out what works?" The clear implication of her discussion is that we don't now know what works. She proposes that we devise means to that end: "Unless we begin searching for improvements and experimenting with them in a systematic way, it is hard to see how we will make much progress in increasing the effectiveness of our social services."[28] As Dr. Rivlin notes, "the key word is 'systematic'." We have already reviewed means by which various decision makers collect and analyze information on what works. None of these is very systematic, however, in the sense of employing anything approaching scientific methods.

Edward A. Suchman distinguishes between "evaluation"—our more general processes by which programs are judged—and "evaluative research"—"the specific use of the scientific method for the purpose of making an evaluation."[29] He cites with approval, and more general application, the six steps for evaluative research in mental health. These include:

1. Identification of the goals to be evaluated.
2. Analysis of the problems with which the activity must cope.
3. Description and standardization of the activity.
4. Measurement of the degree of change that takes place.
5. Determination of whether the observed change is due to the activity or to some other cause.

6. Some indication of the durability of the effects.[30]

He also identifies several of the questions which must be answered if program objectives—presumably the directing force of evaluation—are to be made operational for research purposes.

1. *What* is the nature of the content of the objective?
2. *Who* is the target of the program?
3. *When* is the desired change to take place?
4. Are the objectives *unitary or multiple*?
5. What is the desired *magnitude* of effect?
6. *How* is the objective to be attained?[31]

One can see from this list how important the problem definition activity becomes. Failure to define the problem makes it difficult to set clear objectives and therefore impossible to conduct evaluative research. That does not mean, of course, that people will not try. Congress can and does require evaluation studies whether or not programmatic objectives have been clearly specified. And so something called "program evaluation" is carried out—typically with poor results.

As is suggested from the preceding discussion, description of methods seldom coincides with description of realities. Yet one can hardly proceed any other way. Evaluative research must be developed as though it really could be carried out—as though conditions would always favor an objective and systematic analysis. The effect for present purposes is a variant on the "rules-are-made-to-be-broken" theme. That is, just as with many legislative procedures, compromises have to be made in order to get the job done. Further, the job to be done may itself be at variance with what is publicly stated, in part because certain goals are not publicly acceptable (or so certain people think) or because people differ on the goals to be achieved. I stress this point to illustrate that even the scientific method may be incorporated into the functional charade that frequently characterizes a human policy process.

The foregoing is also a useful preface to a review of evaluation study designs—useful in the sense of a warning not to be overimpressed with the potential effectiveness of some very sophisticated models. Let's turn now to a review of those designs. Carol H. Weiss catalogues three experimental options and then discusses other design features which may or may not be associated with each of the options. First is the *experimental design* in which a systematic effort is made to select an experimental and control group.

> Out of the target population, units (people, work teams, precincts, classrooms, cities) are randomly chosen to be in either the group that gets the program or the "control group" that does not. Measures are

taken of the relevant criterion variable . . . before the program starts and after it ends. Differences are computed, and the program is deemed a success if the experimental group has improved more than the control group.[32]

The problems in carrying out this design are legion. It is one thing to conduct experiments in the laboratory or in a relatively short time period in a controllable environment. It is quite another to pursue this method in the dynamics of ongoing social life where the experiment itself is but one of many competing forces. Still advances are being made with this approach and imaginative adaptations have produced some interesting results.[33]

Second are the *quasi-experimental designs* which are less conscious efforts to "protect against the effects of extraneous variables. . . ."[34] Dr. Weiss wisely observes that this does not simply mean "sloppy experiments" but rather an acknowledgement of what can and cannot be controlled. Techniques include time-series analysis (measurements before, during and after implementation of a program) or use of a so-called nonequivalent control group (individuals with similar characteristics but not strictly a control group). The advantages of this method are obvious. Without abandoning systematic research methods, one has a more flexible and feasible instrument for evaluating effects.

Third are the *nonexperimental designs* of which the three most common are: "before-and-after study of a single program, after-only study of program participants, or after-only study of participants and [a comparison group]."[35] By definition, these studies are less rigorous but they may still provide insight into the operation and effects of a program. And, in fact, such a design may be necessary as a first step to a more scientific study.

Why conduct nonexperimental designs? Weiss notes two important reasons beyond the obvious one of feasibility: (1) They may provide "a preliminary look at the effectiveness of a program," and (2) there may be no other choice. The second point is worth expanding on since it involves political considerations.

> Many government agencies tend to demand one-time ex post facto investigations; they are responding to political pressures and short-term needs, and they want quick results. The system of competitive contracting for evaluation leaves the major decisions in their hands. . . . the agency develops a "request for proposal" (RFP) for evaluation of its program. . . . Research organizations are invited to submit applications . . . and after review, one applicant organization is selected.[36]

In this system, the evaluator must accept the conditions as specified in the RFP and the agency is left with whatever is possible given the constraints identified. In short, the nonexperimental design may be the best that can be produced in this situation.

Weiss also discusses various analytic techniques which may be employed in program evaluation whether or not one relies on one of the designs above. *Comparative evaluation* among projects in a program or among programs has the advantage of providing a broader perspective for drawing conclusions. Systematic comparison is always a profitable exercise if resources are plentiful. *Replication* too is often very useful for developing greater confidence in research results, but, as with comparative program evaluation, it is costly. *Cost-benefit analysis* can be applied in evaluative research as well as in program planning. Weiss accurately reports that it has been used prospectively, "assessing the likely costs and benefits of alternative strategies being proposed for the future," but it can and has been "applied retrospectively to calculate the returns on investment in past programs."[37]

While there are many question marks concerning the current status of evaluative research, there seems little doubt that we will witness many future developments in this sphere. It is presently experiencing the kind of faddishness that often eventually produces routine processes. We may look forward, then, to further testing of evaluative research design and methods, particularly if Rivlin's judgment is accepted that "the federal government should follow a systematic experimentation strategy in seeking to improve the effectiveness of social action programs."[38] Her observations on this point are worthy of fuller exposition.

> The process will not be easy or quick or cheap. Nor can one look forward to an end to it. It would be a mistake to adopt systematic experimentation in the hope that it would "tell us what works." The phrase suggests that there is some all-time optimum way of organizing social services and that we are going to find it and then quit. Clearly the world is not like this. What works for one place or one generation will not work for another. The process of developing new methods, trying them out, modifying them, trying again, will have to be continuous. But unless we begin searching for improvements and experimenting with them in a systematic way, it is hard to see how we will make much progress in increasing the effectiveness of our social services.[39]

So systematic evaluative methods too must be judged in the context of the continuous and incremental adjustment toward elusive goals often themselves in the process of being redefined.

Policy Cycles

In the remarks quoted above, Rivlin refers to a continuous process by which methods are tested, modified, tested again, etc. The same might be said about the policy process overall—at least as portrayed in this book.

And that observation brings us to consider cycles of policy—that is, the ongoing patterns of accommodation in which various institutional actors play various roles in accomplishing the functional activities of the policy process. "Policy cycles" is not the best term for what I want to discuss because it implies more neatness of pattern than I mean to suggest. I do, however, want to build on the notion of a "round of events or phenomena that recur regularly and in the same sequence" (a dictionary definition of "cycle").

In his discussion of the appraising function in decision making, Harold D. Lasswell limits the function to the making of factual statements about the causes and effects of public policy. He notes that "strictly speaking, no applications, prescriptions, or recommendations are part of it."[40] That is a narrower concept than the evaluating function as it has been discussed here. I assume definite output as a result of evaluation. The whole purpose of evaluation is to judge programs applied to problems—to determine whether objectives are being realized and, if so, which ones.

The specific output of evaluation may take several forms—often dependent on who has evaluated, how, and why. Thus, for example, if evaluators are intent on justifying a program and find any evidence to that end, then support for the program and the methods of implementation may be the result. On the other hand, evaluators may identify the need for minor adjustment in either program or procedures. Perhaps the corrective will take the form of a reorganization, a personnel action of some kind (reassignment, removal, reprimand), or a reinterpretation or clarification of program intent.

If evaluators conclude that the program is simply not doing the job, then more extensive change may be required—again depending on what is to be achieved and whether change can, in fact, be effected. It may be that administrators have enough authority to reformulate and reorganize. Or perhaps they will have to seek new authorization, in which case majority coalition building may once again be involved.

Another variation in output is that associated with discovering that the existing program is based on an erroneous interpretation of the problem. In this case policy makers may have defined the problem vastly different from those most affected. Perhaps policy makers assumed that physical conditions in slum areas constituted the real problem for slum dwellers. Clearing of slums and construction of large public housing units would alleviate this need. Thorough evaluation (which in fact has hardly occurred even today) might well reveal, however, that slum dwellers view their problems quite differently. Actual physical conditions may be less important in the short run than job opportunities, transportation to employment sites, or educational opportunities. Clearing the slums will not alleviate these needs. Alleviation of these needs, however, may result in improved physical conditions in the slums. Minor procedural adjustments in policy will not make a difference in this case. What evaluators may call for is a completely new policy approach (though, in assessing the probability and form of change, you should recall the earlier discussion of bureaucratic commitment to existing programs).

Another possibility is that new problems are discovered in the process of evaluating certain programs. The output in this case affects agenda setting as new demands are brought to the attention of government decision makers. Evaluation results in a kind of spin-off of another cycle. These various situations of possible output from evaluation suggest different types of policy cycles, or "rounds of events." First is the very simple and frequently occurring cycle of support.

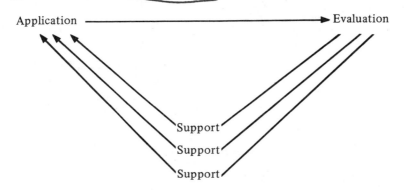

Second is the incremental adjustment cycle, occurring within the functional activities of application and evaluation.

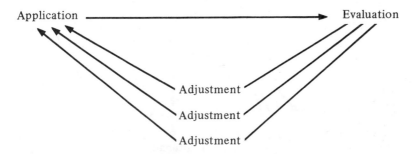

The third type of cycle is more complex. It may involve other functional activities beyond application and evaluation and two or more revolutions. I suggest two variations among many which might be proposed. The first involves programmatic shifts, either within existing authority or where new authority is required. The second captures those cases where the problem is redefined or new problems are identified.

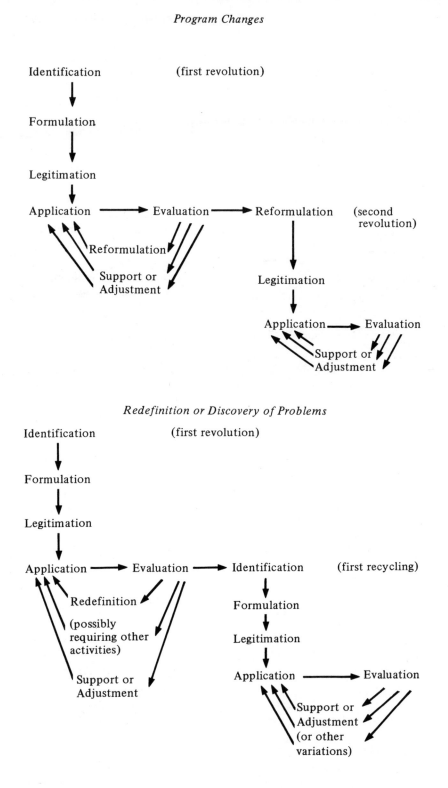

Program Changes

Identification   (first revolution)

Formulation

Legitimation

Application ⟶ Evaluation ⟶ Reformulation   (second revolution)

Reformulation

Support or Adjustment

Legitimation

Application ⟶ Evaluation

Support or Adjustment

Redefinition or Discovery of Problems

Identification   (first revolution)

Formulation

Legitimation

Application ⟶ Evaluation ⟶ Identification   (first recycling)

Redefinition

(possibly requiring other activities)

Support or Adjustment

Formulation

Legitimation

Application ⟶ Evaluation

Support or Adjustment (or other variations)

I assume it goes without saying that these cycles are illustrative only. The variations are virtually limitless. The point is not to identify all combinations but to encourage you to discover the patterns appropriate to public policies being studied.

Two Cases of Evaluation

The cases offered illustrate the two types of evaluation I have stressed— that is, the less systematic and more political evaluation that occurs with any major government program and the more systematic and administrative effort to measure the effects of a program. The public housing program will serve as an example of the first; the community mental health program as an example of the second. Necessarily the first case takes a broader view, and focuses on a longer time span. The second case concentrates more on specific evaluation efforts.

Public Housing Meets the Housing Public

Massive mobilization of resources for the war effort in the early 1940s interrupted the normal course of economic affairs. One of the many effects was to create a housing shortage at war's end. With millions of servicemen returning to civilian life, replenishing the nation's housing supply became a major priority. What better time, then, to set a national housing goal? The Housing Act of 1949 (a major amendment to the Housing Act of 1937) did just that—and in the boldest of terms:

> The Congress hereby declares that the general welfare and security of the Nation and the health and living standards of its people require housing production and related community development sufficient to remedy the serious housing shortage, the elimination of substandard and other inadequate housing through the clearing of slums and blighted areas, and the realization as soon as feasible of the goal of a decent home and suitable living environment for every American family....
>
> Policy Statement in the Housing Act of 1949

To this end, the act authorized federal support for 810,000 housing units for low-income families to be built locally over a period of six years. This came to be known as the public housing program and its history has been marked with struggle. In part, the conflict can be attributed to a growing lack of support among the housing public. By definition the low-income housing program would positively touch a small portion of the total housing public. While a social welfare program can survive without strong support, it has difficulty accomplishing grand goals without that backing. And the Housing Act of 1949 had set a noble goal.

The political evaluation of the public housing program then was not likely to ignore the reactions of the large and powerful housing public, including the construction industry, real estate dealers, bankers, and the huge middle- and upper-income groups not directly benefiting from the program. In fact, the decision-making units involved in the continuous political monitoring of the program were much more likely to reflect these affluent and active interests than the poorly articulated housing interests of the low-access poor. Further, since implementing the national public housing program involved all layers of government (national, state, local), one could expect an overlapping network of assessment, which, while never killing the program, produced enough uncertainty to prevent steady progress.

The population for the more political evaluation of the public housing program was drawn primarily from the following units:

National Government

Executive:

Department of Housing and Urban Development (formerly Housing and Home Finance Agency)
Department of Commerce (notably the Bureau of the Census)
Office of Management and Budget (formerly the Bureau of the Budget)
Council of Economic Advisers
Domestic Council (created under the Nixon administration)
White House Office (special advisers to the president)

Congress:

House Committee on Banking, Currency and Housing; Subcommittee on Housing and Community Development
House Committee on Appropriations; Subcommittee on Housing and Urban Development—Independent Agencies
Senate Committee on Banking, Housing, and Urban Affairs; Subcommittee on Housing and Urban Affairs
Senate Committee on Appropriations; Subcommittee on Housing and Urban Development—Independent Agencies

State and Local Governments

Local housing authorities
Other public and quasi-public local bodies (e.g., planning agencies)
Local governing units (e.g., city councils, county commissions)
State legislatures

State departments of community affairs (a relatively recent organizational unit in some states)

Private Groups

Real estate, construction, business, labor, banking, architect, civil rights, neighborhood, citizen groups.
The press

Several points should be emphasized about this imposing list. First, we are speaking here of an evaluation process occurring over a period of over twenty-five years. During that time many organizational changes have occurred. Thus, for example, the program was at one time administered in Washington by a specific agency—the Public Housing Administration—located within the Housing and Home Finance Agency (later the Department of Housing and Urban Development). Reorganizations now make it difficult to locate the program per se within the executive. Second, not all of these units are continuously involved in evaluating the public housing program. Rather the list represents sources of potential participants. A review of the period will show individuals circumstantially and episodically involved in judging the program. Third, and perhaps most obvious, these units have not been engaged in producing formal evaluation reports which then serve as a basis for comprehensive interaction and decision making. Rather, we are identifying a network within which individual and often segmented evaluation-type activities take place. This characterization also suggests that specification, measurement, and analysis are not well programmed. Finally, these various units clearly have different types of authority which may affect whether and how they get involved in evaluation in the first place, as well as determining what actions they might take as a result of their assessments. This difference is perhaps most clearly illustrated with the congressional committees. Whereas the House Committee on Banking, Currency, and Housing can authorize an extension of the public housing program, the House Committee on Appropriations can refuse to provide the money for it. Both must make judgments about the program—often relying on similar information, but reacting to different pressures.

Given the description so far, it is not surprising to learn that the public housing program has not fared too well. It proved extremely difficult to get funding for the original 810,000 units authorized. In fact, this program is a classic case of the proposition that authorization does not necessarily lead to appropriation. The Public Housing Administration in the 1950s had the authority to support the construction of public housing units at the local level; they just did not have the funds to do so! In 1951 a ceiling of 50,000 units was set on contracts for new housing in appropriations bills—85,000 below the annual authorization in the 1949 act. In 1952 the ceiling was set at 35,000, in 1953 at 20,000, in 1954 no funds at all were appropriated for new starts. As a result of these restrictions, less than one-fourth of the number of units authorized by the 1949 act were completed at the end of the six years. Indeed, the 810,000 figure was not even reached after twenty-five years.

Meanwhile implementation of the public housing program and general analysis of the nation's housing problems were resulting in other types of programs. These efforts were either directed at a special group in the society (e.g., the elderly) or were designed to assist low-income groups between the poverty level and the lowest levels of the middle-income bracket (as with rent supplements and interest subsidies).[41] In addition, other government programs contributed to the housing problem by supporting urban renewal projects and highway construction. Further, the middle-income and high-access groups in the society were solving their post-World War II housing problems. As the statistics in Table 8-1 show, private housing starts increased dramatically during the first five years after the war, dipped, and then leveled off at a high mark. Public housing surged slightly, fell off in the mid-1950s, and then leveled off at a modest amount.

A poorly organized clientele, solution of housing problems for well-organized publics, attractiveness of other programs (particularly urban renewal), negative feedback—all combined to prevent the emergence of a policy cycle of support leading to incremental growth of the public housing program. Those adjustments which were made *reduced* the program. Far from realizing growth, it was all the public housing program could do to maintain itself. As Catherine Bauer Wurster described it:

> . . . Public housing, after more than two decades, still drags along in a kind of limbo, continuously controversial, not dead but never more than half alive. . . . No obituary is yet in order for the U.S. Housing Act of 1937 [as amended by the Housing Act of 1949]. . . . It is more a case of premature ossification.[42]

By contrast, urban renewal enjoyed considerable positive feedback. A definite policy cycle of support with upward increments emerged after 1949. In 1954, when the public housing program was being emasculated, urban renewal was extended. Though the uncertain public housing program continued to exist—administered by the Public Housing Administration through countless local agencies—"the slum clearance provisions of the Housing Act of 1937 [were] slowly transformed into a large-scale program to redevelop the central city."[43] The effect of a successful urban renewal program, administered by a different agency in the Housing and Home Finance Agency, the Urban Renewal Administration, was to in-

Table 8-1. New Housing Starts

| | (000s) | |
	Private	Public (under PHA)
1945	325	0
1946	1,015	0
1947	1,265	0
1948	1,344	0
1949	1,430	.8
1950	1,908	27
1951	1,420	65
1952	1,446	53
1953	1,402	31
1954	1,532	14
1955	1,627	9
1956	1,325	5
1957	1,175	17
1958	1,314	20
1959	1,517	14
1960	1,252	27
1961	1,313	28
1962	1,463	20
1963	1,603	24
1964	1,529	23
1965	1,473	30
1966	1,165	29
1967	1,292	25
1968	1,508	31
1969	1,467	27
1970	1,434	29

Source: U.S. Department of Commerce, Bureau of the Census, *Historical Statistics of the United States*, Part 2. (Washington: U.S. Government Printing Office, 1975), pp. 639, 641.

crease the need for an expanded public housing program. One of the most severe critics of urban renewal, Martin Anderson, calculated that urban renewal projects destroyed 126,000 homes between 1950 and 1960—101,000 of which were substandard. Since the public housing program atrophied during that decade, the effect was devastating. Anderson estimates that 28,000 housing units were built—most of them in high-rent apartments. His conclusions?

More homes were destroyed than were built.

Those destroyed were predominantly low-rent homes.

Those built were predominantly high-rent homes.

Housing conditions were made worse for those whose housing conditions were least good.

> Housing conditions were improved for those whose housing conditions were best.[44]

These two intimately related programs were applied by different populations but evaluated by many of the same people. The significance of support, organization, and resources during these stages is highlighted by this contrast. Scott Greer summarizes:

> The LPAs [local authorities] move toward a program of downtown development and the upgrading of residential districts nearby because this is effective propaganda of the deed. They produce the positive response of relevant publics, including the political officials of the central city and the downtown businessmen. As it succeeds in this sense, it tends to set the precedent for other programs, in this and other cities. In the center of the city many persons can see the program's effects; and they are influential persons. Tall towers and green malls have a disproportionate intellectual appeal because of their esthetic effect. Meanwhile, most of the substandard homes, neighborhoods, and districts may remain exactly what they were before—substandard.[45]

So considerable doubt is expressed that local units would have been anxious to apply the program, even if public housing had been expanded during the 1950s. The fact is that when public housing was introduced to the housing public, it simply was not well received. And, however arcane the evaluation system might appear, it did reflect these negative signals.

The black ghetto riots of the 1960s rekindled interest in low-income housing programs. As they watched the cities burn, those in positions of influence and authority concluded that they might have a stake in slum *improvement* as well as slum *clearance*. Even the public housing program benefited. Almost as many units were constructed, 1965–1970, as had been built in the previous decade (see Table 8-1). There are some lessons in the unsystematic political evaluations of this program in the past, however, which suggest that it will continue to face problems in the future. A program which must depend on street rioting for support is not likely to fare well in the long run.

I offer a specific case to conclude this discussion. In May of 1974 the last of the residents in the massive Pruitt-Igoe public housing project in St. Louis moved out and a seven-foot-high fence sealed off the 67 acre area. At one point, 12,000 persons were housed at Pruitt-Igoe—the great majority of them on welfare. While the public housing program was designed to solve a basic social problem for the poor, this particular project, as with many like it, only made matters worse.

> Within 18 months of its opening, small children had fallen from its upper windows, assaults became commonplace and vandals attacked and stripped vacant apartments abandoned by terrorized residents.

> Entire buildings became vacant as crime spread throughout the projects. Frozen pipes burst in winter, flooding apartments of those families that remained. . . .
>
> Those who remained in those final years were subjected almost nightly to gun battles between drug-running gangs fighting to establish their "territories" in the vacant, deteriorating buildings.[46]

Not every project has met the fate of Pruitt-Igoe. But it does not take very many such cases in an unsystematic, impressionistic evaluation network to elicit a negative reaction. As noted earlier, this more political evaluation is not necessarily either objective or comprehensive. Rather it proceeds under the pressure of those with resources and access—and that has not included the presumed beneficiaries of public housing.

To summarize, here was a program for which evaluation criteria were available—both in general terms ("a decent home and suitable living environment for every American family . . .") and in specific, quantitative goals (810,000 housing units in six years). Yet as the program was implemented, other less public criteria were obviously being applied in a seemingly amorphous evaluation process controlled, if at all, by those unsympathetic to or disinterested in the original goals. An important lesson to be drawn from this case is that the clientele group for a particular policy must be strong enough (or develop the organizational strength) to influence the evaluation of that policy. I have stressed throughout that the poor in this society face difficulty in organizing for gaining access to any of the decision-making processes (problem definition through to evaluation). As a consequence, and as is illustrated here, programs designed for their benefit meld into an environment which is unlikely to be supportive in the long run. Thus, a further lesson would appear to be that unless programs of this type provide means by which those affected can organize and speak for themselves—that is, provide meaningful reactions pro and con—they will remain essentially gratuitous in nature, a bit of patronizing from the affluent majority.

The Many Faces of Evaluation in Mental Health Policy

In an essay presumably directed to evaluating the national mental health program, Dr. Stanley F. Yolles, former director of the National Institute of Mental Health, pointed out that:

> At its best, public policy in the United States is a reflection of the will of the people. At our best, we can serve that will by learning as much as we can about why man behaves as he does and by suggesting methods of intervention to change the way people act, think, work, and live. If we succeed, we need not worry about evaluating the na-

tional health program. The people of the United States will do it for us.[47]

Through this bit of convoluted logic, Dr. Yolles essentially dismisses the need for evaluation as long as "we" do "our" job and democracy is allowed to work its will. That evaluation is necessary just to determine whether the job itself is appropriate apparently was not considered by Yolles. The statement does illustrate one of the many faces of evaluation, however. By this view programs are developed and implemented in accordance with prevailing professional goals and values. This process somehow reflects the will of the people, who in turn will evaluate its products favorably (or so the statement seems to imply).

I begin with this statement not because it represents a misguided, minority view, but rather because it tends to dominate much of the thinking among professional staff in government agencies. Essentially it is a rationale for doing what you have been trained to do—not an uncommon tendency in any endeavor. It also warns us that evaluations conducted within agencies or by committed professionals are likely to justify what is. Critical internal reviews leading to significant change in organization, procedures, or purposes are likely to be rare.

Two levels of evaluation will be described here—that within the national policy-making apparatus and that at the local level where services are delivered. The primary focus of attention is the Community Mental Health Centers program, first authorized in the Mental Retardation Facilities and Community Mental Health Centers Construction Act of 1963. Hopefully the discussion will illustrate the variety of the more systematic evaluations which can occur and, by inference, suggest that evaluation, like all policy processes, depends very much on the initial assumptions, breadth and depth of analysis, political and organizational context, and, of course, programmatic commitment.

Before proceeding further, it is useful to distinguish among several kinds of questions which might serve as the basis for evaluation. Paul Binner distinguishes among such questions as: "What is being done by this program?"; "How much is being done?"; "How much is being accomplished?"; and "Are the accomplishments of the program worthwhile?"[48] The first two questions simply ask for descriptive data without any particular attention paid to the ends to be achieved. Many so-called evaluations are of this type. The third question asks about goal achievement. Is what is being done accomplishing anything—that is, in the direction of program purposes? And the last question raises the more fundamental point of whether the purposes themselves are useful.

Binner also distinguishes between program and procedural evaluations. Essentially this is a distinction between goals and methods for achieving them.

> The program evaluation model is concerned primarily with progress toward a goal and requires a clear enough conception of the goals to provide milestones that indicate relative distances from it. The procedure evaluation model is primarily concerned with establishing cause-and-effect relationships between procedures and their outcomes. As such, the two answer related but different questions and the answer to one does not necessarily provide the answer to the other.[49]

We will see in the first instance described below that program and procedural evaluations did result in quite different sets of proposals. We will also see that, just as with public housing, the context of evaluation is important. In this case, however, an active and supportive clientele was able to resist critical, independent evaluations of their program.

Evaluation from the Top.   The Community Mental Health Centers (CMHC) program has met one of the principal tests for congressional support—that is, it distributed facilities throughout the nation, potentially a little something for every congressional district. Perpetuity is not necessarily guaranteed for such programs (the poverty program also spread largesse liberally among constituencies), but they begin with a definite advantage. Dr. Marc Fried identified another edge for programs—a further advantage in meeting the challenge of critical evaluations. It simply sounded like a good idea. Those familiar with the "snake pit" image of state mental hospitals were susceptible to what appeared to be a more humane method for treating the mentally ill.

> The vast and rapid impact of community mental health programs suggests that the spread of interest was as much ideological as it was a realistic response to realistic gaps in services. Thus, we are confronted with a movement rather than with a theory or empirical data or methods. We remain uncertain about what has been wrong with previous approaches to mental health and illness, except at the grossest level, and we are unclear about the range of options opened up by a new conception of the relationship between communities and professional mental health services and facilities.[50]

So what serves as an advantage in resisting threats from the outside also makes more difficult an objective evaluation within. Fried observes that evaluation of services has traditionally been informal and unsystematic. Therefore: "In view of our deep reluctance to confront problems of service evaluation . . . it is hardly surprising that the development of community mental health programs and centers has far outstripped our capacity to assess their benefits and deficiencies."[51]

Here then was a generally supportive environment for the extension and expansion of the community mental health program. At the same time, however, the Nixon administration was formulating a philosophical approach to the proper role of the federal government in domestic policy issues. Dubbed the "new federalism," this approach placed a great deal of stress on state and local decision making, with national financial support through general revenue sharing. The expiration of the CMHC Act in 1973 and the prospect of a national health insurance program (possibly including mental health) were sufficient stimuli for a full-scale policy evaluation of community mental health.

Two analyses were produced—one by the National Institute of Mental Health (NIMH) working with the staff of the secretary of Health, Education and Welfare (HEW), and one independently by those in the office of the HEW secretary who were sympathetic to the new federalism concept. Not unexpectedly, the reports come to quite different conclusions. Joseph L. Falkson, a participant in the second evaluation, describes the NIMH effort as reducing the scope of the study by "bringing it down from the big question . . . to a series of limited, safe questions, the answers to any of which would not prove inimical to its [NIMH's] interests."[52] The result then was supportive. The document itself was huge and simply directed attention to individual programs without comparative analysis or comprehensive evaluation of whether the accomplishments were worthwhile (see Binner's question above).

> It covered virtually every program service area run by NIMH. Its pages were flooded with data. Each separate section on programs conveyed a series of . . . budgetary options (i.e., how many more projects could be set up under alternative levels of funding). The message came through loud and clear: NIMH is doing a fine job, except for its continuing financial problems. More money for its programs will prove highly beneficial to society.[53]

The second study began with a different set of specifications—those drawn from the framework of the new federalism. According to Falkson, this led them to a set of large questions which the community mental health fraternity was unlikely ever to face directly.

1. Should CMHCs be permanently subsidized by the federal government? If not, how long should grant subsidies be retained for a given project?
2. If permanent federal subsidy should prove necessary, which allocative tools available to the federal government would best serve to finance CMHCs (e.g., insurance premiums covering primary mental health services, continued reliance on federal grants, or allocations to the states as part of a health revenue sharing program)?
3. How effective have CMHCs been in (a) ameliorating mental illness and promoting mental health, and (b) distributing mental health services to the poor and to others in need but not receiving services?[54]

These questions obviously broadened the evaluation. While equally subjective in nature ("Should CMHCs be permanently subsidized . . .?" sets the boundaries for analysis just as surely as does "How can we do even better than we already are?"), this second set of analysts made their normative framework quite explicit, and therefore could specify the kinds of data required. The group studied the distribution of benefits among the states and concluded that:

> While project grants have expanded the absolute supply of services, they have tended to reinforce preexisting maldistributive tendencies of the private sector by flowing more to resource-dense than resource-scarce areas.[55]

Five options were offered as a result of this analysis—ranging from permanent federal support to CMHCs to a phasing out of CMHC grants and funding through health insurance. According to Falkson, the group hoped that the last option would ultimately prevail.

To make a long story short, the Nixon administration recommended still another option—the *immediate* end to the CMHC program. Congress was not impressed with this choice, however. It proposed an extension of the program, merely changing the labels to suit the circumstances. The president was presented with the Health Revenue Sharing and Health Services Act of 1974.[56] Falkson argued that "health revenue sharing was a euphemism . . . which could not hide the categorical nature of the legislation."[57] President Ford vetoed the legislation; Congress passed it again in 1975; President Ford vetoed it again, and Congress overrode the second veto.

Falkson concluded that "the New Federalist mental health services policy options were lost in an atmosphere of ideological commitment and the evangelical rhetoric of the community mental health lobby."[58] Marc Fried's conclusions about the "movement" (see above) appear to find support in this statement. But one might note further that ideology combined with practical constituency benefits presents a particularly tough adversary for those supporting a contrary view. As Falkson realistically observes, this second evaluation report "could not have prevailed through the cogency of its logic alone."[59]

Evaluation Below. However complex the evaluation of programs might be in terms of the "big questions" asked by decision makers in Washington, the process becomes incomprehensibly muddled when state and local administration is added. As Wholey, et al., note:

> The evaluation of federal social programs is complicated by the fact that most are administered by state and local governments or other public agencies. . . . A long tradition of local autonomy and the lack of precedents for federal monitoring of local efforts . . . often leads

to reluctance on the part of federal managers to insist on evaluation of such programs, even when the federal input is substantial.[60]

Given the increasing pressure to evaluate, often in the form of a congressional mandate, review exercises must be carried out. As noted above, Carol Weiss, among others, has identified several designs for systematic evaluation—experimental, quasi-experimental, nonexperimental designs, etc.—but any such efforts require a common methodology and comparable resources if they are to facilitate comparative analysis and be additive for comprehensive program evaluation. While efforts are being made in these directions, the present state of "evaluation below" is primitive.[61]

Even if the methods and resources were facilitative of systematic evaluation, however, Bruce A. Rocheleau identifies organizational problems in guaranteeing useful results. Rocheleau studied fourteen mental health organizations in Florida in order to judge the extent to which they might accommodate any form of evaluation of their work. He interviewed clinicians, directors, and evaluators and found support of general evaluations of programs, but considerable opposition to evaluations of individuals who implement the program. Yet "all groups were agreed that the performance of the individual clinician is a key to the success of the programs and to the overall quality of service provided by the organization."[62] In a sense, therefore, the local psychology of evaluation was to depersonalize it as much as possible in order to protect those actually doing the job.

Rocheleau also found that evaluation was viewed as a means for insuring organizational survival and security. His interviews revealed the following functions which might be served:

1. Evaluation as a defensive strategy in anticipation of future requirements for . . . accountability by funding agencies and other bodies. . . .
2. Evaluation as a means of providing justification of the worth of the mental health services to the community.
3. Evaluation as a method of securing grants and other resources for the organization. . . .
4. The use of evaluation staff to carry out "nonevaluative" activities necessary or useful to the organization's survival.[63]

And finally, Rocheleau describes the role of the in-house evaluator as being highly sensitized to his or her organization's social life. He stressed the need for evaluators to have more than one source of authority and found relatively high turnover in this most difficult and demanding position. They "placed a high priority on obtaining the trust and respect of operational personnel," which often led them to "activities and pursuits quite different from those they had originally planned" (e.g., simple descriptive data collection).[64]

It is clearly difficult for internal evaluators to fight their organization's ethos. As Carol H. Weiss concludes: "Organizations tend to find the status quo a contentedly feasible state."[65] Thus, evaluations below do not look too different from in-house evaluations above. What this brief excursion into evaluation by local mental health organizations suggests, however, is that they possess a capacity to accommodate to, even anticipate, demands to justify their existence. And because of this capacity they can conduct evaluations on their own terms. This suggests that any effort to appraise the evaluation function outside its organizational and political context leads to misunderstanding.

Summary

A great deal of stress is being placed on program and policy evaluations these days—both as a critical exercise for determining what choices to make in the future and as a research emphasis for students of the policy process. The discussion and cases presented here have sampled the richness of this dynamic and potentially comprehensive functional activity. The word "sampled" is used advisedly and the reader should take special note of that fact. It is probable that, just as with this edition, this chapter will again require the most revision in a few years. For despite its fundamental nature, those in government and the academy are still just exploring the dimensions and methods of evaluating public policies.

Notes

1. Jerry W. Lansdowne, "An Appraisal of a National Policy: The Employment Act of 1946," unpublished Ph.D. dissertation, University of Arizona, 1968, p. 244.

2. Carol H. Weiss, *Evaluation Research* (Englewood Cliffs, N.J.: Prentice-Hall, 1972), p. 1. Students will find this a most useful presentation of the purposes, procedures, and pitfalls of program evaluation.

3. Weiss, p. 18.

4. Carl H. Weiss, "The Politicization of Evaluation Research," *Journal of Social Issues*, vol. 26, no. 4 (Autumn 1970), p. 58. See also Weiss, "Where Politics and Evaluation Research Meet," *Evaluation*, vol. 1, no. 3, 1973, pp. 37–45.

5. Weiss, "The Politicization of Evaluation Research," *Journal of Social Issues*, p. 58.

6. Donald T. Campbell, "Reforms as Experiments," *American Psychologist*, vol. 24, no. 4 (April 1969), p. 410.

7. Weiss, *Evaluation Research*, pp. 11-12.

8. Joseph S. Wholey, et al., *Federal Evaluation Policy* (Washington: The Urban Institute, 1973), p. 28.

9. Wholey, et al., p. 28.

10. Peter H. Rossi, "Testing for Success and Failure in Social Action," in Peter H. Rossi and Walter Williams, eds., *Evaluating Social Programs* (New York: Seminar Press, 1972), pp. 17-18.

11. Rossi, p. 18.

12. Edward A. Suchman, *Evaluative Research* (New York: Russell Sage Foundation, 1967), p. 11.

13. Morris S. Ogul, "Legislative Oversight of Bureaucracy," in U.S. Congress, House of Representatives, Select Committee on Committees, *Committee Organization in the House*, 93rd Cong., 1st sess., 1973, vol. 2, pp. 701-702.

14. U.S. Congress, Senate, *A Compilation of the Legislative Reorganization Act of 1946*, Document No. 71, 83rd Cong., 1st sess., 1953, p. 16.

15. Carol Goss, "Congressional Committee Oversight: The Case of the Office of Saline Water," unpublished M.A. thesis, University of Arizona, 1968, p. 8.

16. Aaron Wildavsky, "Rescuing Policy Analysis from PPBS," *Public Administration Review*, vol. 29 (March-April 1969), p. 193.

17. Wildavsky, p. 194.

18. Allen Schick, "A Death in the Bureaucracy: The Demise of Federal PPB," *Public Administration Review*, vol. 33 (March-April 1973), p. 155.

19. Schick, pp. 148-149.

20. Daniel Bell, "Government by Commission," *The Public Interest*, vol. 1 (Spring 1966), pp. 3-9.

21. See Alan L. Dean, "Advantages and Disadvantages in the Use of Ad Hoc Commissions for Policy Formulation," a paper presented at the

annual meeting of the American Political Science Association, New York, September 5–7, 1957, and reprinted in Thomas E. Cronin and Sanford D. Greenberg, eds., *The Presidential Advisory System* (New York: Harper & Row, 1969), pp. 101–116.

22. Dean, pp. 104–106.

23. Thomas R. Wolanin, *Presidential Advisory Commissions* (Madison: University of Wisconsin Press, 1975), p. 193.

24. For a review of the Hatch Act Commission's work, see Charles O. Jones, "Reevaluating the Hatch Act: A Report on the Commission on Political Activity of Government Personnel," *Public Administration Review*, vol. 29 (May–June 1969), pp. 249–254.

25. For examples of literature evaluating policies of the federal government, see the bibliography—for example, the works of Nader, Charles Abrams, Rachel Carson, Donald E. Carr, Michael Harrington, Edward Higbee, Jane Jacobs, Wesley McCune, Martin Anderson, James Conant, and Daniel P. Moynihan.

26. See Bruce L. R. Smith, *The RAND Corporation: A Case Study of a Nonprofit and Advisory Corporation* (Cambridge, Mass.: Harvard University Press, 1966).

27. See, for example, Barry M. Blechman, et al., *Setting National Priorities: The 1976 Budget* (Washington: The Brookings Institution, 1975).

28. Alice M. Rivlin, *Systematic Thinking for Social Action* (Washington: The Brookings Institution, 1971), p. 119.

29. Suchman, p. 31.

30. Suchman, p. 31.

31. Suchman, pp. 39–41. Emphasis his.

32. Weiss, *Evaluation Research*, p. 61.

33. See in particular Campbell's discussion in "Reforms as Experiments," *American Psychologist*, vol. 24, no. 4 (April, 1969) pp. 409–429.

34. Weiss, p. 67.

35. Weiss, p. 73.

36. Weiss, p. 74.

37. Weiss, p. 85.

38. Rivlin, p. 118.

39. Rivlin, p. 119.

40. Harold D. Lasswell, "The Decision Process: Seven Categories of Functional Analysis," reprinted in Nelson W. Polsby et al., eds., *Politics and Social Life* (Boston: Houghton Mifflin, 1963), p. 102.

41. See Robert Taggart III, *Low-Income Housing: A Critique of Federal Aid* (Baltimore: The Johns Hopkins Press, 1970), pp. 18–20, for a review of these programs.

42. Catherine Bauer Wurster, "The Dreary Deadlock of Public Housing" in William L. C. Wheaton et al., eds., *Urban Housing* (New York: The Free Press, 1966), p. 246.

43. Scott Greer, *Urban Renewal and American Cities* (Indianapolis: Bobbs-Merrill, 1965), p. 32.

44. Martin Anderson, "The Federal Bulldozer," in James Q. Wilson ed., *Urban Renewal* (Cambridge, Mass.: MIT Press, 1967), p. 495.

45. Greer, *Urban Renewal*, p. 34. The reasons why urban renewal does not result in better housing for the poor—despite the intention of the law—are too complex to discuss here. Suffice it to say that urban renewal specializes in knocking down housing units and replacing them primarily with government buildings, shopping centers, office buildings, malls, and high-rent apartments.

46. *The Christian Science Monitor*, May 30, 1974.

47. Stanley F. Yolles, "The Comprehensive National Mental Health Program: An Evaluation," in Leigh M. Roberts, et al., eds., *Comprehensive Mental Health* (Madison: University of Wisconsin Press, 1968), p. 287.

48. Paul Binner, "Program Evaluation," in Saul Feldman, ed., *The Administration of Mental Health Services* (Springfield, Ill.: Charles C. Thomas, 1973), p. 345.

49. Binner, p. 349.

50. Marc Fried, "Evaluation and Relativity of Reality," in Roberts, et al., p. 42.

51. Fried, p. 42.

52. Joseph L. Falkson, "Minor Skirmish in a Monumental Struggle: HEW's Analysis of Mental Health Services," *Policy Analysis*, vol. 2 (Winter 1976) p. 106.

53. Falkson, p. 106.

54. Falkson, p. 107.

55. Falkson, p. 112. For a critical review of other outside evaluation studies contracted for by NIMH, see Franklin D. Chu and Sharland Trotter, *The Madness Establishment* (New York: Grossman, 1974), pp. 110–120.

56. Actually President Nixon signed the first temporary extension of the program in 1973.

57. Falkson, p. 116.

58. Falkson, p. 118.

59. Falkson, p. 119.

60. Wholey, et al., p. 73.

61. See Rivlin, *passim*.

62. Bruce A. Rocheleau, "The Organizational Context of Evaluation Research," in Charles O. Jones and Robert D. Thomas, eds., *Public Policy Making in a Federal System* (Beverly Hills, Calif.: Sage Publications, 1976), p. 245.

63. Rocheleau, p. 248.

64. Rocheleau, p. 254.

65. Weiss, p. 114.

9

Conclusion as Prelude

Functional Activities	Categorized in Government	and as Systems	with Output
Resolution/ Termination	Problem Resolution or Change	Program Termination	Solution or Change

A s will soon become apparent, this is a last chapter that isn't absolutely essential as far as the framework of study is concerned. For, in fact, much of what is to be discussed here is implicit in the explication of other functional activities. In particular, it should be apparent that one seldom has a sense of closure in studying the policy process. I have judged that an explicit discussion of this point is useful, however, and in addition I wish to draw your attention to other matters which seem properly placed in a concluding chapter. First, then, I discuss the nature of resolution and termination as functional activities in the policy process. Second, I offer a set of categories for decision making and policy which hopefully increase understanding. Third, I introduce some difficult problems in what one might call "the morality of choice." And finally I recap the framework in somewhat more elaborate form.

Resolution for Whom?

In his discussion of policy analysis, Robert Eyestone points out that:

> Policy questions are questions of differing values, and policy decisions are the result of some kind of settlement among people whose preferences are somewhat different. A choice usually satisfies some people more than others because it comes closer to what they wanted than to the wishes of others.[1]

One of the major lessons to be derived from this book is that public problems aren't comprehensively or universally "solved." In fact, the term "solution," which has a ring of finality to it, comes to be so highly relative as to distort its more common usage. This explains the reliance on "resolution," a word which literally refers to an "act or process of resolving, or reducing to simpler form." Specifically, resolution is viewed here as *a process in which public problems undergo change.* In this text we have directed particular attention to the contributions of government toward that end, recognizing that actions of many other public and private institutions likewise affect the nature of public problems. And at this point I am suggesting simply that one study the effects of various government programs rather than attempt to establish objective criteria for determining whether a solution is at hand.

There are any number of practical justifications for this approach. First and foremost, one cannot simply hold the problem and its environment constant for some of the following reasons:

1. Events interfere to alter people's perceptions of their needs.
2. Other problems emerge for some people that are of a higher priority than those for which a program has been developed.
3. Pressures from some sources are reduced or dispersed.
4. Private actions relieve needs, often influencing how people define problems and react to programs.
5. Programs themselves have unanticipated outcomes which may influence how people define problems.

This list represents a small sample of the factors which constitute the dynamic social world into which government programs are introduced. The most we can do is identify the effects of particular programs and decisions through observation (e.g., 100 new housing units, 120 fewer substandard housing units), inference (e.g., reduced rioting less press attention), and more or less systematic measurements (e.g., surveys, field research, experimentation).

Second, even if the world were more static, with few changes occurring between the perception of problems and the implementation of programs, determining when and whether a solution was at hand would be difficult. What measures would one rely on? What criteria would one use to determine when a particular public's needs were being met? What of the case in which problems are defined for others (the "others" not able to or interested in defining problems for themselves)? And don't forget such complicating "initial realities" as "Policy makers are not faced with a given problem" and "Many programs are developed and implemented without the problems ever having been clearly defined" (see Chapter 1). I have already discussed many of these problems as associated with evaluation. Normally policy actors do no more than keep the channels open for feedback and make imprecise judgments about how satisfied the customers are. While congressmen pay attention to their mail and executives are sensitive to the need for public support for programs, very little conscious effort is made to determine whether problems are "solved" or not.

Third, whether or not the policy environment remains static, it is difficult to know what other outcomes might have been realized had a different program been developed and implemented. Put differently, social change by one means may or may not be similarly achieved by other means. Alice M. Rivlin illustrates the point in discussing the popular Headstart program.

> After the fact, an evaluation attempted to uncover whether the program had had an *average* effect, discernible in test scores at the first and second grade levels. But the program was not designed to answer the really important and interesting questions: Were some approaches more successful than others? Were some more successful with particular types of children?[2]

In this case solutions not only appear to be very much in the eye of the beholder, but the viewing itself is limited.

As stressed earlier, we come very close here to repeating material discussed earlier (particularly in the evaluation chapter). Nowhere is this more the case than when measuring problem resolution or change in terms of program or organizational effectiveness and efficiency. Yet the perspective is sufficiently different to merit brief mention.

Yehezkel Dror defines effectiveness as the "extent to which direct goals are achieved." Efficiency is defined as a "cost-benefit ratio." As he points out, a program can be effective and inefficient where costs are ignored, or efficient and very ineffective where the scale of benefits is ignored.[3] The tidiness of these definitions disappears as soon as one asks: "What or whose goals, costs, benefits?" Until these are determined, one can hardly proceed to measure either quality of a program or organization. When these are determined, one is faced with complexities inherent in the discovery that there are several types of goals, costs, and benefits, and varying interpretations of any one type. Further, some of these ends are directed more consciously toward organizational survival than problem resolution. As Fremont J. Lyden and his colleagues observe:

> The process of goal definition should not be taken for granted. Operating goals are not self-evident in an organization's official goal statement. And real, or operative, goals must be ascertained for development of an effective design for the operation of the organization, and realistic criteria for measuring organizational accomplishment.[4]

The Bureau of the Budget (now the Office of Management and Budget) sought to develop measures for organizational accomplishment in a study of productivity in 1963. The results are of direct relevance to our discussion here. The specific concern was to "compare the amount of resources used with the volume of products or services." The study was careful to point out "that measurement of output is different in nature and in objectives from work measurement on the one hand and from measurement of social benefit or the impact of programs on the other."[5] Still, measures of volume of production or service surely provide a basis for analyzing social benefit. The problem comes in developing those measures.

Five agencies were used in the Bureau of the Budget study—the Division of Disbursement of the Department of the Treasury, the Department of Insurance of the Veterans Administration, the Post Office Department, the Systems Maintenance Service of the Federal Aviation Agency, and the Bureau of Land Management of the Department of the Interior. Systems for developing productivity data were developed in four of the five agencies—those whose service lent itself to quantitative description. In the case of the Bureau of Land Management, however, measurement proved difficult due to "limited time, unavailability of strategic data, and severe difficulties of interpretation and analysis."[6] Relating manpower units to volume of airmail handled, postage stamps sold, and postcards delivered is one thing; developing similar measures for the management of 160 million acres of forests and woodlands (one function of the Bureau of Land Management) is quite another. But the Bureau of Land Management was selected because it was thought quantitative measures *could be developed*. Think of the problems associated with measuring the productivity of the Environmental Protection Agency or the National Science Foundation. As the report concluded:

> The basic requirement for productivity measurement in an organization is that both its outputs and its inputs be measurable. Valid measurement of the end-product output may be more or less difficult in various organizations and in some instances, especially where the nature, quality, and purpose of output undergo rapid change, or where the output is otherwise undefinable or nonhomogeneous, it may be practically impossible.[7]

It should also be noted that the study sought to measure effects of agencies rather than programs, which might involve several agencies, or policies, which would present an even more complex measuring problem.

In summary, reference should be made to another of the "initial realities" listed in Chapter 1: "Most problems aren't solved by government though many are acted on there." That statement allows for those problems which are solved, by someone's criteria, but advises the student to concentrate analysis more on what is done than on what is solved.

Termination as a Process

In an oversimplified model of policy making and implementation, the problem is defined, a program developed and implemented, the problem or problems solved, and the program and its organizational components terminated. Since it is most difficult to determine when public problems are solved (see above), however, it follows that termination is seldom a simple matter of course. I offer the following generalizations as relevant to an understanding of this functional activity:

1. Those programs and their interactive organizational elements which go out of existence seldom do so as a result of the problem or problems being solved.
2. Termination is typically a process of organizational adjustment in which policy actors shift to consider related matters.

The first generalization requires little discussion. If you think about those specific units of government—agencies, committees, bureaus—which have gone out of business, seldom is it a result of having solved the problems of an issue-area. More important seem to be loss of support and/or significant changes in the nature of the problems. Thus many agencies were terminated at the end of World War II—agencies which served as major populations for implementation and evaluation systems in certain issue-areas. One of the first to go was the Office of Price Administration (OPA). The OPA had the unenviable task during the war of regulating prices and rationing commodities and services. No one liked them very much, as consumers had to stand in line to receive their ration stamps and sellers were frustrated in not being able to set prices as high as the market would bear. Still, the country was at war, and OPA developed into a large agency with 73,000 employees. With the end of the war, however, came a clamor for goods and for profits. Though the need to prevent run-away inflation was evident, the pressure on the price-regulation policy system to relax controls was overwhelming. In 1946 Congress enacted legislation severely crippling enforcement by OPA. President Truman vetoed the bill, and OPA was allowed to go out of business. As for those who thought price controls should have continued as a curb on inflation, OPA Administrator Paul A. Porter expressed their feelings in his irreverent renaming of the defunct organization—the Office for Cessation of Rationing and Priorities—OCRAP![8]

More impressive than the number of policy systems that go out of existence is the number that survive and expand. Herbert Kaufman found that nearly 85 percent of the government organizations he studied still existed in 1973 (148 of 175 agencies in his sample).[9] Once policy cycles have developed in a particular issue-area, interrupting them becomes a major assignment. Too many commitments by too many people exist at that point for a clean cut-away to occur. So termination—defined by Harold D. Lasswell as "the ending of prescriptions and of arrangements entered into within their framework"[10]—typically is a process itself, wherein those committed try to survive, at least until other arrangements can be made. Anthony Downs is most helpful in explaining this phenomenon as he discusses the death of bureaus.

> The older a bureau is, the less likely it is to die. This is true because its leaders become more willing to shift major purposes in order to keep the bureau alive.
> The best time to "kill" a bureau is as soon as possible after it comes into existence.[11]

Bureaus, congressional committees, and lobbyists populate the systems which apply policy, evaluate results, make adjustments, renew authority, and so on. Termination of a particular pattern may occur in this shifting, adjusting, and renewal, but it is usually subtle and almost never a clean break. Again Downs provides some of the reasons: bureaus are often willing to shift functions; bureau clients are willing to offer support despite reduced usefulness because they get something for little or no cost; it is extremely difficult to know just how useful and effective a bureau is (as we have noted); bureaus are less willing than private firms to try to kill each other off; some bureaus survive by getting an aggrandizing bureau to swallow them.[12]

Consider, for example, the enormously complex policy systems for agricultural problems. Drawn from the Department of Agriculture, the Committees on Agriculture in the House and Senate, and the many large farm groups, these systems have proved to be impressively adaptable to new circumstances through reorganizations, sensitivity to change, bargaining. The Department of Agriculture remains one of the largest departments despite (or perhaps because of) the success of American farmers in producing food. A review of the various divisions, agencies, and units of the department reveals an impressive array of functions. A cynic would have a field day. Consider that the Soil Conservation Service and other research agencies help to increase production; stabilization units regulate production to protect the farmer's prices; the Commodity Credit Corporation manages the surpluses; the Marketing and Consumer Services protects the customer; the Rural Development Bureau offers loans to farmers for many purposes besides farming. The department also has a large international affairs division, has electricity and telephone programs under the Rural Electrification Administration, is in the housing business, and manages gigantic national forest preserves. Coordinating all of these programs—some of which appear to be in conflict with one another—is a massive, perhaps impossible task. In 1962 one cynical congressman did review this elaborate machinery and, during the debate on the farm bill, introduced an amendment to the effect that "at no time shall the number of employees in the Department of Agriculture exceed the number of farmers in America." The amendment passed by a voice vote, only to be defeated when someone called for a division of the House.

Adaptability toward survival is not unique to agriculture policy systems. It is a universal characteristic in the policy process. In a world in which human needs are never fully met, it doesn't take a very clever chap to adapt his talents in the direction of some needs somewhere. Consider these examples. Even though the "man on the moon" project has terminated, the National Aeronautics and Space Administration remains hale and hearty. Its budget for fiscal 1977 exceeds that of many departments. As noted earlier, the Office of Economic Opportunity survived long after its loss of political support. And termination was characterized by a distribution of the poverty programs to other federal bureaus. The federal highway program, supported by the Highway Trust Fund, continues apace despite clear warnings that petroleum shortages may force major changes in transportation by the year 2000. The Subversives Activities Control Board existed long after its functions had all but disappeared. Charged with responsibility of maintaining a list of communist-associated organizations, the board was successful in listing only eight in its 22-year existence (others listed were negated by the courts). Even at its death an effort was made in Congress to expand its functions and change the name to the Federal Internal Security Board. And the so-called break-up of the Atomic Energy Commission was in fact the creation of two agencies—the Nuclear Regulatory Commission and an Energy Research and Development Administration dominated by a nuclear-oriented staff.

I emphasize again that these survivals and adaptations are not unexpected. In fact, while I have selected among the agencies for simple illustrations, the more common adaptations are made within the complex of specialized interacting bureaucratic, congressional, and interest group subpopulations. There the sharp and persistent eye will pick up continuous adjustments which, over time, may amount to termination of both program and organizational interaction.

Types of Decision Making

In their book, *A Strategy of Decision*, David Braybrooke and Charles E. Lindblom rely on two important dimensions—understanding and change in identifying four types of decision making.[13]

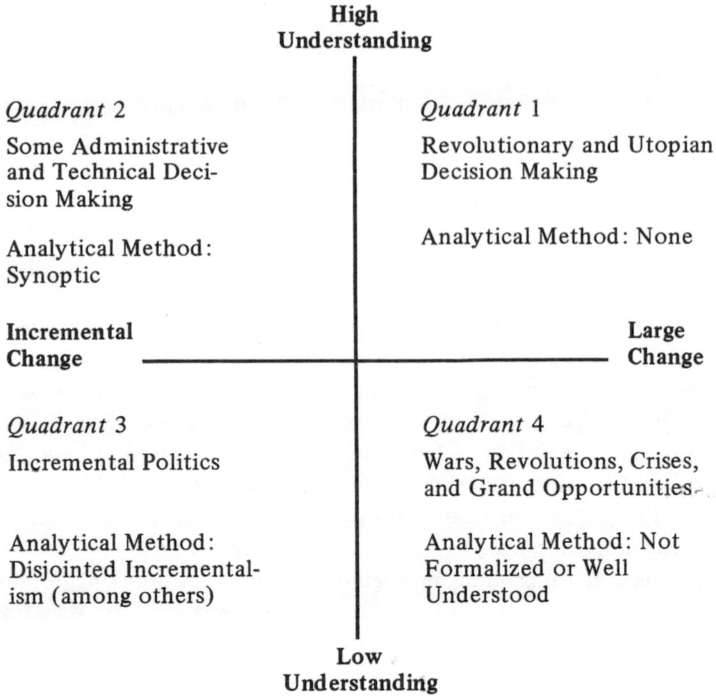

High
Understanding

Quadrant 2	*Quadrant* 1
Some Administrative and Technical Decision Making	Revolutionary and Utopian Decision Making
Analytical Method: Synoptic	Analytical Method: None

Incremental Change ——————————————— **Large Change**

Quadrant 3	*Quadrant* 4
Incremental Politics	Wars, Revolutions, Crises, and Grand Opportunities
Analytical Method: Disjointed Incrementalism (among others)	Analytical Method: Not Formalized or Well Understood

Low
Understanding

Figure 9-1. Lindblom's Four Quadrants of Decision Making. *Source*: David Braybrooke and Charles E. Lindblom, *A Strategy of Decision* (New York: The Free Press, 1963), p. 78.

Primarily Lindblom's formulation, this set of categories is most suggestive for policy study (see Figure 9-1). Of course, Lindblom argues persuasively that most democratic decision making fits within the third quadrant. The 1960s in particular have provided us with examples of fourth quadrant decision making, however, and the other quadrants are worth further pondering as well. Given his principal judgment and interest, Lindblom is considerably more explicit on describing the conditions for the third quadrant than the other three. Therefore, in accepting the utility and potential of this framework, I was motivated to conceptualize further.

First, it is of some importance that I justify the dimensions used. Acknowledging that decision making is multidimensional, I think a good case can be made for beginning one's analysis with knowledge (or understanding) and change. I prefer the term "knowledge" to "understanding" for its slightly broader meaning, at least as used by one of my personal gods—John Dewey. In *The Public and Its Problems*, Dewey points out that "knowledge is communication as well as understanding."[14] Thus, as used here, knowledge refers to the degree of understanding which is communicated and therefore shared among particular publics (primarily those involved in decision making).

The relationship of knowledge (as communication and understanding) to change in a democratic society is intimate. And in a fundamental sense this connection constitutes the agenda of study for scholars of democratic policy making. We want to know how it is that public (used in a pluralistic sense) awareness, interpretation, reaction, and cognition contribute to or result in social change. Therefore, while many factors obviously influence what happens between enlightenment and public action, we are well advised to begin analysis within those parameters.

Let us turn then to a reformulation of Lindblom's four quadrants—one which seeks to fill in some of the gaps and provide a bit more parallelism. While Figure 9-2 more or less speaks for itself, a few words of explanation might prove helpful. First note that I have used an even more expansive term than "knowledge" for the vertical dimension. By "estimated capacities" I refer to the principal policy actors' estimates of knowledge as defined above as well as administrative and political capabilities for effecting social change. Second, change itself requires a referent. Several possibilities suggest themselves—for example, change in existing policy or law, change in social behavior or physical condition, institutional change, etc. Granting the importance of all of these and the need for study and analysis of each, the present reference relied on for assigning characteristics is an estimate of *intended* social change (behavioral, institutional, physical) by those identified as principal actors.

A third point to keep in mind is simply that the quadrants are, in fact, collections of an inestimable number of variations in decision making. This conclusion derives from the fact that the knowledge and change dimensions are presented as continuua. It follows that literally hundreds of intersections might be identified by a comprehensive study of public policy. Thus the full conceptualization of decision making by these dimensions would be charted as an enormous grid rather than a single intersection, as is indicated by the light dotted lines on the chart. Fourth, it bears emphasis that the framework presented in this book should be useful in a full explication of the characteristics of each quadrant, or any one variation within a quadrant. That is, one expects to find operating within each a complex network of functional activities (problem definition, program formulation, legitimation, implementation) that in probability will vary in population, nature of interaction, output, etc. At least these are the types of hypotheses well worth pursuing. Finally, comprehension of the complexity of the American policy system can be facilitated by understanding that it is characterized by all these decisional styles.

Turning now to the individual quadrants, it should be noted first that

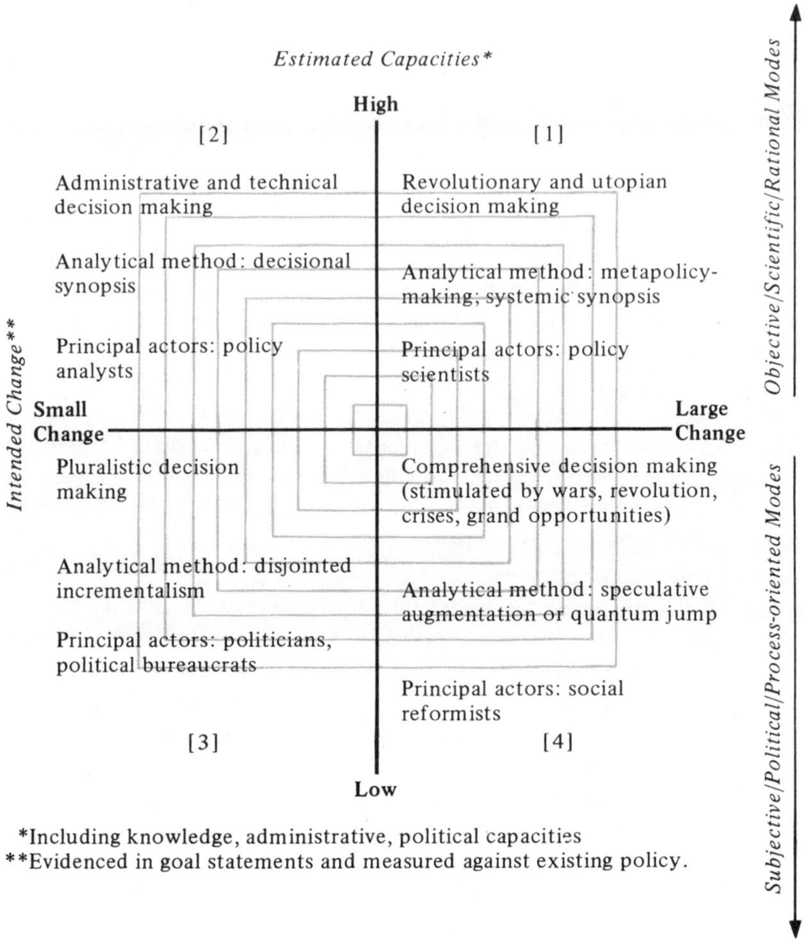

Figure 9-2. Four Modes of Decision Making. *Variations on a Theme of Charles E. Lindblom.*

those on the high side of estimated capacities are characterized as "objective/scientific/rational modes"; those on the low side as "subjective/political/process-oriented modes." These are general characteristics indicating the effect of confidence in available capacities. Quadrant 1 is the least familiar to us. Policy scientists might wish to prepare us for it, but even they recognize the serious limits in realizing a high degree of public knowledge and consequent large social change.[15] The analytical method referred to in this quadrant focuses on change in the whole political order—what Yehezkel Dror calls "metapolicymaking," i.e., "policy making on how to make policy."[16]

Quadrant 2 is less ambitious. The effort there is toward comprehensive-
ness within specialized issue-areas or institutions (referred to as "decisional
synopsis" as compared to "systemic synopsis" in Quadrant 1). As noted,
the principal actors constitute a rising class of policy analysts who do not
have the grand designs of the policy scientists. Rather they possess a professional desire to bring their own particular skills and high knowledge to
bear on public issues. Arnold J. Meltsner describes this group as follows:

> Analysts know that policy making is a big pot which many stir. But
> they are not intimidated by the complexity of the process or by the
> lack of immediate success. Each wants to be one of the stirrers. . . .
>   Intellectually, analysts perceive that the output of analysis should
> be measured in terms of implementation or actual social and be-
> havioral change. But given their distance from the executors of
> policy, many are happy when the client accepts their recommenda-
> tions and acts on them.[17]

Quadrant 3 remains highly descriptive of what happens in American policy making (both in terms of output and strategies employed). Disjointed
incrementalism has been criticized as not sufficiently discrete—i.e., one
often finds a large variation in what gets labeled as a policy or budgetary
increment. Still as a summary of the style of knowledge availability and
use, and the nature and size of intended policy change, disjointed incrementalism continues to convey an accurate picture of ordinary decision
making.

That brings us to perhaps the most interesting quadrant of all—that in
which estimated capability remains relatively low but an opportunity to
act presents itself to those intending large change in policy. As noted in
the chart, this opportunity may come in the form of war or revolution
but more typically in a democracy as a result of a crisis, massive expression of public opinion on some issue, or possibly a landslide election for
one party. Whatever the cause, a policy breakthrough is achieved despite
the limits of knowledge. In this instance the style of knowledge use is
"speculative," the nature of policy change "augmentative," if not actually
quantum.[18] My final comments turn briefly to the matter of responsiveness in these various modes of decision making. In paraphrasing Lester
M. Salamon and Gary L. Wamsley (as they discuss bureaucratic responsiveness): "The real issue concerning [institutional] responsiveness . . . may
not be *whether* [an institution] is responsive, but *to whom* and *under
what circumstances*."[19] As we know, knowledge has both objective and
subjective dimensions. In this political system we have sought to be responsive to both—to the facts and how they are interpreted. I believe it
may be a fair characterization to suggest the following:

1. The policy scientists prefer responsiveness to an elite core of objec-

tive scientists who specify what is the "best" policy and the means to achieve it.

2. The policy analysts prefer responsiveness to expertise but acknowledge the subjective context within which policy is developed and implemented in a democratic system.

3. The politicians prefer responsiveness to public opinion whether or not it is informed by available knowledge and willingly accept compromise of both.

4. The social reformists prefer responsiveness to particular subjective interpretations and are typically unwilling to accept compromise.

5. Each group is likely to experience discomfort if dominated by any one of the others.

Again one cannot help but be impressed with the assignment of describing and analyzing this mix of populations as they act on public issues within and between the layers of government in the United States. And what are the results? That is the next topic.

Types of Policy Effects

The Apollo "man on the moon" project of the National Aeronautics and Space Administration (NASA) represented a huge commitment of national resources (over 25 billion dollars during the period of 1965-1970). What were the effects? What needs were met? What problems were solved? One thinks immediately of national pride, international goodwill, sectional economic gain (in Florida and Texas), technological breakthroughs, etc., but these represent only the most obvious, first-order effects which in many cases are no more than the promotional efforts of NASA and its supporters. More difficult to determine are the secondary and tertiary, intended and unintended effects and consequences of having pursued a particular government program. Certainly policy intentions or goals are not always synonymous with policy effects, even when they are clearly specified. And even if they were, Lindblom points out that analysts typically "identify situations or ills from which to move *away* rather than goals *toward* which to move."

> Even short-term goals are defined largely in terms of reducing some observed ill rather than in terms of a known objective of another sort. . . . Policy aims at suppressing vice even though virtue cannot be defined, let alone concretized as a goal; at attending to mental illness even though we are not sure what attitudes and behavior are most healthy; at curbing the expansion of the Soviet Union even

though we do not know what positive foreign policy objectives to
set against the Kremlin's; at reducing the governmental inefficien-
cies even though we do not know what maximum level of compe-
tence we can reasonably expect. . . .[20]

This set of observations further illustrates the complexity of identifying
and measuring policy effect, suggesting as it does the need to analyze a full
range of changes and movements resulting from a government program.
For in studying outcomes one is faced with the fact that some are expected, others are not; some are manifest, others are latent; some are short-
run, others long-run; some are easily identifiable, others are not; some
propagate, others terminate; some are fed back into the government,
others are either fed into other institutions or simply absorbed out there.
These differences once again emphasize the need to specify the basis for
any one classification of policy effects. Though all too common an exercise, it is not enough merely to create categories and label the entries
"policy" or "policy effects" or "policy outcomes." As stressed in Chapter 1, "whatever we learn must be specified in terms of the questions we
sought to answer, the time frame within which our research was conducted, the institutional units studied. . . ."

Perhaps the most frequently cited public policy categories are those developed by Theodore J. Lowi—distribution, regulation, and redistribution.
In what sense are these "public policies?" The discussion of the term "policy" in Chapter 1 advises that such a question must be asked in order to
delineate the focus of study. In this case Lowi responds by defining policies "in terms of their impact or expected impact on the society."[21] He
speaks of three types of policy impacts noted above—distributive, regulatory, and redistributive. By distributive he refers to the effects of programs which give somebody something. The land distribution program of
the federal government during the nineteenth century would be a classic
example. But many subsidy programs would also classify. By regulatory
he refers to those government standards and controls which seek to influence our behavior. Typically these regulations develop in response to
practices which are deemed unacceptable for some reason (e.g., polluting
the environment, price fixing, endangering the public health). Redistributive is not quite so simple since, as Lowi points out, "in the long run,
all governmental policies may be considered redistributive . . . some people
pay in taxes more than they receive in services."[22] What he means to convey, however, is that some programs more than others take from a group
and give to another. It is a matter of degree, of course, and an important
determinant in distinguishing "distributive" from "redistributive" appears
to be the extent of group involvement and conflict in policy development
and implementation. The less a group contributes and the more it gets

from government, the more redistributive the policy. Randall B. Ripley and Grace A. Franklin also suggest that it is a matter of intention—that "redistributive policy involved a *conscious* attempt by the government to manipulate the allocation of wealth, property, rights, or some other value among broad classes or groups in society."[23]

Robert H. Salisbury has extended Lowi's categories to include self-regulation—a necessary addition. Obviously, self-regulation also involved limits on what certain people may do, but the group itself is authorized to set these limits (for example, professional licensing of lawyers, physicians, engineers). Salisbury also distinguishes between policy which is primarily allocative and that which is primarily structural. Allocative is just as it implies—a policy which confers benefits (distributive and redistributive). Structural policies, on the other hand, create units and guidelines for future allocations.[24] It is the distinction between whether, for example, the law specifically allocates money to a group for some purpose (e.g., veterans through the GI Bill of Rights) or whether some unit of government is given authority by law to allocate resources under certain circumstances (e.g., secretary of Agriculture in raising price supports).

Ripley and Franklin have begun the arduous task of identifying the manifold characteristics of the Lowi "policy types." They attempt to specify how certain broad features and core relationships differ among the three. Further, they assume the existence and importance of "subgovernments" in policy development and implementation, stressing the cross-institutional nature of most government decision making. Subgovernments emerge as collections of actors directing their attentions and efforts to particular issues. These actors are drawn from various institutional units—agencies, committees, interest groups. They interact frequently around the subject matter—for example, agriculture, veterans' benefits, medicare, minimum wage, etc.

It is not possible, nor necessary, to repeat the details of this fine effort to encourage students of public policy to venture from the more institution-bound analysis. It is sufficient for present purposes to note that Ripley and Franklin find different patterns of relationships among various institutional units for programs with distributive, regulative, and redistributive effects. They generalize these relationships in Figure 9-3.

One of the more obvious conclusions from reviewing these charts is that they represent a global mapping of relationships. Research will likely show variation within as well as between these three types of policies.

The effort by Ripley and Franklin also supports a point frequently made in these pages. An effort to explore policy effects, like any other feature or output, inevitably draws one back to consider events and how they are variously interpreted as needs, problems, issues. In short, what comes out is related to what goes in. It should also be noted in concluding this sec-

Relative Importance of Relationships for Determining Policy Actions
in Distributive Domestic Policy

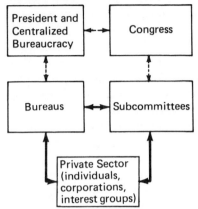

Relative Importance of Relationships for Determing Policy Actions
in Regulatory Domestic Policy

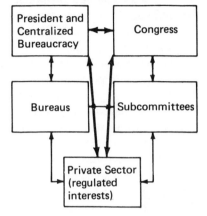

Relative Importance of Relationships for Determining Policy Actions
in Redistributive Domestic Policy

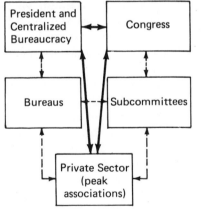

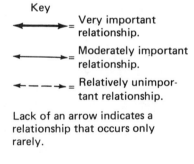

Figure 9-3. **Institutional Relationships Among Different Policies.** *Source*:
Randall B. Ripley and Grace A. Franklin, *Congress, the Bureaucracy,
and Public Policy*, (Homewood, Ill.: Dorsey, 1976), pp. 167–168.

tion that very little research has yet been conducted on policy effects,
either in determining what those effects are or in analyzing the causes.
Since many of these effects are social, economic, ecologic, even sometimes
psychological, it seems clear that an interdisciplinary research effort is
called for.

The Morality of Choice

What should come out of the policy process? What are the effects we are seeking? And how should these favored outcomes be achieved? One measure of our national choices is, of course, the budget. At the writing of the first edition of this book (1970), the budget dollar was still heavily committed to national defense (over 41 cents, with 13 cents going to Vietnam) and the amount allocated to human resources (education, health, income security programs) was increasing steadily. At this writing (the fiscal 1977 budget), national defense accounts for approximately one-fourth of the budget dollar (a decrease of some 15 percent since 1970), whereas the human resource programs now account for over half of the budget dollar. Given this trend, can we safely conclude that we are now making more moral choices? Maybe yes, maybe no. It clearly depends on who is drawing conclusions and by what moral standards. There are those who argue that the principal function of the national government is to provide a stout defense so that the citizenry can realize its potential. Human resources programs by this view are not only unnecessary, they are dysfunctional for the realization of a diverse and dynamic society. Others argue that large defense expenditures do no more than guarantee immorality. Preparation for war, they believe, leads to war. Governments should serve those whom society has not rewarded. By this view equality is not a passive process in which individuals are merely guaranteed freedom from interference. It is an active process in which serious attention and sizeable resources are directed toward adjusting imbalances in society.

In fact, the morality of choice in a democratic system appears to depend on maintaining such diverse views, thus complicating the smooth flow of public policy. Abraham Kaplan points out that "an absolutistic morality cannot take hold on democratic politics, for politics in a democracy is essentially pluralistic, tolerant, compromising."[25] Democratic public choice then cannot avoid certain human limitations—indeed, as E. E. Schattschneider and others argue, it is founded and structured on the human condition.

> Democracy is based on a profound insight into human nature, the realization that all men are sinful, all are imperfect, all are prejudiced, and none knows the whole truth. That is why we need liberty and why we have an obligation to hear all men. Liberty gives us a chance to learn from other people, to become aware of our own limitations, and to correct our bias. Even when we disagree with other people we like to think that they speak from good motives, and while we realize that all men are limited, we do not let ourselves imagine that any man is bad. *Democracy is a political system for people who are not too sure that they are right.*[26]

This conclusion should not be interpreted as downgrading the intelligence of democrats. Quite the reverse. Democratic public choice carries with it a heavy burden of community awareness and knowledge. Scientific inquiry and understanding are not only to be encouraged in democracy, they are essential for the operation and survival of that form of government. As T. V. Smith aptly observed: ". . . democracy succeeds in proportion as it discovers a form of education calculated to get at the bases of physical and social living and then makes this education accessible to all its citizens."[27] By this view, the morality of choice is corrupted when the citizenry fails to engage in or support inquiry and/or refuses to acknowledge or integrate its results. No small social experiment this! And the temptations to abandon the effort are many. For the ultimate challenge is to realize a humane, but human, government; to achieve social justice without determining and enforcing absolute values.

It is important to point out, of course, that whereas democracy cannot countenance an absolutistic morality, it must sustain, even protect, moralists. And, in fact, Kaplan finds Americans susceptible to moralization that "sentimentalizes the people," on the one hand, and pragmatism that seeks to make democracy effective on the other. The inevitable conflicts keep politics interesting, if slightly unsettling, to the tidy mind. Kaplan's comments, written in the late 1950s, are remarkably appropriate for the 1960s and 1970s, and, in all likelihood, for some future period as well.

> The American morality of power is under continuous tension between our moralization and our vulgar pragmatism. The uneasy equilibrium between what we think of as "idealism" and "realism" periodically gives way to the one tendency or the other. Like a character in Dostoevski, we hang suspended between bursts of religious ecstacy and drunken debauchery. Power is to be used by men of conscience and integrity for the common good, and its exercise guided always by the ideals of justice and humanitarianism, sympathy and fair play. At the same time, power is intrinsically immoral, corrupting those who have it, and in its very nature destroying the freedom of those subjected to it. Politics, in short, we regard as a succession of necessary evils; we play with words to make virtues of these necessities, rather than apply our energies to reconstituting either the facts that make them necessary or the valuations that make them evil.[28]

The 1960s and 1970s have been characterized by high moralism—and for good reason. Civil rights and environmental insults, the tragedies of Vietnam and Watergate have had the combined effect of increasing cynicism, if not destroying the underlying support for the system. Our pragmatic oriented decision makers have had to join in the broad philosophical and moral debate about what has gone wrong. While this form of discourse has its place and can, in fact, influence the future course of events, a major lesson derived from this book is that big decisions effecting large social change are infrequent. Translating the conclusions of grand national debates into effective policy development and implementation is no simple matter. Typically decision makers are faced with proximate choices and limited, often conflicting, information; not a linear decision path from a consensus on ultimate values and goals. And "political morality," according to Kaplan, "lies in the everyday shaping of policy, not merely in the heroic stand at a time of crisis."[29]

All of this is not to downgrade the role of criticism and national debates, or to suggest that they have no function or impact. Indeed, the criticism of American foreign and domestic policies in Vietnam and the moral fervor expressed over presidential excesses in Watergate and related matters have surely influenced American politics and policy making. But unless such dramatic expressions of public outrage cause revolution, they tend to result more in turning corners, making adjustments, and preventing the next increment. Even where large change is intended, the programs designed to achieve it are fitted within an organizational and programmatic setting which may be resistant to sudden movement.

"What should come out?" is a basic question that will, and should, require extensive discussion among students of public policy. I think it is important (1) to consider the problems of applying absolute moral principles in a democratic policy process, (2) to evaluate one's own values and policy biases, and (3) to acknowledge the fact that most choices in the policy process are highly constrained. These recommendations are designed to improve understanding of the policy process. They are not meant to dissuade anyone from critically analyzing American public policies and how they are developed. I value criticism myself as essential in politics and social life. My credo is "constructive criticism is better than negative criticism," but "negative criticism is better than no criticism."

In this connection, one should be forewarned that the study of how things really work can sometimes blunt critical drive. Several things can happen. One may become enamored with the process as a result of studying it—seeing a reasonable function for everything that goes on, "understanding" every bit-and-piece decision that is made. Or one finds the process so complicated, so lengthy, and so unmanageable that all reform seems hopeless. Since every aspect of the overall process is so extraordinarily intricate, another possibility is that one never has enough information to evaluate and criticize. Students of public policy should guard against all of these. We can't afford to have our scholars "neutralized" in politics. I agree with David Easton, in his presidential address to the American Political Science Association:

We need to accept the validity of addressing ourselves directly to the the problems of the day to obtain quick, short-run answers with the tools and generalizations currently available, however inadequate they may be. We can no longer take the ideal scientific stance of behavioralism that because of the limitations of our understanding, application is premature and must await future basic research.[30] Application is always premature, information is always incomplete, choices are never the best possible. Certainly the fact that you are aware of these limitations of man should not cause your withdrawal from social and political processes. "To know is to bear the responsibility for acting and to act is to engage in reshaping society."[31]

Conclusion as Prelude

And now to the final order of business. I have sought in these pages to provide "an introduction to the study of public policy." My purpose has been to suggest a set of concepts to guide inquiry. In so doing, I have consciously tried to raise questions rather than answer them, and to acknowledge rather than ignore or gloss over the incredible complexities of democratic decision making. I have also tried to identify certain biases I have so that the reader can take those into account in using this framework (see Chapter 1). Just as the policy process (Table 9-1, p. 230) itself ends with a beginning, so also this book will have served its central purpose if it launches further study of American public policy. A final and somewhat more elaborate summary of the framework is offered as a prelude to that effort.

Table 9-1. The Policy Process

System	Activities	Output
	Problem to Government Phase	
Problem Identification Event	Perception (receiving and registering an event)	Problem
	Definition (bringing into sharp relief the effect of an event)	
	Aggregation (grouping)	
	Organization (developing structure)	
	Representation (developing and maintaining access)	Demand
	Agenda setting (theories, strategies)	Agendas 1. Problem Definition 2. Proposal 3. Bargaining 4. Continuing
	Action in Government Phase	
Program Development	Formulation (developing a plan, a method, a prescription for acting on a problem): Includes routine, analogous and creative formulation.	Proposal
	Legitimation (approving a proposal by an accepted means—importance of majority coalition building)	Program
Legitimacy (authorizing and supporting government)	Appropriation (approving program funds) 1. Formulation 2. Legitimation	Budget

Government to Problem Phase

Program Implementation	Organization (establishing administrative methods and units)	Structure
	Interpretation (translating authorization into acceptable feasible directives—importance of discretion)	Working rules/Standards
	Application (routine provision of services, payments, controls—importance of "mutual role taking")	Varies (depends on program)

Program to Government Phase

Program Evaluation	Evaluation (judging the merit of programs—as functional activity in all systems; as a systematic endeavor for specific programs) 1. Specification (setting purposes, criteria) 2. Measurement (collecting data—systematic, unsystematic) 3. Analysis (reviewing data—systematic, unsystematic) 4. Recommendation (proposing change)	Varies (depends on findings)

(Emergence of policy cycles of support, incremental adjustment, program change, redefinition or discovery of problems).

Problem Resolution or Change Phase

Program Termination	Resolution (effecting change in public problems)	Relative solution; social change
	Termination (organization adjustment)	

Notes

1. Robert Eyestone, *Political Economy* (Chicago: Markham, 1972), p. 80.

2. Alice M. Rivlin, *Systematic Thinking for Social Action* (Washington: The Brookings Institution, 1971), p. 85.

3. Yehezkel Dror, *Ventures in Policy Sciences* (New York: Elsevier, 1971), p. 2.

4. Fremont J. Lyden, et al., eds., *Policies, Decisions and Organization* New York: Appleton-Century-Crofts, 1969), p. 137.

5. Bureau of the Budget, *Measuring Productivity* (Washington, D.C.: U.S. Government Printing Office, 1964), p. 4. Emphasis added.

6. Bureau of the Budget, p. 304.

7. Bureau of the Budget, p. 17.

8. Told in Cabell Phillips, *The Truman Presidency* (New York: Macmillan, 1966), p. 111. On postwar conversion, see Fritz M. Marx, ed., "The American Road from War to Peace: A Symposium," *American Political Science Review*, vol. 38 (December 1944), pp. 1114–1191.

9. Herbert Kaufman, *Are Government Organizations Immortal?* (Washington, D.C.: The Brookings Institution, 1976), p. 34.

10. Harold D. Lasswell, "The Decision Process: Seven Categories of Functional Analysis," reprinted in Nelson W. Polsby et al., eds., *Politics and Social Life* (Boston: Houghton Mifflin, 1963), p. 93.

11. Anthony Downs, *Inside Bureaucracy* (Boston: Little, Brown, 1967), p. 20.

12. Downs, pp. 22–23. See also Kaufman, Ch. 1 for a full treatment of the factors favoring and threatening agency life.

13. David Braybrooke and Charles E. Lindblom, *A Strategy of Decision* (New York: The Free Press, 1963), p. 78.

14. John Dewey, *The Public and Its Problems* (Denver: Swallow, 1927; 1954), p. 176.

15. See, for example, Yehezkel Dror, *Public Policymaking Re-examined* (San Francisco: Chandler, 1968) and Harold D. Lasswell, *A Pre-View of Policy Sciences* (New York: Elsevier, 1971).

16. Dror, pp. 8, 160.

17. Arnold J. Meltsner, "Bureaucratic Policy Analysts," *Policy Analysis*, vol. 1 (Winter 1975), pp. 116–117.

18. See Charles O. Jones, *Clean Air* (Pittsburgh: University of Pittsburgh Press, 1975), for an analysis of the effect of this type of decision making.

19. Lester M. Salamon and Gary L. Wamsley, "The Federal Bureaucracy: Responsiveness to Whom?" in LeRoy N. Rieselbach, ed., *People vs. Government: The Responsiveness of American Institutions* (Bloomington: Indiana University Press, 1975), p. 152.

20. Braybrooke and Lindblom, p. 102.

21. Theodore J. Lowi, "American Business, Public Policy Case Studies, and Political Theory," *World Politics*, vol. 16 (July 1964), p. 689.

22. Lowi, p. 690.

23. Randall B. Ripley and Grace A. Franklin, *Congress, the Bureaucracy, and Public Policy* (Homewood, Ill.: Dorsey, 1976), p. 18.

24. See Robert H. Salisbury, "The Analysis of Public Policy: A Search for Theories and Roles," in Austin Ranney, ed., *Political Science and Public Policy* (Chicago: Markham, 1968), pp. 151–175; and "A Theory of Policy Analysis and Some Preliminary Applications," paper written with John P. Heinz and presented at the 1968 Annual Meeting of the American Political Science Association, Washington, D.C.

25. Abraham Kaplan, *American Ethics and Public Policy* (New York: Oxford University Press, 1963), p. 50.

26. E. E. Schattschneider, *Two Hundred Million Americans in Search of a Government* (New York: Holt, Rinehart and Winston, 1969), p. 53. Emphasis added.

27. T. V. Smith, *The Democratic Way of Life* (Chicago: University of Chicago Press, 1926), p. 192.

28. Kaplan, p. 77.

29. Kaplan, p. 103.

30. David Easton, "The New Revolution in Political Science," *American Political Science Review*, vol. 63 (December 1969), pp. 1055–1056.

31. This statement is central to what David Easton calls the "Credo of Relevance"—a set of tenets subscribed to by a large group of political scientists in the late 1960s because of their concern about the relevance of political research and teaching. See Easton, p. 1052.

Bibliography

A complete bibliography on American public policy would include most works written on economics, politics, history, sociology, anthropology, psychology, geography, and many written on the natural sciences. I have been somewhat more selective. After directing you to some sources which are essential to any study of public policy, I provide listings of books in several categories that you will find very useful in studying various aspects of policy.

Certain journals, magazines, and newspapers are particularly rich in material relevant to the study of public policy. Journals such as *Social Forces, Urban Affairs Quarterly, Public Policy, The Public Interest, Policy Studies Journal, Policy Sciences, Policy Analysis, Publius,* and *Public Administration Review* have several articles in every issue. The *Annals* of the American Academy of Political and Social Science, *The American Behavioral Scientist, Society,* and *Law and Contemporary Problems* frequently devote whole issues to particular policy areas. Other more popular journals such as *Commentary, The New Republic, The National Review,* and *The Nation* are designed to provide intelligent analysis of contemporary public problems. Among the national newspapers, *The New York Times, The Christian Science Monitor, The Wall Street Journal,* and *The Washington Post* provide the best coverage and analysis of issues and the policy process. The *American Political Science Review* and the various regional political science journals—*Polity* (Northeast), *Journal of Politics* (South), *American Journal of Political Science* (Midwest), and *Western Political Quarterly*—have occasional articles of major interest.

One should also draw upon the many publications of the Congressional Quarterly, Inc. The *Weekly Reports,* the *Almanacs, Congress and the Nation,* and the many special reports are invaluable sources. Also useful are the *Editorial Research Reports* devoted to specific issue-areas. A similar publication, *The National Journal,* provides additional analysis of the national scene.

Another important source is the fantastic array of government documents. No country in the world has so many documentary sources.

Particularly rich are the congressional documents. Committee hearings, reports, special staff studies, the *Congressional Record*, and the *Journals* are indispensable for studying the role of representatives and senators in the policy process. Further, they are of great value in studying the dimensions of problems, the development of existing policy, the evaluation of policy, and the role of the executive.

The following list includes books that expand on the points made here (regarding both the policy process in general and the role of specific institutions), provide good descriptions of major issue-areas, and give you detailed analyses of specific policy processes in operation.

General Works on Public Policy— Theory, Framework, Analysis

Agger, Robert E., et al. *The Rulers and the Ruled*. New York: Wiley, 1964.

Anderson, James E. *Public Policy-Making*. New York: Praeger, 1975.

Bauer, Raymond A., and Kenneth J. Gergen, eds. *The Study of Public Formation.* New York: The Free Press, 1968.

Braybrooke, David, and Charles E. Lindblom. *A Strategy of Decision*. New York: The Free Press, 1963.

Caputo, David A. *Politics and Public Policy in America*. Philadelphia: Lippincott, 1974.

Charlesworth, James C., ed. *Contemporary Political Analysis*. New York: The Free Press, 1967.

Cobb, Roger W. and Charles D. Elder. *Participation in American Politics: The Dynamics of Agenda-Building*. Boston: Allyn and Bacon, 1972.

Coleman, James S. *Policy Research in the Social Sciences*. Norristown, N.J.: General Learning Press, 1972.

Dahl, Robert A. *Modern Political Analysis.* Englewood Cliffs, N.J.: Prentice-Hall, 1963.

——. *A Preface to Democratic Theory*. Chicago: University of Chicago Press, 1956.

——. *Who Governs?* New Haven, Conn.: Yale University Press, 1961.

——, and Charles E. Lindblom. *Politics, Economics, and Welfare*. New York: Harper & Row, 1953.

——. *Polyarchy*. New Haven, Conn.: Yale University Press, 1971.

Davies, James, *Human Nature in Politics*. New York: Wiley, 1963.

Deutsch, Karl W. *The Nerves of Government*. New York: The Free Press, 1963.

Dewey, John. *The Public and Its Problems*. New York: Holt, Rinehart and Winston, 1927.

Dolbeare, Kenneth, ed. *Public Policy Evaluation*. Beverly Hills, Calif.: Sage, 1975.

Donovan, John C. *The Policy Makers*. New York: Pegasus, 1970.

Downs, Anthony. *An Economic Theory of Democracy*. New York: Harper & Row, 1957.

Dror, Yehezkel. *Design for Policy Sciences*. New York: Elsevier, 1971.

——. *Public Policymaking Reexamined*. San Francisco: Chandler, 1968.

——. *Ventures in Policy Sciences*. New York: Elsevier, 1971.

Dye, Thomas R. *Understanding Public Policy*. Englewood Cliffs, N.J.: Prentice-Hall, 1975.

Easton, David. *A Framework for Political Analysis*. Englewood Cliffs, N.J.: Prentice-Hall, 1965.

——. *A Systems Analysis of Political Life*. New York: Wiley, 1965.

Edelman, Murray. *The Symbolic Uses of Politics*. Urbana, Ill.: University of Illinois Press, 1964.

Etzioni, Amitai. *The Active Society*. New York: The Free Press, 1968.

Eulau, Heinz, and Kenneth Prewitt. *Labyrinths of Democracy*. Indianapolis: Bobbs-Merrill, 1973.

Eyestone, Robert. *Political Economy*. Chicago: Markham, 1972.

——. *The Threads of Public Policy*. Indianapolis: Bobbs-Merrill, 1971.

Freeman, J. Leiper. *The Political Process*. New York: Random House, 1955.

Galbraith, John K. *Economics and the Public Purpose*. Boston: Houghton Mifflin, 1973.

——. *The Affluent Society*. Boston: Houghton Mifflin, 1958.

——. *The New Industrial State*. Boston: Houghton Mifflin, 1967.

Gaus, John M. *Reflections on Public Administration*. University, Ala.: University of Alabama Press, 1947.

Gerth, H. H., and C. Wright Mills. *From Max Weber: Essays in Sociology*. London: Routledge & Kegan Paul, 1948.

Greenberg, Edward S. *Serving the Few: Corporate Capitalism and the Bias of Government Policy*. New York: Wiley, 1974.

Greenstein, Fred I., and Nelson W. Polsby, eds. *The Handbook of Political Science*. Reading, Mass.: Addison-Wesley, 1975.

Heclo, Hugh. *Modern Social Politics in Britain and Sweden*. New Haven, Conn.: Yale University Press, 1974.

Hennessy, Bernard C. *Public Opinion*. Belmont, Calif.: Wadsworth, 1965.

Hofferbert, Richard I. *The Study of Public Policy*. Indianapolis: Bobbs-Merrill, 1974.

Holden, Matthew, Jr., and Dennis L. Dresang, eds. *What Government Does*. Beverly Hills, Calif.: Sage, 1975.

Hoos, Ida R. *Systems Analysis in Public Policy: A Critique*. Berkeley: University of California Press, 1972.

Ilchman, Warren F., and Norman T. Uphoff. *The Political Economy of Change*. Berkeley: University of California Press, 1971.

Jones, Charles O., and Robert D. Thomas, eds. *Public Policy Making in a Federal System*. Beverly Hills, Calif.: Sage, 1976.

Kaplan, Abraham. *American Ethics and Public Policy*. New York: Oxford University Press, 1963.

Key, V. O., Jr. *Public Opinion and American Democracy*. New York: Knopf, 1961.

Lasswell, Harold D. *A Pre-View of Policy Sciences*. New York: Elsevier, 1971.

——. *The Future of Political Science*. New York: Atherton, 1963.

——, and Abraham Kaplan. *Power and Society*. New Haven, Conn.: Yale University Press, 1950.

Lerner, Daniel, and Harold D. Lasswell, eds. *The Policy Sciences*. Stanford, Calif.: Stanford University Press, 1951.

Lindblom, Charles E. *The Intelligence of Democracy*. New York: The Free Press, 1965.

——. *The Policy-Making Process*. Englewood Cliffs, N.J.: Prentice-Hall, 1968.

Lowi, Theodore. *The End of Liberalism.* New York: Norton, 1969.

———. *The Politics of Disorder.* New York: Basic Books, 1971.

MacRae, Duncan, Jr. *The Social Function of Social Science.* New Haven, Conn.: Yale University Press, 1976.

McConnell, Grant. *Private Power and American Democracy.* New York: Knopf, 1966.

Meehan, Eugene J. *The Theory and Method of Political Analysis.* Homewood, Ill.: Dorsey, 1965.

Mitchell, Joyce and William C. *Political Analysis and Public Policy.* Chicago: Rand McNally, 1969.

Mitchell, William C. *The American Polity.* New York: The Free Press, 1962.

Nagel, Stuart S. *The Legal Process from a Behavioral Perspective.* Homewood, Ill.: Dorsey, 1969.

———, ed. *Policy Studies in America and Elsewhere.* Lexington, Mass.: Lexington Books, 1975.

Parenti, Michael. *Democracy for the Few.* New York: St. Martin's, 1974.

Pitkin, Hanna F. *The Concept of Representation.* Berkeley: University of California Press, 1967.

Polsby, Nelson, et al., eds. *Politics and Social Life.* Boston: Houghton Mifflin, 1963.

Presthus, Robert. *Elites in the Policy Process.* London: Cambridge University Press, 1974.

Price, Don K. *The Scientific Estate.* Cambridge, Mass.: Harvard University Press, 1965.

Raiffa, Howard. *Decision Analysis: Introduction to Making Choices Under Uncertainty.* Reading, Mass.: Addison-Wesley, 1968.

Ranney, Austin, ed. *Political Science and Public Policy.* Chicago: Markham, 1968.

Reagan, Michael D. *The Managed Economy.* New York: Oxford University Press, 1963.

Redford, Emmette S. *Democracy in the Administrative State.* New York: Oxford University Press, 1969.

Riker, William. *The Theory of Political Coalitions.* New Haven, Conn.: Yale University Press, 1962.

Rivlin, Alice M. *Systematic Thinking for Social Action.* Washington, D.C.: Brookings Institution, 1971.

Rogers, Harrell R., Jr., and Charles S. Bullock, III. *Law and Social Change.* New York: McGraw-Hill, 1972.

Rose, Arnold M. *The Power Structure.* New York: Oxford University Press, 1967.

Rossi, Peter H., and Walter Williams. *Evaluating Social Programs.* New York: Seminar Press, 1972.

Schattschneider, E. E. *The Semisovereign People.* New York: Holt, Rinehart, and Winston, 1960.

———. *Two Hundred Million Americans in Search of a Government.* New York: Holt, Rinehart, and Winston, 1969.

Schneier, Edward V., ed. *Policy-Making in American Government.* New York: Basic Books, 1969.

Smith, T. Alexander. *The Comparative Policy Process.* Santa Barbara, Calif.: ABC-CLIO, 1975.

Straayer, John A., and Robert D. Wrinkle. *American Government, Policy, and Non-Decision.* Columbus, Ohio: Merrill, 1972.

Suchman, Edward. *Evaluative Research.* New York: Russell Sage, 1967.

Thayer, Frederick C. *An End to Hierarchy! An End to Competition!* New York: New Viewpoints, 1973.

Truman, David. *The Governmental Process.* New York: Knopf, 1951.

Van Dyke, Vernon. *Political Science: A Philosophical Analysis.* Stanford, Calif.: Stanford University Press, 1960.

Wade, Larry L. *The Elements of Public Policy.* Columbus, Ohio: Merrill, 1972.

Wade, Larry L., and R. L. Curry, Jr. *A Logic of Public Policy.* Belmont, Calif.: Wadsworth, 1970.

Weiss, Carol H. *Evaluation Research.* Englewood Cliffs, N.J.: Prentice-Hall, 1972.

Williams, Walter L. *Social Policy Analyses and Research.* New York: Elsevier, 1971.

Wilson, James Q. *Political Organizations.* New York: Basic Books, 1973.

Young, Roland, ed. *Approaches to the Study of Politics.* Evanston, Ill.: Northwestern University Press, 1958.

General Works on Political Institutions

Altshuler, Alan, ed. *The Politics of the Federal Bureaucracy.* New York: Dodd, Mead, 1968.

Barber, James D. *The Presidential Character.* Englewood Cliffs, N.J.: Prentice-Hall, 1972.

Bernstein, Marver H. *The Job of the Federal Executive.* Washington, D.C.: Brookings Institution, 1958.

———. *Regulating Business by Independent Commission.* Princeton, N.J.: Princeton University Press, 1955.

Brewer, Garry D. *Politicians, Bureaucrats, and the Consultant.* New York: Basic Books, 1973.

Cater, Douglass. *The Fourth Branch of Government.* Boston: Houghton Mifflin, 1959.

———. *Power in Washington.* New York: Random House, 1964.

Cronin, Thomas E., and Sanford D. Greenberg, eds. *The Presidential Advisory System.* New York: Harper & Row, 1969.

Davis, James W., Jr. *The National Executive Branch.* New York: The Free Press, 1970.

Davis, Kenneth C. *Discretionary Justice.* Baton Rouge, La.: Louisiana State University Press, 1970.

Downs, Anthony. *Inside Bureaucracy.* Boston: Little, Brown, 1967.

Fenno, Richard F., Jr. *Congressmen in Committees.* Boston: Little, Brown, 1973.

———. *The President's Cabinet.* Cambridge, Mass.: Harvard University Press, 1959.

Froman, Lewis A., Jr. *The Congressional Process.* Boston: Little, Brown, 1967.

Gawthrop, Louis. *Bureaucratic Behavior in the Executive Branch.* New York: The Free Press, 1969.

Grodzins, Morton. *The American System.* Chicago: Rand McNally, 1966.

Gross, Bertram. *The Legislative Struggle.* New York: McGraw-Hill, 1953.

Herring, E. Pendleton. *Group Representation before Congress.* Baltimore: The Johns Hopkins Press, 1929.

———. *The Politics of Democracy.* New York: Holt, Rinehart and Winston, 1940.

Horn, Stephen. *Unused Power: The Work of the Senate Committee on Appropriations.* Washington, D.C.: Brookings Institution, 1970.

Hyneman, Charles. *Bureaucracy in a Democracy.* New York: Harper & Row, 1950.

Jacob, Charles E. *Policy and Bureaucracy.* Princeton: Van Nostrand, 1966.

Jacob, Herbert, and Kenneth N. Vines, eds. *Politics in the American States.* Boston: Little, Brown, 1976.

Jewell, Malcolm E., and Samuel C. Patterson. *The Legislative Process in the United States.* New York: Random House, 1973.

Kaufman, Herbert. *Are Government Organizations Immortal?* Washington, D.C.: Brookings Institution, 1976.

Keefe, William J. *Parties, Politics and Public Policy.* Hinsdale, Ill.: Dryden, 1976.

Keefe, William J., and Morris S. Ogul. *The American Legislative Process.* Englewood Cliffs, N.J.: Prentice-Hall, 1973.

Kingdon, John W. *Congressmen's Voting Decisions.* New York: Harper & Row, 1973.

Koenig, Louis W. *The Chief Executive.* New York: Harcourt Brace Jovanovich, 1975.

Kohlmeier, Louis J. *The Regulators.* New York: Harper & Row, 1969.

Krislov, Samuel. *The Supreme Court in the Political Process.* New York: Macmillan, 1965.

Leach, Richard H. *American Federalism.* New York: Norton, 1970.

Mainzer, Lewis C. *Political Bureaucracy.* Chicago: Scott, Foresman, 1973.

Manley, John F. *The Politics of Finance.* Boston: Little, Brown, 1970.

Martin, Roscoe. *The Cities and the Federal System.* New York: Atherton, 1965.

Matthews, Donald R. *U.S. Senators and Their World.* Chapel Hill, N.C.: University of North Carolina Press, 1960.

Mayhew, David R. *Congress: The Electoral Connection.* New Haven, Conn.: Yale University Press, 1974.

Milbrath, Lester W. *The Washington Lobbyists.* Chicago: Rand McNally, 1963.

Monsen, R. Joseph, Jr., and Mark W. Cannon. *The Makers of Public Policy.* New York: McGraw-Hill, 1965.

Neustadt, Richard E. *Presidential Power*. New York: Wiley, 1960.

Ornstein, Norman J., ed. *Congress in Change*. New York: Praeger, 1975.

Ott, David J., and Attiat F. Ott. *Federal Budget Policy*. Washington, D.C.: Brookings Institution, 1969.

Peabody, Robert L., and Nelson W. Polsby, eds. *New Perspectives on the House of Representatives*. Chicago: Rand McNally, 1963.

Peltason, Jack. *The Federal Courts in the Political Process*. New York: Random House, 1955.

Polsby, Nelson W. *Congress and the Presidency*. Englewood Cliffs, N.J.: Prentice-Hall, 1976.

Pressman, Jeffrey L. *House vs. Senate: Conflict in the Appropriations Process*. New Haven, Conn.: Yale University Press, 1966.

Price, David. *Who Makes the Laws?* Cambridge, Mass.: Schenkman, 1972.

Reagan, Michael D. *The New Federalism*. New York: Oxford University Press, 1972.

Rieselbach, Leroy N. *Congressional Politics*. New York: McGraw-Hill, 1973.

——, ed. *People vs. Government: The Responsiveness of American Institutions*. Bloomington, Ind.: Indiana University Press, 1975.

Ripley, Randall B. *Congress: Process and Policy*. New York: Norton, 1975.

Ripley, Randall B., and Grace A. Franklin. *Congress, the Bureaucracy, and Public Policy*. Homewood, Ill.: Dorsey, 1976.

Rourke, Francis E. *Bureaucracy, Politics and Public Policy*. Boston: Little, Brown, 1976.

Schooler, S. Dean. *Science, Scientists, and Public Policy*. New York: The Free Press, 1971.

Schubert, Glendon. *Judicial Policy-Making*. Chicago: Scott, Foresman, 1965.

Shapiro, Martin. *Law and Politics in the Supreme Court*. New York: The Free Press, 1964.

Smith, Bruce L. R. *The RAND Corporation*. Cambridge, Mass.: Harvard University Press, 1966.

Smith, T. V. *The Democratic Way of Life*. Chicago: University of Chicago Press, 1926.

Smithies, Arthur. *The Budgetary Process in the United States.* New York: McGraw-Hill, 1955.

Sorauf, Frank J. *Party Politics in America.* Boston: Little, Brown, 1972.

Sorensen, Theodore C. *Decision-Making in the White House.* New York: Columbia University Press, 1963.

Sundquist, James L. *Making Federalism Work.* Washington, D.C.: Brookings Institution, 1969.

Wallace, Robert Ash. *Congressional Control of Federal Spending.* Detroit, Mich.: Wayne State University, 1960.

Wasby, Stephen L. *The Impact of the United States Supreme Court.* Homewood, Ill.: Dorsey, 1970.

Wolanin, Thomas R. *Presidential Advisory Commissions.* Madison: University of Wisconsin Press, 1975.

Woll, Peter. *American Bureaucracy.* New York: Norton, 1963.

Zeigler, Harmon. *Interest Groups in American Society.* Englewood Cliffs, N.J.: Prentice-Hall, 1964.

Selected Analyses of Domestic Issue-Areas

Abrams, Charles. *The Future of Housing.* New York: Harper & Row, 1946.

Banfield, Edward C. *The Unheavenly City Revisited.* Boston: Little, Brown, 1974.

Barker, Lucius J., and Jesse J. McCorry, Jr. *Black Americans and the Political System.* Cambridge, Mass.: Winthrop, 1976.

Battan, Louis J. *The Unclean Sky.* Garden City, N.Y.: Doubleday, 1966.

Blechman, Barry M., et al. *Setting National Priorities: The 1975 Budget.* Washington, D.C.: Brookings Institution, 1974.

——, et al. *Setting National Priorities: The 1976 Budget.* Washington, D.C.: Brookings Institution, 1975.

Brown, Harrison. *The Challenge of Man's Future.* New York: Viking, 1954.

——, et al. *The Next Hundred Years: Man's Natural and Technological Resources.* New York: Viking, 1957.

Burch, Philip H., Jr. *Highway Revenue and Expenditure Policy in the United States.* New Brunswick, N.J.: Rutgers University Press, 1962.

Carmichael, Stokley, and Charles V. Hamilton. *Black Power.* New York: Random House, 1967.

Carson, Rachel. *The Silent Spring.* Boston: Houghton Mifflin, 1962.

Christenson, Reo M. *Challenge and Decision.* New York: Harper & Row, 1973.

Chu, Franklin D., and Sharland Trotter. *The Madness Establishment.* New York: Grossman, 1974.

Dales, J. H. *Pollution, Property, and Prices.* Toronto: University of Toronto Press, 1968.

Davis, David. *Energy Politics.* New York: St. Martin's, 1974.

Downs, Anthony. *Who Are the Urban Poor?* New York: Committee for Economic Development, 1968.

Dupre, Stefan, and Sanford Lakoff. *Science and the Nation.* Englewood Cliffs, N.J.: Prentice-Hall, 1962.

Esposito, John. *Vanishing Air.* New York: Grossman, 1970.

Fitch, Lyle C., et al. *Urban Transportation and Public Policy.* San Francisco: Chandler, 1964.

Freeman, S. David. *Energy: The New Era.* New York: Random House, 1974.

Fried, Edward R., et al. *Setting National Priorities: The 1974 Budget.* Washington, D.C.: Brookings Institution, 1973.

Garvey, Gerald. *Energy, Ecology, Economy.* New York: Norton, 1972.

Glazer, Nathan. *Affirmative Discrimination.* New York: Basic Books, 1975.

Gordon, Kermit, ed. *Agenda for the Nation.* Washington, D.C.: Brookings Institution, 1968.

Halperin, Morton H. *Bureaucratic Politics and Foreign Policy.* Washington, D.C.: Brookings Institution, 1974.

Harrington, Michael. *The Other America.* New York: Macmillan, 1963.

Herber, Lewis. *Crises in Our Cities.* Englewood Cliffs, N.J.: Prentice-Hall, 1965.

Herfindahl, Orris C., and Allen V. Kneese. *Quality of the Environment.* Baltimore: The Johns Hopkins Press, 1965.

Higbee, Edward. *Farms and Farmers in an Urban Age.* New York: Twentieth Century Fund, 1963.

Holloman, J. Herbert, and Michel Grenon. *Energy Research and Development.* Cambridge, Mass.: Ballinger, 1975.

Jacobs, Jane. *The Death and Life of Great American Cities.* New York: Random House, 1961.

Jencks, Christopher. *Inequality.* New York: Basic Books, 1972.

Krasnow, Erwin G., and Lawrence D. Longley. *The Politics of Broadcast Regulation.* New York: St. Martin's, 1973.

Levy, Lillian, ed. *Space: Its Impact on Man and Society.* New York: Norton, 1965.

Manvel, Allen D. *Housing Conditions in Urban Poverty Areas.* Washington, D.C.: U.S. Government Printing Office, 1968.

Mechanic, David. *Mental Health and Social Policy.* Englewood Cliffs, N.J.: Prentice-Hall, 1969.

——. *Politics, Medicine, and Social Science.* New York: Wiley, 1974.

Murphy, Earl F. *Governing Nature.* Chicago: Quadrangle Books, 1967.

Nadel, Mark V. *The Politics of Consumer Protection.* Indianapolis: Bobbs-Merrill, 1971.

Nader, Ralph. *Unsafe at Any Speed.* New York: Grossman, 1965.

Nathan, Richard P. *Monitoring Revenue Sharing.* Washington, D.C.: Brookings Institution, 1975.

Ng, Larry K. Y., ed. *The Population Crisis.* Bloomington, Ind.: Indiana University Press, 1975.

Noll, Roger. *Reforming Regulation.* Washington, D.C.: Brookings Institution, 1971.

Owen, Henry, and Charles L. Schultze, eds. *Setting National Priorities: The Next Ten Years.* Washington, D.C.: Brookings Institution, 1976.

Owen, Wilfred. *Transportation for Cities.* Washington, D.C.: Brookings Institution, 1976.

Pechman, Joseph A. *Federal Tax Policy.* New York: Norton, 1971.

President's Commission on National Goals. *Goals for Americans.* Englewood Cliffs, N.J.: Prentice-Hall, 1960.

Reagan, Michael. *Science and the Federal Patron.* New York: Oxford University Press, 1969.

Redford, Emmette S. *The Regulatory Process.* Austin: University of Texas Press, 1969.

Ripley, Randall B. *The Politics of Economic and Human Resource Development.* Indianapolis: Bobbs-Merrill, 1972.

Roberts, Leigh M., et al., eds. *Comprehensive Mental Health.* Madison: University of Wisconsin Press, 1968.

Rosenbaum, Walter A. *The Politics of Environmental Concern.* New York: Praeger, 1973.

Schultze, Charles L. *The Politics and Economics of Public Spending.* Washington, D.C.: Brookings Institution, 1968.

——, et al. *Setting National Priorities: The 1971 Budget.* Washington, D.C.: Brookings Institution, 1970.

——, et al. *Setting National Priorities: The 1972 Budget.* Washington, D.C.: Brookings Institution, 1971.

——, et al. *Setting National Priorities: The 1973 Budget.* Washington, D.C.: Brookings Institution, 1972.

Seligman, Ben B. *Permanent Poverty: An American Syndrome.* Chicago: Quadrangle Books, 1968.

Silberman, Charles. *Crisis in Black and White.* New York: Random House, 1964.

——. *Crisis in the Classroom.* New York: Random House, 1970.

Steiner, Gilbert Y. *The State of Welfare.* Washington, D.C.: Brookings Institution, 1971.

Stevens, Robert, and Rosemary Stevens. *Welfare Medicine in America.* New York: The Free Press, 1974.

Stockwell, Edward G. *Population and People.* Chicago: Quadrangle Books, 1968.

Taggart, Robert III. *Low-Income Housing: A Critique of Federal Aid.* Baltimore: The Johns Hopkins Press, 1970.

Thomas, Norman. *Education in National Politics.* New York: McKay, 1975.

Watts, William, and Lloyd A. Free. *State of the Nation, 1974.* Washington, D.C.: Potomac Associates, 1974.

Wheaton, William L. C., et al., eds. *Urban Housing.* New York: The Free Press, 1966.

Wholey, Joseph S., et al. *Federal Evaluation Policy.* Washington, D.C.: Urban Institute, 1970.

Wise, Arthur E. *Rich Schools, Poor Schools.* Chicago: University of Chicago Press, 1968.

Selected Studies of the Policy Process

Alford, Robert R. *Health Care Politics.* Chicago: University of Chicago Press, 1975.

Allison, Graham T. *Essence of Decision: Explaining the Cuban Missile Crisis.* Boston: Little, Brown, 1971.

Amrine, Michael. *The Great Decision: The Secret History of the Atomic Bomb.* New York: Putnam, 1959.

Anderson, James E., ed. *Cases in Public Policy-Making.* New York: Praeger, 1976.

Anderson, Martin. *The Federal Bulldozer.* Cambridge, Mass.: MIT Press, 1964.

Art, Richard. *The TFX Decision.* Boston: Little, Brown, 1968.

Bachrach, Peter, and Morton S. Baratz. *Power and Poverty: Theory and Practice.* New York: Oxford University Press, 1970.

Bailey, Stephen K. *Congress Makes a Law.* New York: Columbia University Press, 1950.

——, and Edith K. Mosher. *ESEA: The Office of Education Administers a Law.* Syracuse, N.Y.: Syracuse University Press, 1969.

Baldwin, Sidney. *Poverty and Politics: The Rise and Decline of the Farm Security Administration.* Chapel Hill, N.C.: University of North Carolina Press, 1968.

Bardach, Eugene. *The Skill Factor in Politics.* Berkeley: University of California Press, 1972.

Bauer, Raymond, et al. *American Business and Public Policy.* New York: Atherton, 1963.

Bellush, Jewell, and Stephen M. David, eds. *Race and Politics in New York City.* New York: Praeger, 1971.

Bendiner, Robert. *Obstacle Course on Capitol Hill.* New York: McGraw-Hill, 1965.

Bibby, John, and Roger Davidson. *On Capitol Hill.* New York: Holt, Rinehart and Winston, 1972.

Caputo, David A., and Richard L. Cole. *Urban Politics and Decentralization: The Case of General Revenue Sharing.* Lexington, Mass.: Heath Lexington, 1974.

Carroll, Holbert N. *The House of Representatives and Foreign Affairs.* Pittsburgh, Pa.: University of Pittsburgh Press, 1958.

Chamberlain, Lawrence H. *The President, Congress, and Legislation.* New York: Columbia University Press, 1946.

Cleaveland, Frederick, ed. *Congress and Urban Problems.* Washington, D.C.: Brookings Institution, 1969.

Crecine, John P. *Governmental Problem Solving.* Chicago: Rand McNally, 1969.

Crenson, Matthew A. *The Un-Politics of Air Pollution.* Baltimore: The Johns Hopkins Press, 1971.

Dahl, Robert A. *Congress and Foreign Policy.* New York: Norton, 1950.

Danhof, Clarence H. *Government Contracting and Technological Change.* Washington, D.C.: Brookings Institution, 1968.

Danielson, Michael. *Federal-Metropolitan Politics and the Commuter Crisis.* New York: Columbia University Press, 1965.

Davidson, Roger H. *Coalition-Building for Depressed Areas Bills: 1955–1965.* Indianapolis: Bobbs-Merrill, 1966.

——. *The Politics of Comprehensive Manpower Legislation.* Baltimore: The Johns Hopkins Press, 1972.

Davies, J. Clarence, III, and Barbara S. Davies. *The Politics of Pollution.* Indianapolis: Bobbs-Merrill, 1975.

Davis, James W., Jr., and Kenneth M. Dolbeare. *Little Groups of Neighbors: The Selective Service System.* Chicago: Markham, 1968.

Dommel, Paul R. *The Politics of Revenue Sharing.* Bloomington, Ind.: Indiana University Press, 1974.

Donovan, John D. *The Politics of Poverty.* New York: Pegasus, 1967.

Dye, Thomas R. *Politics, Economics, and the Public.* Chicago: Rand McNally, 1966.

Eidenberg, Eugene, and Roy D. Morey. *An Act of Congress.* New York: Norton, 1969.

Engler, Robert. *The Politics of Oil.* New York: Macmillan, 1961.

Etzioni, Amitai. *Demonstration Democracy.* New York: Gordon and Breach, 1970.

Fenno, Richard F., Jr. *The Power of the Purse.* Boston: Little, Brown, 1966.

Freedman, Leonard. *Public Housing: The Politics of Poverty.* New York: Holt, Rinehart and Winston, 1969.

Friedman, Lawrence M. *Government and Slum Housing.* Chicago: Rand McNally, 1968.

Fritschler, A. Lee. *Smoking and Politics.* New York: Appleton-Century-Crofts, 1969.

Gans, Herbert. *The Urban Villagers.* New York: The Free Press, 1962.

Green, Harold P., and Alan Rosenthal. *Government of the Atom.* New York: Atherton, 1963.

Greenberg, Stanley. *Politics and Poverty.* New York: Wiley, 1974.

Greenstone, J. David, and Paul E. Peterson. *Race and Authority in Urban Politics.* New York: Russell Sage, 1973.

Greer, Scott. *Urban Renewal and American Cities.* Indianapolis: Bobbs-Merrill, 1965.

Hadwiger, Don, and Ross B. Talbot. *Pressures and Protests.* San Francisco: Chandler, 1965.

Hardin, Charles. *The Politics of Agriculture.* New York: The Free Press, 1952.

Huntington, Samuel. *The Common Defense.* New York: Columbia University Press, 1961.

James, Dorothy B. *Poverty, Politics, and Change.* Englewood Cliffs, N.J.: Prentice-Hall, 1972.

Jones, Charles O. *Clean Air: The Policies and Politics of Pollution Control.* Pittsburgh, Pa.: University of Pittsburgh Press, 1975.

Kash, Don E., and Irwin L. White. *Energy Under the Oceans.* Norman, Okla.: University of Oklahoma Press, 1973.

Latham, Earl. *The Group Basis of Politics.* Ithaca, N.Y.: Cornell University Press, 1952.

Logsdon, John M. *The Decision to Go to the Moon.* Cambridge, Mass.: MIT Press, 1970.

Maass, Arthur. *Muddy Waters.* Cambridge, Mass.: Harvard University Press, 1951.

Marmor, Theodore R. *The Politics of Medicare.* Chicago: Aldine, 1973.

Masters, Nicholas A., et al. *State Politics and the Public Schools: An Exploratory Analysis.* New York: Knopf, 1964.

Meranto, Philip. *The Politics of Federal Aid to Education in 1965.* Syracuse, N.Y.: Syracuse University Press, 1967.

Meyerson, Martin, and Edward Banfield. *Politics, Planning, and the Public Interest.* New York: The Free Press, 1955.

Mitroff, Ian L. *The Subjective Side of Science.* New York: Elsevier, 1974.

Moynihan, Daniel P. *Maximum Feasible Misunderstanding.* New York: The Free Press, 1969.

——. *The Politics of a Guaranteed Income.* New York: Random House, 1973.

Munger, Frank J., and Richard F. Fenno, Jr. *National Politics and Federal Aid to Education.* Syracuse, N.Y.: Syracuse University Press, 1962.

Oppenheimer, Bruce I. *Oil and the Congressional Process.* Lexington, Mass.: Lexington Books, 1974.

Peabody, Robert L., et al. *To Enact a Law: Congress and Campaign Financing.* New York: Praeger, 1972.

Pierce, Lawrence C. *The Politics of Fiscal Policy Formation.* Pacific Palisades, Calif.: Goodyear, 1971.

Piven, Frances Fox, and Richard A. Cloward. *Regulating the Poor.* New York: Pantheon Books, 1971.

Pressman, Jeffrey L., and Aaron B. Wildavsky. *Implementation.* Berkeley: University of California Press, 1973.

Rainwater, Lee, and William Yancey. *The Moynihan Report and the Politics of Controversy.* Cambridge, Mass.: MIT Press, 1967.

Robinson, James A. *Congress and Foreign Policy-Making.* Homewood, Ill.: Dorsey, 1962.

Rossi, Peter, and Robert Dentler. *The Politics of Urban Renewal.* New York: The Free Press, 1961.

Rossi, Peter H., and Katharine C. Lyall. *Reforming Public Welfare.* New York: Russell Sage, 1976.

Ruttenberg, Stanley H., et al. *The American Oil Industry: A Failure of Antitrust Policy.* New York: National Marine Engineers' Beneficial Association, 1973.

Schattschneider, E. E. *Politics, Pressures, and the Tariff.* Englewood Cliffs, N.J.: Prentice-Hall, 1935.

Selznick, Philip M. *T.V.A. and the Grass Roots.* Berkeley: University of California, Press, 1949.

Sharkansky, Ira. *The Politics of Taxing and Spending.* Indianapolis: Bobbs-Merrill, 1969.

Sindler, Alan, ed. *American Political Institutions and Public Policy.* Boston: Little, Brown, 1969.

Spanier, John, and Eric M. Uslaner. *How American Foreign Policy Is Made.* New York: Praeger, 1974.

Steiner, Gilbert Y. *Social Insecurity.* Chicago: Rand McNally, 1966.

Stevenson, Gordon M., Jr. *The Politics of Airport Noise.* North Scituate, Mass.: Duxbury Press, 1972.

Sundquist, James L. *Politics and Policy.* Washington, D.C.: Brookings Institution, 1968.

Westin, Alan F., ed. *The Uses of Power.* New York: Harcourt Brace Jovanovich, 1962.

Wildavsky, Aaron. *Dixon-Yates: A Study in Power Politics.* New Haven, Conn.: Yale University Press, 1962.

——. *The Politics of the Budgetary Process.* Boston: Little, Brown, 1964.

Wilson, James Q., ed. *Urban Renewal.* Cambridge, Mass.: MIT Press, 1967.

Wirt, Frederick. *The Politics of Southern Equality.* New York: Aldine, 1970.

Wirt, Frederick M., and Michael W. Kirst. *The Political Web of American Schools.* Boston: Little, Brown, 1972.

Wolman, Harold, *Politics of Federal Housing.* New York: Dodd, Mead, 1971.

Index